PHOTOGRAPHY FILM & TELEVISION

[THINK AGAIN]

NATIONAL MUSEUM
PHOTOGRAPHY
FILM & TELEVISION

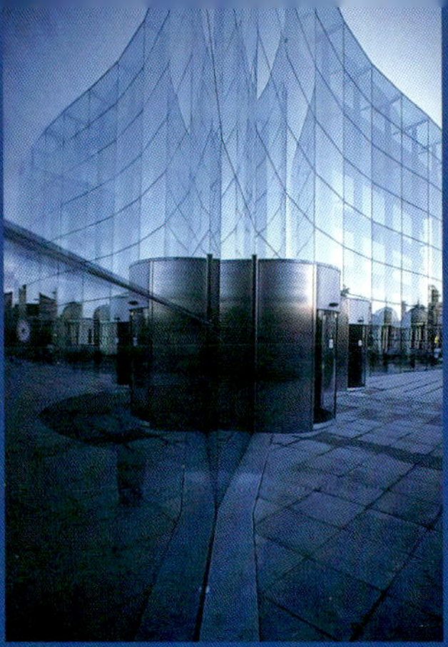

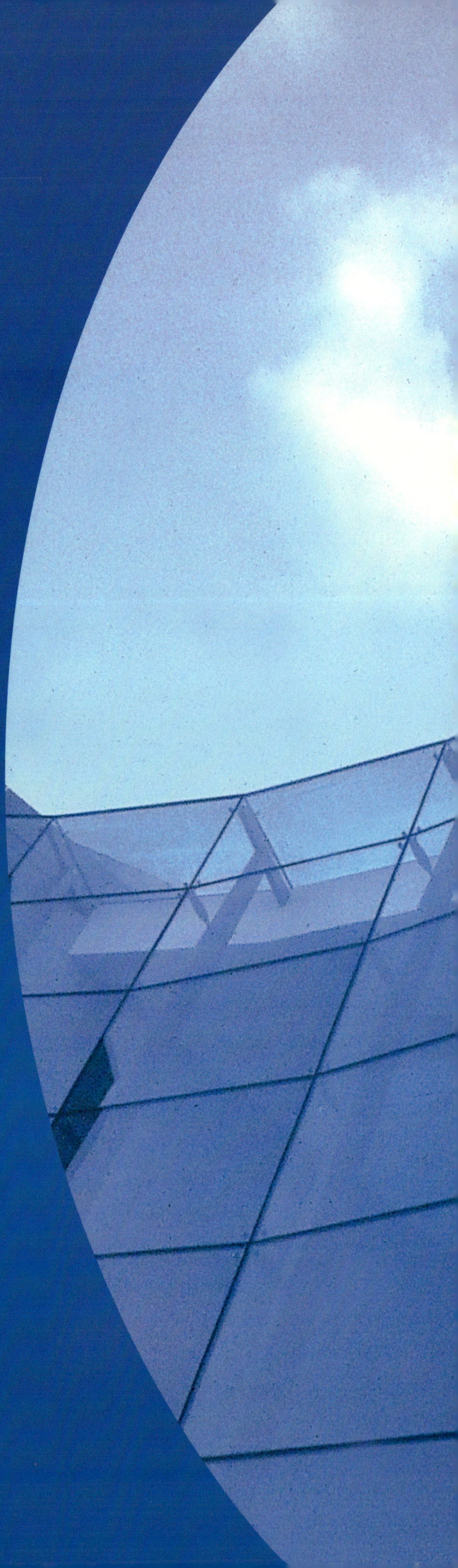

First published 1999 by the Science Museum, Exhibition Road, London SW7 2DD for the National Museum of Photography, Film & Television

The NMPFT is part of the National Museum of Science & Industry which includes the Science Museum in London and Wroughton and the National Railway Museum in York.

ISBN 1 900747 13 8

Designed and typeset by DS Print & Redesign
Cover image © The Attik
Production by Ian Wolverson
Printed in Great Britain by DS Print & Redesign

Commissioned photography by Bob Cox and Paul Thompson
Special thanks to Joanne O'Hagan and Nicola O'Shea

National Museum of Photography, Film & Television
Bradford BD1 1NQ

Tel. 01274 202030
Fax 01274 723155
Website http://www.nmsi.ac.uk/nmpft

Contents

Think again!

Amanda Nevill
Head of Museum

Tension has been building in what appears to be a far-flung quarter of the world. The situation is now at stalemate. A military response, we are persuaded, is justified in bringing the baddie down. A war unfolds in full colour on our television screens and in the newspapers. From the comfort and guaranteed safety of home—fire burning, drink in hand—we watch the action develop, much as we might watch *Saving Private Ryan*—but this is a real war being enacted, real people being killed. We can see live coverage of bombs falling, broadcast from the roofs of the city under fire: the reality is palpable.

The front cover of a newspaper shows a Western pilot about to leave on a bombing mission. He is giving a thumbs-up sign. Next to this self-assured photograph is a horrific picture of an injured civilian. The accompanying colour magazine has received heavy sponsorship from a large toiletries and perfume manufacturer, so we are asked to consume a worrying mix of life-and-death issues alongside the comparative trivia of the perfect product to attract the man or woman of our dreams. How are we to assimilate all these messages? Why do pictures of conflict and heroism appear side by side? What was the photographer's intention in taking such images? Did the picture editor deliberately place the photographs to shock, or is it a coincidence? What are the moral implications of being able to watch film fantasy and reality as though they were one? Does a carefully chosen picture sell more perfume? Sell more newspapers?

> *'The winds are always on the side of the ablest navigators.'*
> Edward Gibbon (1737–94), historian

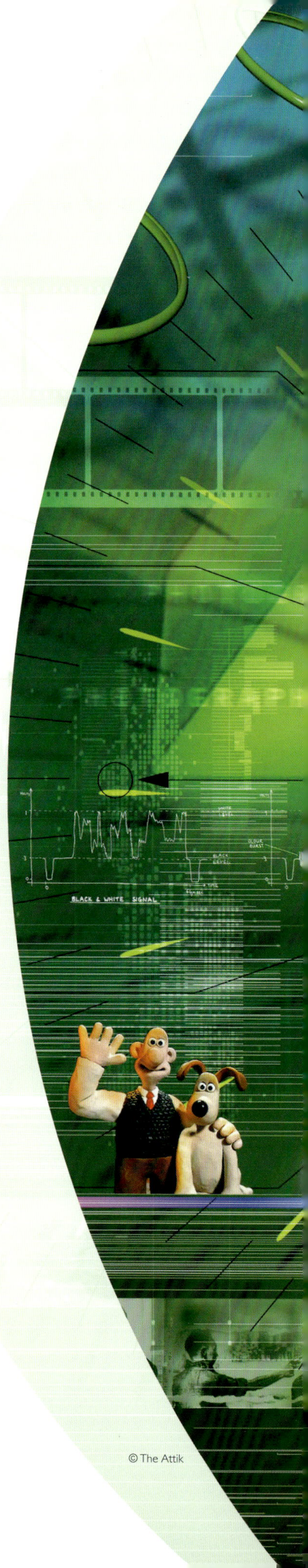

© The Attik

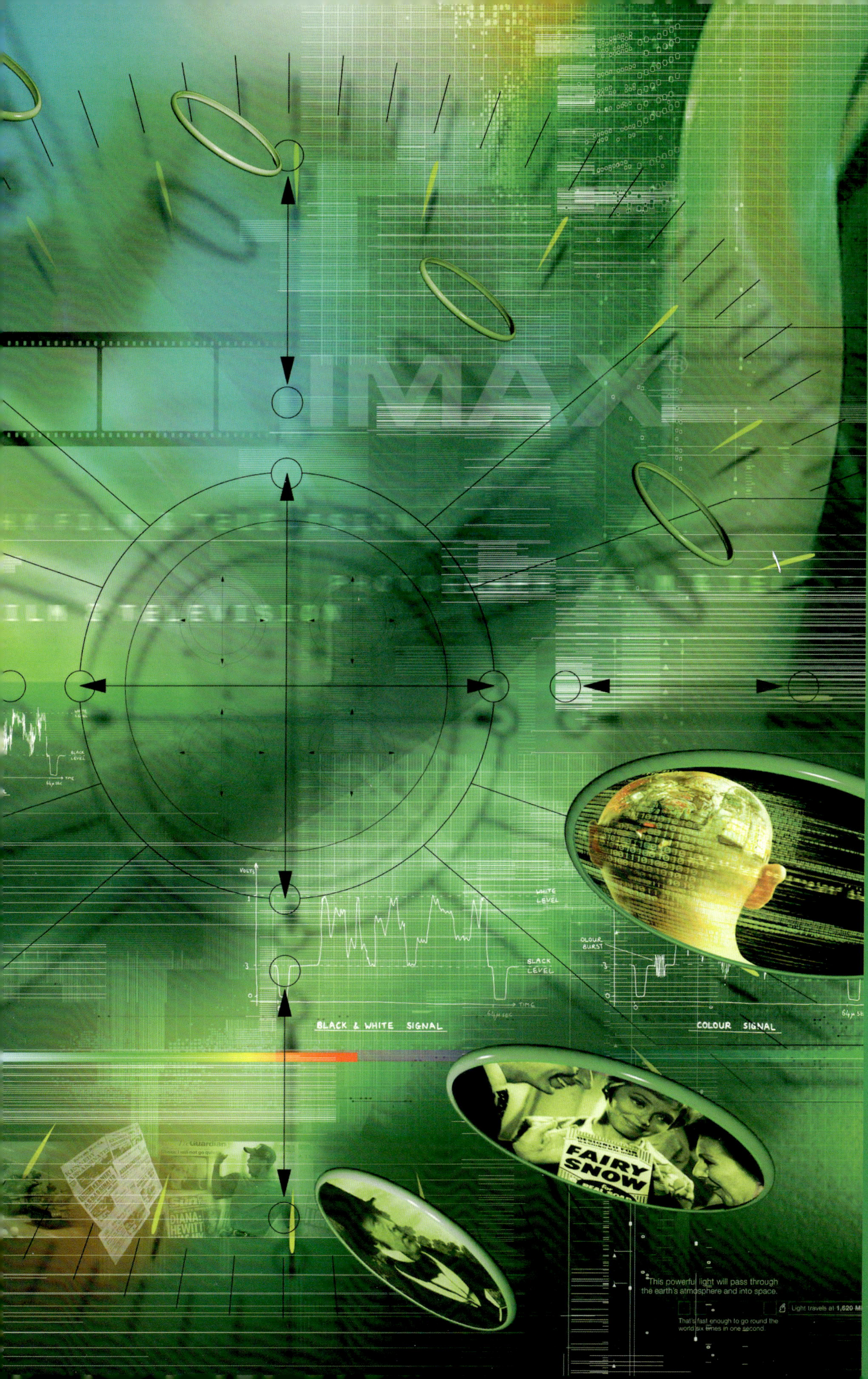
IMAX
BLACK & WHITE SIGNAL
COLOUR SIGNAL
FAIRY SNOW
This powerful light will pass through the earth's atmosphere and into space.
That's fast enough to go round the world six times in one second.

Still and moving images tell us most of what we know about the world. The National Museum of Photography, Film & Television is not simply about looking at photographs, films and television: it is about thinking about what we see and understanding our response. The Museum will challenge your perspectives of the way you view the world, and perhaps even cause you to 'think again'.

Every so often history records a step change of such significance that its impact touches every area of life. The digital revolution has changed photography, film and television completely, opening up a world where they work hand in hand with computers and telecommunications. The Museum itself had to think again as this technological revolution demanded a dramatic response. Backing of £16 million from the Heritage Lottery Fund, the Arts Council of England, the Foundation for Sport and the Arts, the European Union and private industry enabled a major development which has substantially increased the Museum's size, providing innovative galleries where visitors can explore and interact with digital technology. The *new* Museum provides an inspirational and exciting navigational aid for entering into the world of digital imaging.

Just as nineteenth-century economies were revolutionised by the creation of infrastructures which enabled commodities to be physically moved from the manufacturing site to the consumer, so the convergence of computer, telecommunications and imaging technology is precipitating similar revolutions in the twentieth and twenty-first centuries. Fortunes are being made, not just in the physical creation of networks and interfaces, but in the exchange of a new currency whose basic unit is not a manufactured product but a virtual commodity: access to information.

Interestingly, the very technology the Museum is presenting—the digital transfer of information, and multimedia—has shaped and is still shaping a society with new expectations and demands, thus dictating the philosophy behind the new Museum's design and its intellectual mission. The Museum has had to deal with the expectation that information is immediately available, wherever events unfold in the world—or even in space!—and the fact that social opinions and attitudes shift and change much more fluidly, and fluently, than they might have done in the past. A museum with a purely static approach is unlikely to hold the attention of a twenty-first-century audience used to zapping through a multiplicity of television channels. The

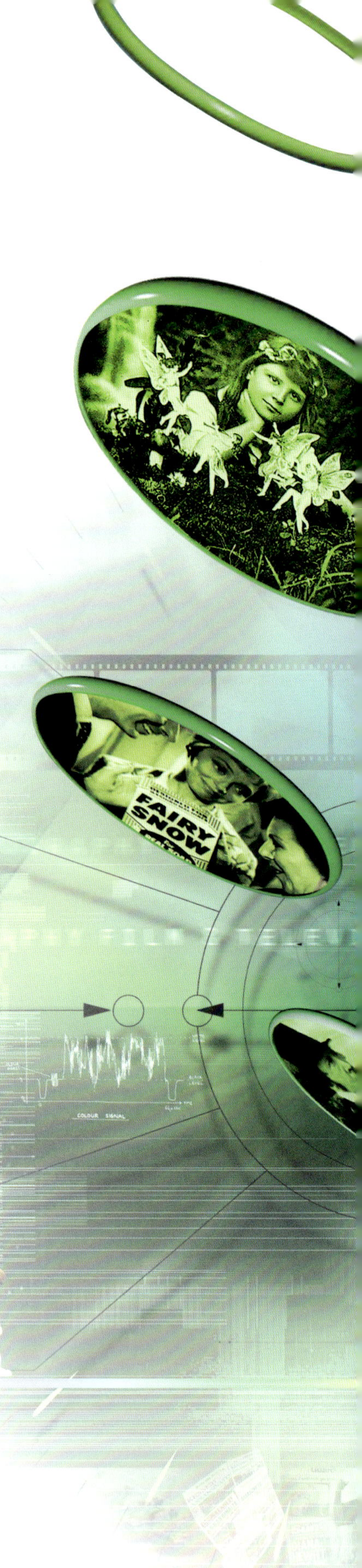

© The Attik

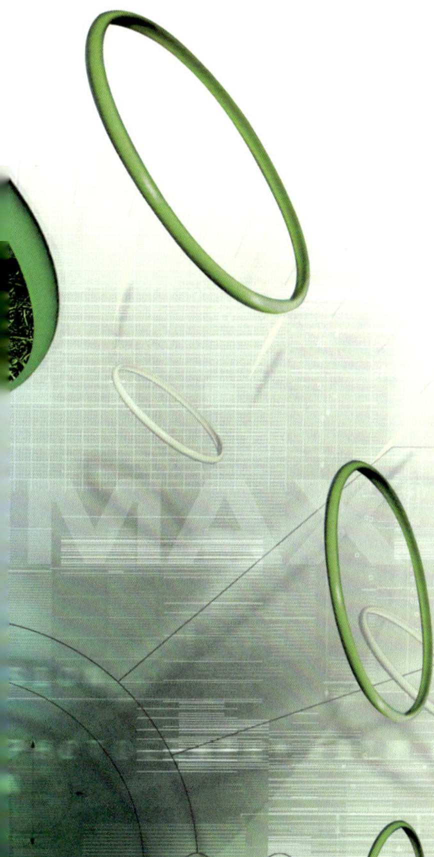

excitement of living in a society where information flows at the same speed as, or even faster than, life itself inevitably means that transition and change are part of the way we live, and any museum engaging with the expectations of today's and tomorrow's audiences needs to reflect this. Digital technology allows our new Museum to do just that.

The Museum has not abandoned the tried-and-tested approach so beloved by our many visitors, but this new direction introduces new galleries and facilities where the driving aim is to put the visitor in charge. Its research and on-line information points, unprecedented and easy access to collections, and its programme of special exhibitions and events provide an experience that will be unique to each individual visitor. We are as excited about showing you the future as celebrating the past. We promise that every time you visit the Museum you will find something new, something topical, something controversial—something which will make you 'think again'.

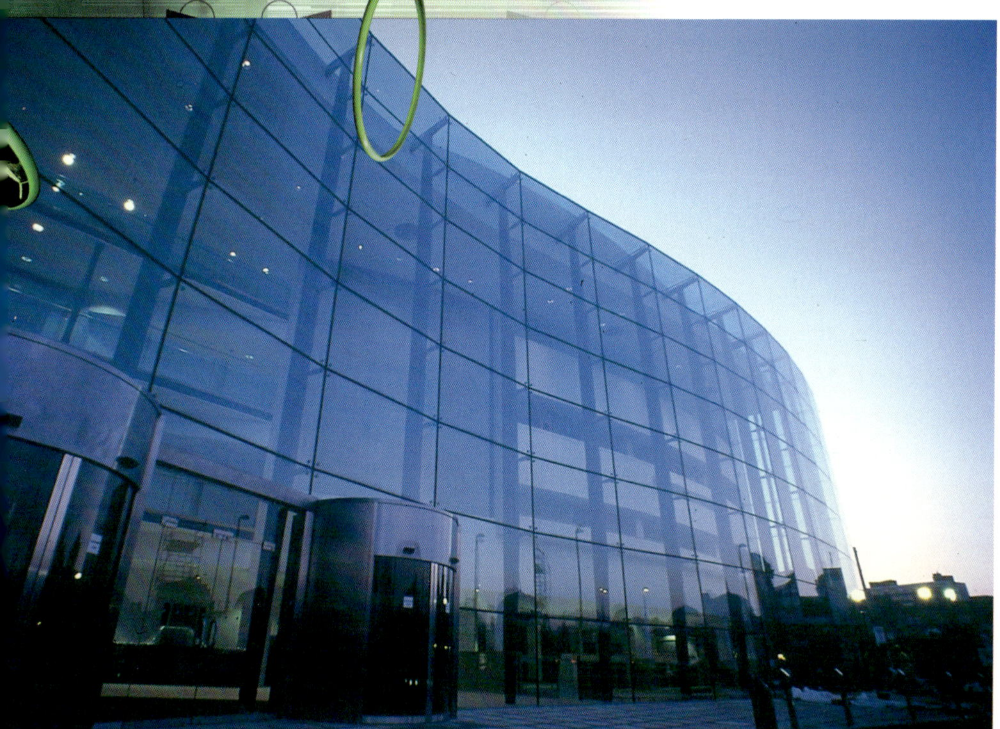

Exterior of the new National Museum of Photography, Film & Television

Pencils, plastic and computers

Michael Harvey
Curator of Cinematography

A grey winter's morning in Manchester. A small group of animators at Cosgrove Hall Films are quietly working at drawing tables. Suddenly one lifts her pencil from the paper and swings it around like a sword. She is acting the movement of the character, working out how to animate the different stages of the action. If you look closely at most animators' drawing boards, you will find a mirror close by at which the animator pulls faces from time to time, just to try out the expression of the character being drawn.

The Comb, *1990. This short film by the Quay Brothers is a homage to the writings of the Swiss author Robert Walser.*

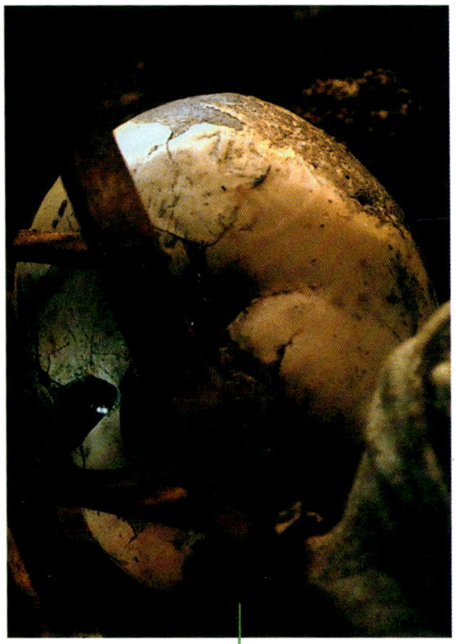

In Bristol, at Aardman Animations, model animators are working in black-tented cubbyholes in one studio, shooting scenes for a series of *Morph*, while in another a huge motion-control camera is being used for an animated shot which will match seamlessly with live action footage in a commercial. Just down the road at Bolexbrothers they're refining the designs for a character in a Woolworth's commercial.

In London, at a studio in a small industrial unit south of the Thames, the American twins Stephen and Timothy Quay are gently adjusting small fragments of mirror to reflect light on to parts of a set for a commercial. Lush red clusters of tomatoes contrast vividly with the browns, blacks and greys of the sets from previous productions which are arranged around the studio. North of the Thames, in crowded Soho, animators are working at computer screens in offices several floors above the bustle of Berwick Street Market or Great Marlborough Street. There is no reason why such artistic activity could not take place out of town, in less expensive accommodation, but they like the buzz of being at the centre of where everything happens in the film and advertising industries. Perhaps it gives their work an extra edge.

'Without art we would die of a surfeit of reality.'
Friedrich Nietzsche (1844–1900), philosopher

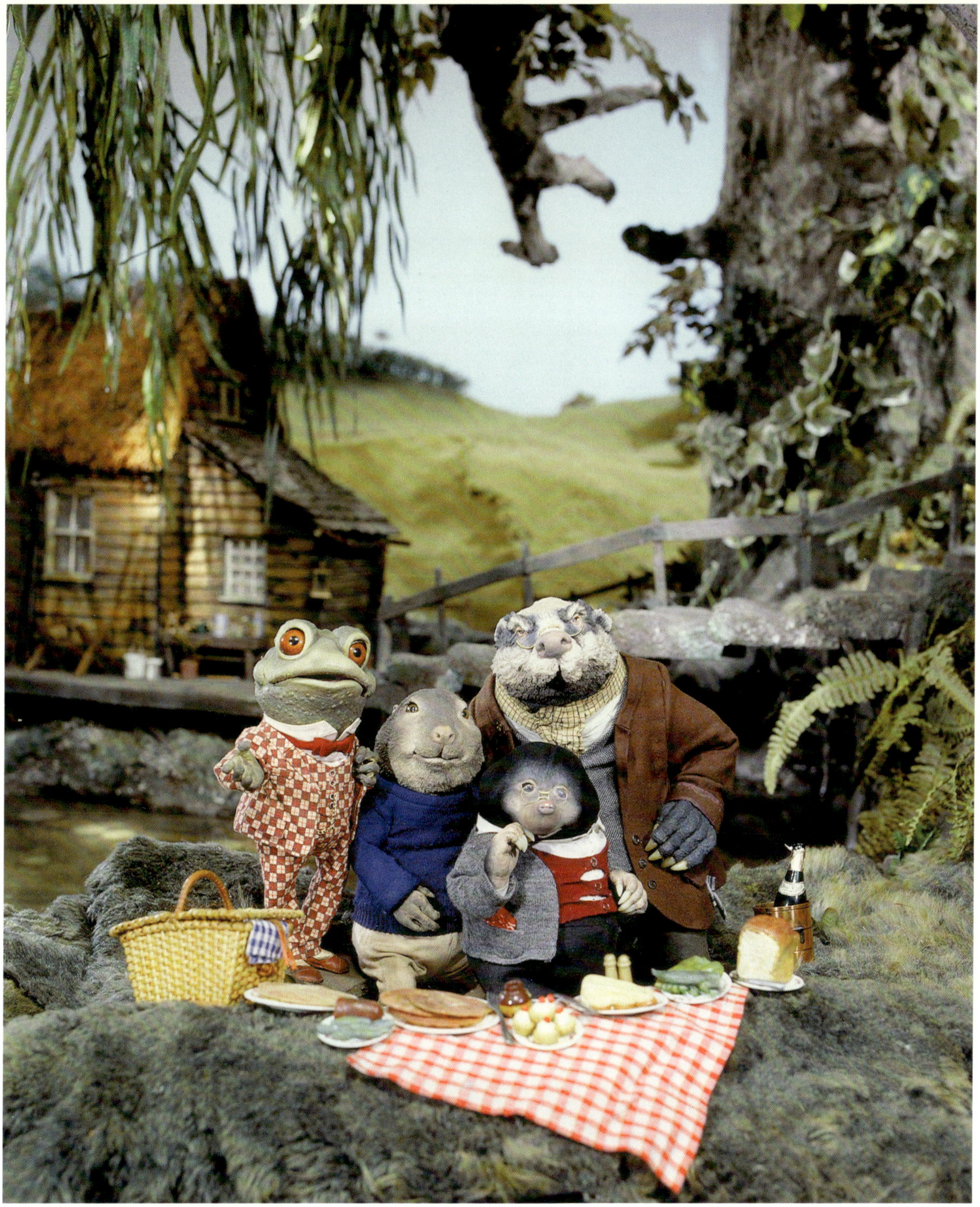

© Cosgrove Hall Films

The Wind in the Willows, *1983. This feature-length model animation, produced by Cosgrove Hall Films, won an International Emmy and a BAFTA award.*

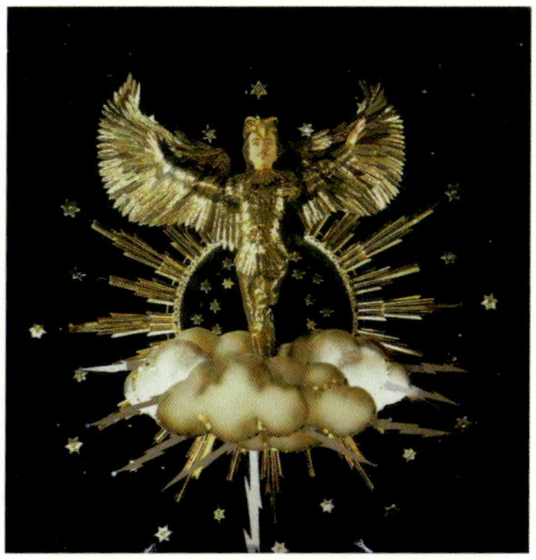

© Aardman Animations Ltd. 1989

Next, *1989, directed and animated by Barry Purves. The film was one of the Lip Sync series produced by Aardman Animations for Channel 4.*

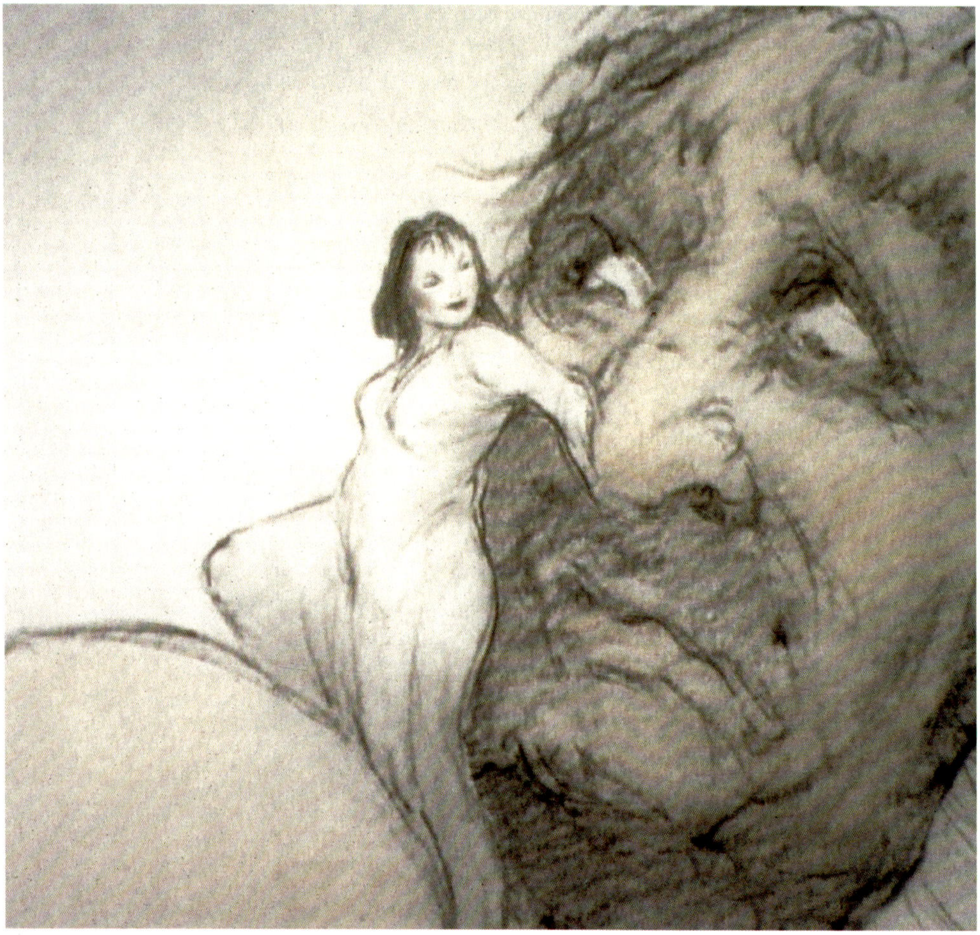

© S4C

The Canterbury Tales, *1998. 'The Wife of Bath's Tale' was animated by Joanna Quinn for the S4C production.*

If you had visited Soho studios in the 1950s or 1960s, you would have seen similar scenes, though everyone at that time was producing hand-drawn animation. Bob Godfrey at Biographic Films was developing his characteristic brand of broad seaside-postcard humour, George Dunning at TV Cartoons was directing the team making The Beatles' *Yellow Submarine*, while over in Soho Square Richard Williams' animation studio was turning out title sequences for *The Charge of the Light Brigade* and *Casino Royale*. The Halas & Batchelor studio was going strong after its success with *Animal Farm* and was producing commercials and television series for British and US television. It had taken over the studio at Stroud where David Hand, lured from the Walt Disney Studios by J Arthur Rank, had attempted to establish a British animation industry along the lines of the American one. The venture failed and British animation settled back to being largely a cottage industry.

Animal Farm, *1954, the first British animation feature, made by Halas & Batchelor.*

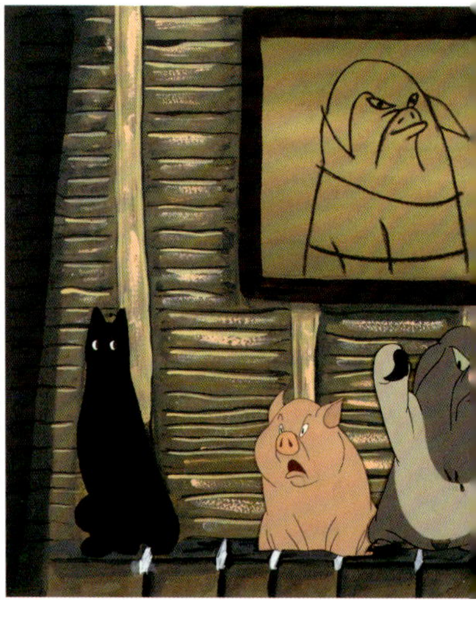

So what has changed since then? For a start, animation is no longer concentrated just in London. There are major studios in Bristol, Manchester and Cardiff, which—and it's no coincidence—are also television production centres. British animation has become a multi-million-pound international business. The most obvious example is Aardman Animations with its Wallace and Gromit characters who, like Disney's Mickey Mouse, are being marketed on a worldwide scale. If anyone doubts the impact of animation, let them reflect on the fact that Wallace and Gromit may be solely responsible for saving the Wensleydale cheese—and the economic infrastructure of Dales farming—from extinction.

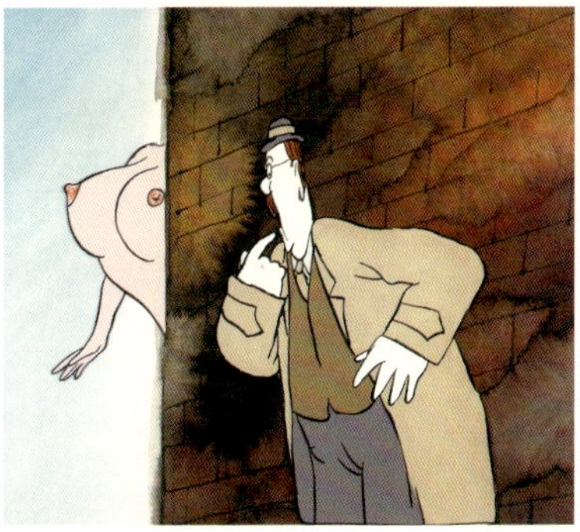

Dream Doll, *1979, a co-production between Bob Godfrey and the Yugoslav animator Zlatko Grgić which was nominated for an Oscar.*

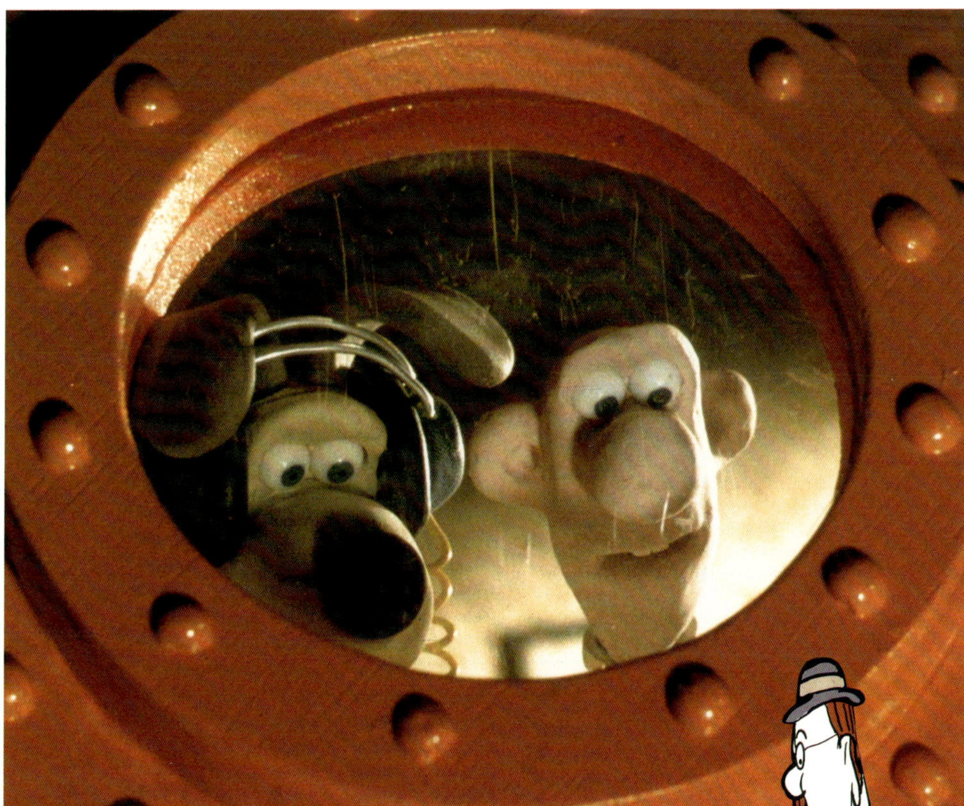

A Grand Day Out, *1989. Directed and animated by Nick Park, this was the first film featuring Wallace and Gromit.*

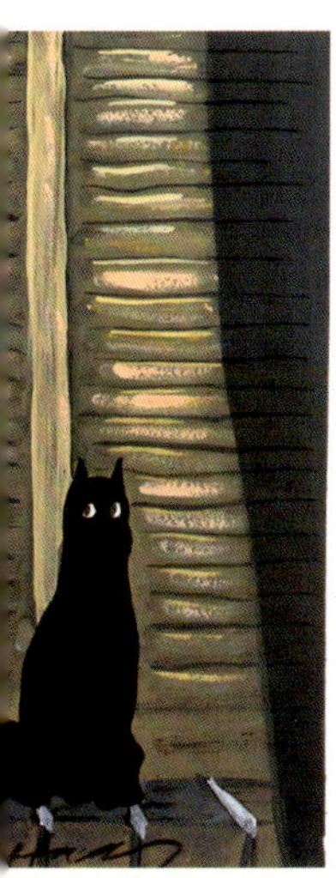

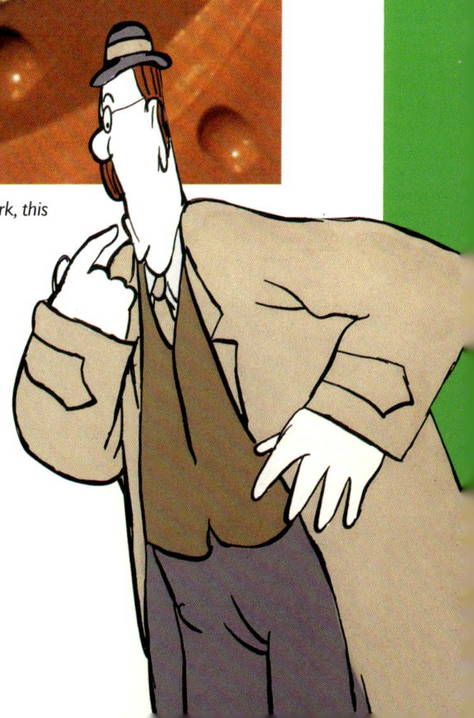

Triangle, 1995. This Oscar-nominated film is one of a trilogy of films devoted to dance, made by Erica Russell for Channel 4.

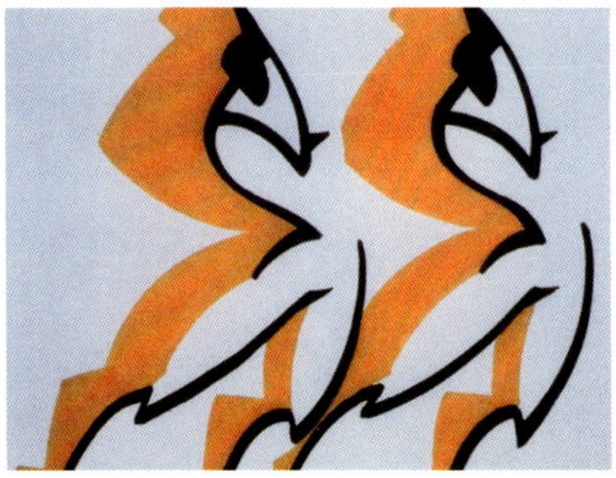

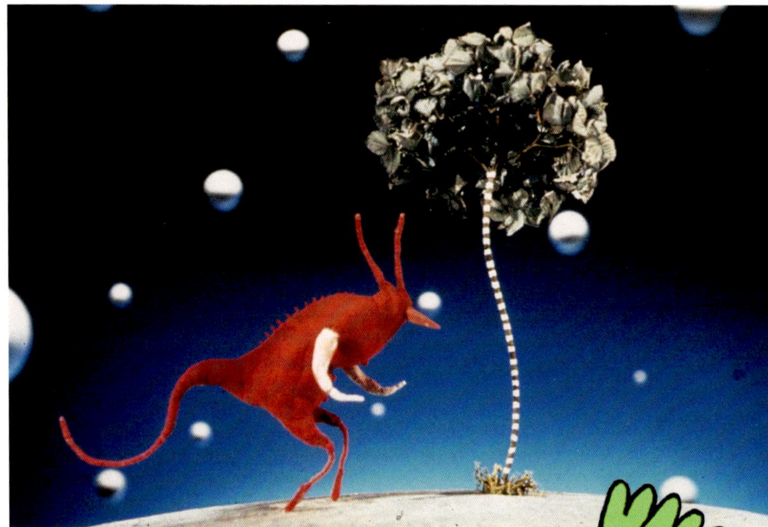

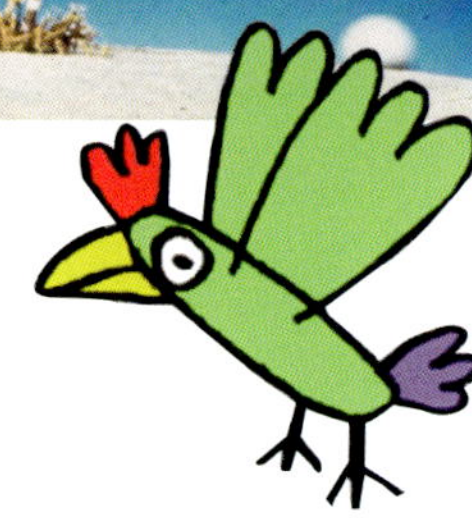

Another difference is that nowadays most animation goes through a computer at some stage, or is computer-generated in the first place. Digital technology is having an increasing impact on animators but, rather than jettisoning time-honoured techniques, they are using it in complex ways, mixing drawn, cut-out or model animation with computer methods. The support of the BBC and Channel 4 Television since the mid 1980s has fostered a renaissance in the industry and widened public appreciation of the variety and scope of animation. For however exhilarating the American cartoon style is—and in the hands of masters like Tex Avery or Chuck Jones it is supremely witty and imaginative—it is still only one aspect of animation. 'If you can't make it good, make it loud and fast,' wryly commented Bill Kroyer, the animator who produced the ground-breaking computer animation for *Tron* in the early 1980s. While he certainly wasn't referring to the classics of American animation, you can see his point: in poor animation, speed and noise can easily replace sensitivity and imagination; in good animation, it never does.

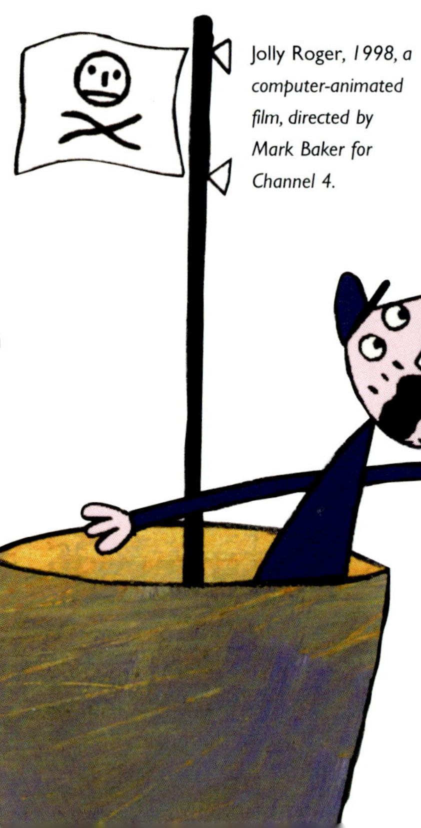

Jolly Roger, 1998, a computer-animated film, directed by Mark Baker for Channel 4.

What British animators have demonstrated, in their uniquely understated British way, is that animation does not always have to be funny nor does it have to pile on lashings of sentiment in order to tug at our heartstrings. There is still a lot of humour in British animation, particularly in commercials where its use has been almost honed to perfection, but it is often subtle or ironic and is used to make social comment. The work of women animators is particularly good in this respect, with Joanna Quinn's Beryl deflating the overweening male ego and Candy Guard revealing the anxieties and fantasies of her thirty-something character Dolly Pond.

Spotless Dominoes, *1991, animated and directed by Philip Hunt while he was a student at the Royal College of Art.*

Peter Lord's work in the early 1980s, in which he animated realistic-looking characters who spoke with the voices of real people, showed that model animation could express the subtle nuances of a character's personality. His series of *Conversation Pieces* are like miniature feature films. It is not surprising that he and the special-effects animator Ray Harryhausen share the view that animation is a form of acting. This opinion is taken further by Barry Purves, the animator responsible for the virtuoso displays of model animation in *Screen Play* and *Rigoletto*. He sees animation as a process of breathing life into inanimate characters, whether they be puppet models or drawings on a celluloid sheet. The animator as a god-like figure or a crazed Frankenstein? Maybe a little of both, though it's hard to decide on a grey winter's morning in Manchester.

On Probation, *1982, directed by Peter Lord and David Sproxton, the two founders of Aardman Animations. It was one of the* Conversation Pieces *series made for Channel 4.*

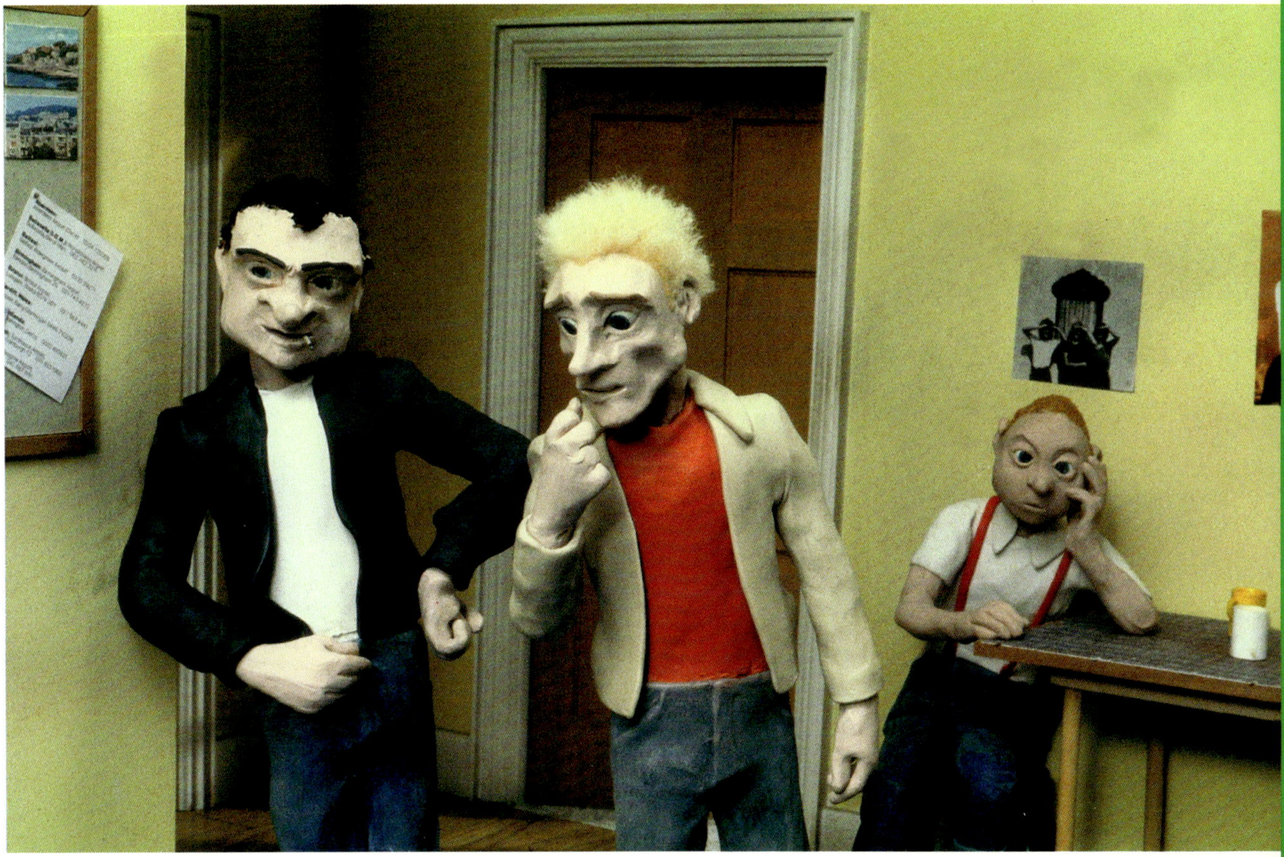

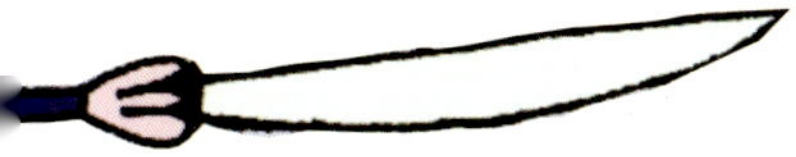

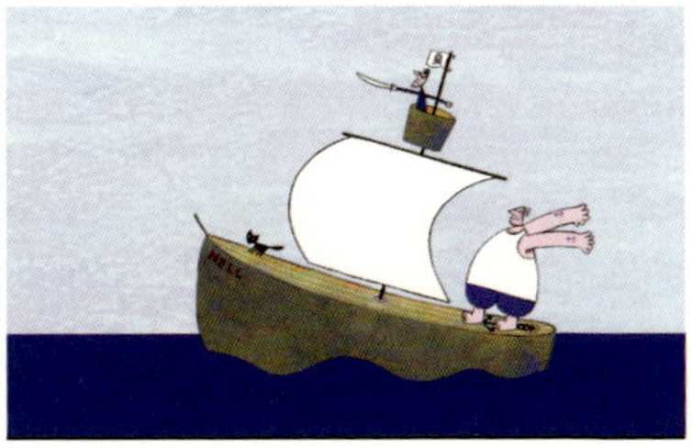

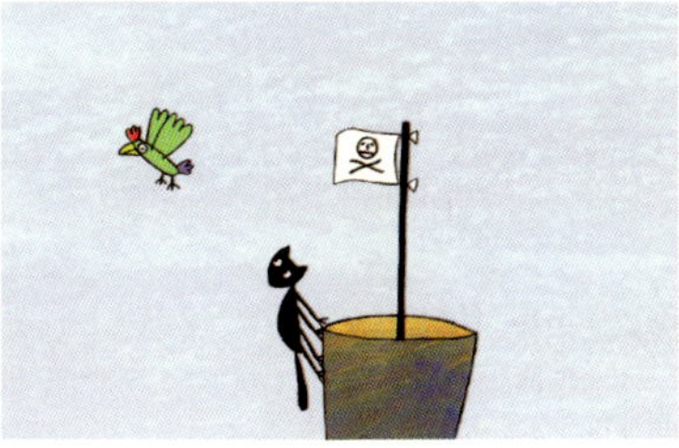

Wired worlds:
exploring the digital frontier

Tony Sweeney
Deputy Head of Museum

'Everything that can be invented has been invented.'
Charles H Duell, Commissioner in the US Office of Patents

The world of images is going digital. Blockbuster movies are created entirely on desktop computers; computer games rival Hollywood for glamour, gore and earnings; robot eyes help us see beyond the limits of human ability; computer screens become windows on to virtual worlds and electronic 'life-forms'. In only a generation since the birth of the computer age we have arrived at a new frontier. Media, computing and telecommunications are converging to create 'wired worlds' where text, images and sounds are flashed around the globe in digital streams of 1s and 0s.

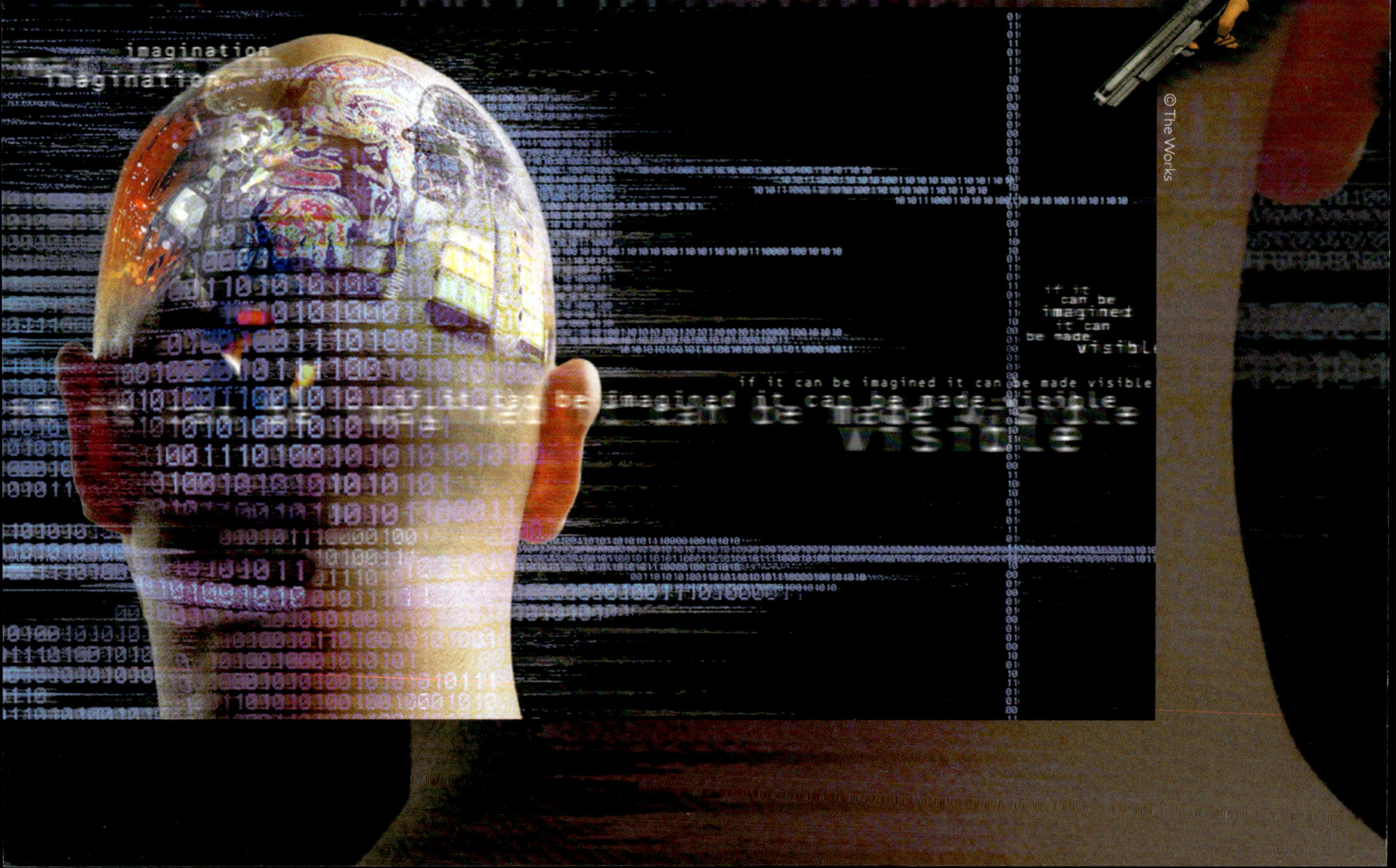

© The Works

Digital electronics power this new information age. Computers may essentially be simple number-crunching tools, but their impact is profound. Computers can represent nearly everything we know about the world—real things and abstract ideas—as digital data. This can be processed, transmitted and shown as still or moving images.

New media have often been disparaged in their early days. In 1876 the US Western Union company said of a new invention: 'This "telephone" has too many shortcomings to be seriously considered as a means of communication…'. Early radio was also summarily dismissed: '…who would pay for a message sent to nobody in particular?' (associates of David Sarnoff, about 1920). Television was seen as 'the biggest time-waster of all time' (Isaac Schoenberg, 1936). Shades of initial reactions to the digital media revolution! Even its own early champions seemed in two minds. In 1977 Ken Olson, founder of the Digital Equipment Corporation, said: 'There is no reason anyone would want a computer in their home'. Perhaps he was thinking about the 1949 prediction in *Popular Mechanics* that: 'Computers in the future may weigh no more than 1.5 tons'! Yet an average household in the industrialised world today contains an abundance of computers or microchip-controlled devices, ranging from CD-audio players and satellite television decoders to pocket calculators and home PCs.

Computers are transforming the ways we work, learn and entertain ourselves, and digital media today are seemingly all-pervasive. We have access to computer-based image capture and manipulation, multimedia information systems, digital animation, interactive games, Internet-based communications, virtual environments and networked communities. The pace of change is breathtaking—new versions of computer hardware and software are launched literally every few months. The same functions could often be performed before through traditional analogue systems, but digital techniques bring new levels of speed and capability, transforming the working practices they affect. Whole new industries are springing up around areas such as interactive computer games, computer-aided design and engineering.

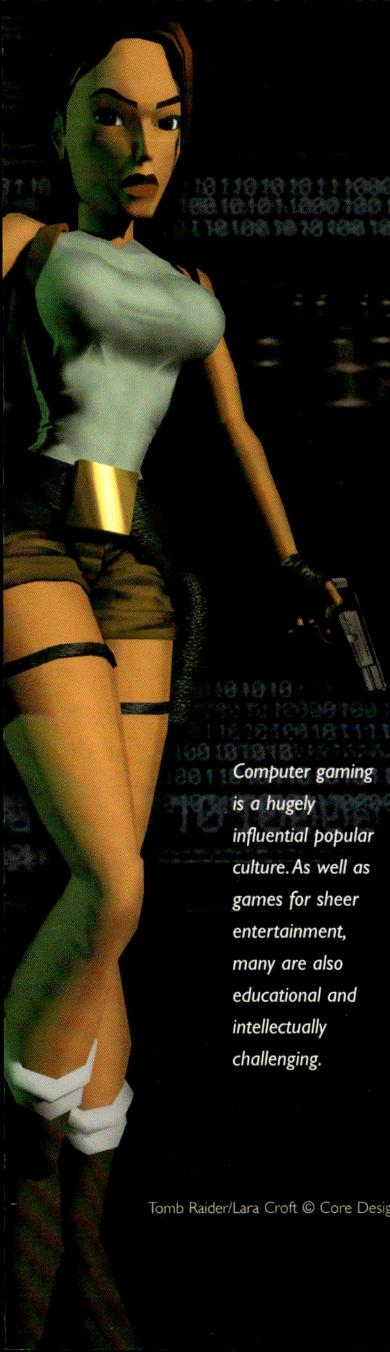

Computer gaming is a hugely influential popular culture. As well as games for sheer entertainment, many are also educational and intellectually challenging.

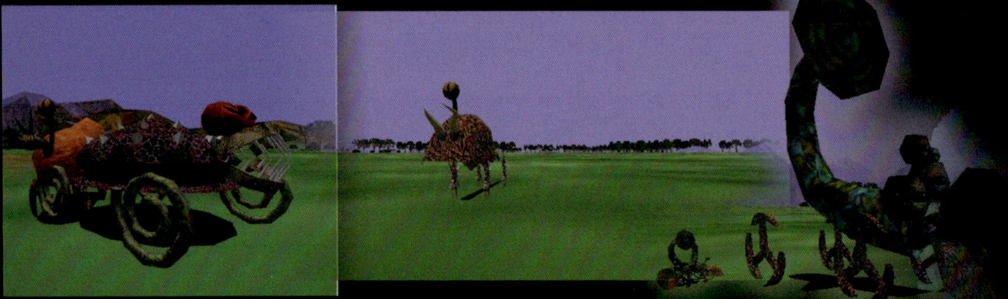

We increasingly record our lives and memories with digital cameras, camcorders and home PCs. The World Wide Web is changing the ways in which we publish and consume information of all kinds, bringing the whole world to our fingertips. Digital technology is driving a massive increase in the choice available to us through many more television channels—of course the question here is, will it also increase programme quality, or just spread it more thinly?

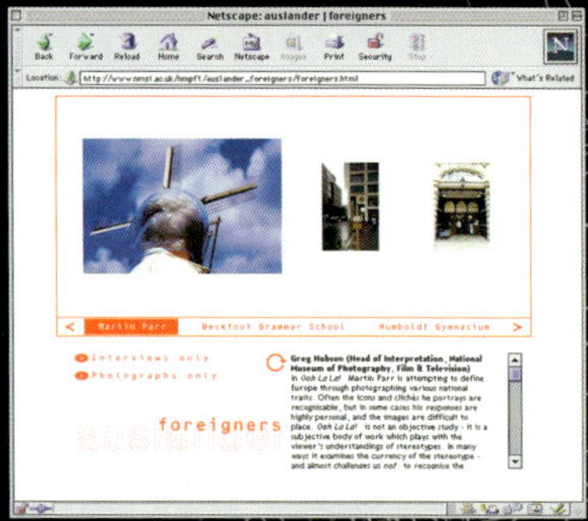

The World Wide Web is transforming how we communicate, educate and entertain ourselves.

Doctors are now able to engage in remote diagnosis, and even perform operations, using cameras and displays coupled to communications networks. Computers are routinely used in advanced medical research: for example, to model the very life processes of the human body and diseases such as cancer.

Digital systems can recreate startlingly real images of destroyed historic buildings and sites in immersive virtual reality displays. The age of the 'virtual actor'—realistic digital animations of humans replacing or supplementing the real thing in films—is upon us. Avatars—personal digital agents on the Web—are becoming more sophisticated and lifelike. The future beckons with the prospect of computers actually embedded in our bodies, automatically responding to our actions and thoughts, acting as intelligent agents of our will.

The digital revolution has more ambiguous aspects, of course. The Internet is often seen as a medium of free speech, enabling communication across virtually all boundaries. It has been used as such by dissidents against authoritarian regimes, for example, to promote resistance campaigns and maintain links to the outside world. Yet the Internet is also a prime means for the distribution of pernicious material such as pornography. News images can be altered in undetectable ways for purposes of propaganda. Individual faces in a crowd can be picked out and tracked automatically by computer-surveillance systems. The ability of computers to store and analyse huge amounts of information raises the spectre of a 'Big Brother' society. It

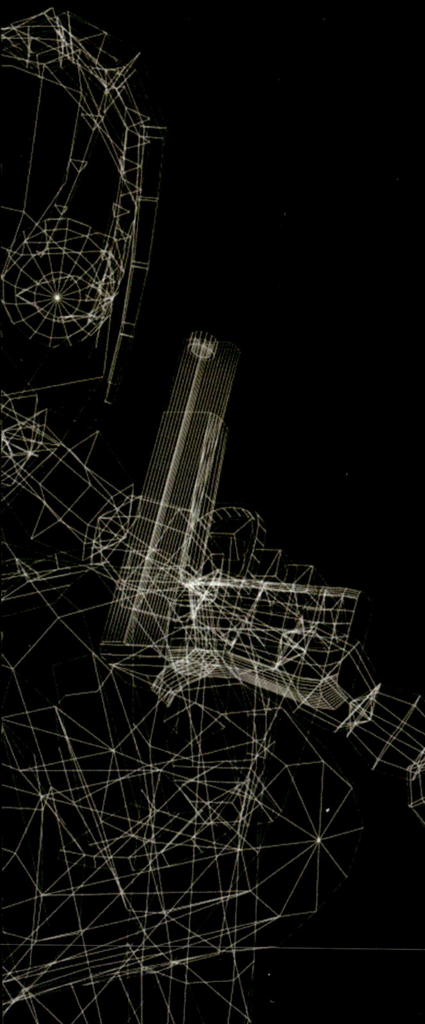

seems impossible to tame or censor the explosive growth and innovation in digital media.

Digital media are affecting society in other ways too. They are increasingly the means through which we communicate, receive information and model events and things. They provide new ways of seeing and exploring the real world; new creative methods to picture the world of the imagination and artificial worlds generated by computer programs. This capacity to make clear the hidden fundamentals of our world, and to make unreal or artificial worlds visible, can open us up to new perspectives on life. Established notions of storytelling, place, time, community and identity are shifting. The very ways in which we understand ourselves and others are changing.

Proponents of the new digital technologies look forward to a bright knowledge-rich future, yet ignore the massive global disparities in access to the media and the skills needed to engage with and benefit from it. Opponents predict a fragmented de-socialised future, but fail to see the dynamic new forms of global interaction and opportunities for creating wealth which are emerging in this new world. Yet, arguably, technology itself is neither good nor bad. Its impact depends on how it is used by producers and consumers, by groups and individuals. By choosing to explore the digital frontier, we can help shape the wired worlds that we increasingly inhabit.

Charles H Duell's assertion that invention is dead was made in 1899. A century on, in the age of cyberspace, humankind's inventiveness seems more vibrant than ever.

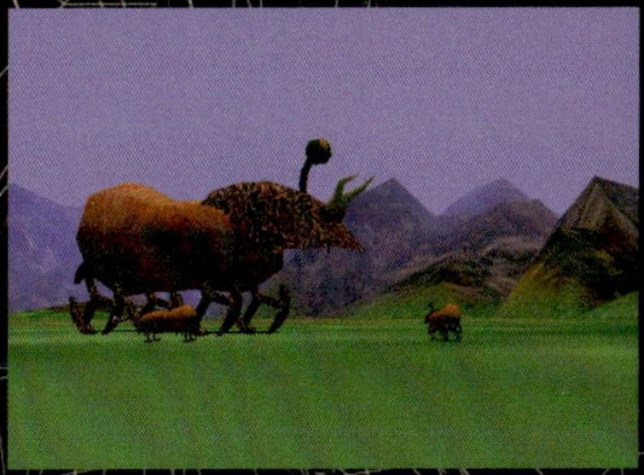

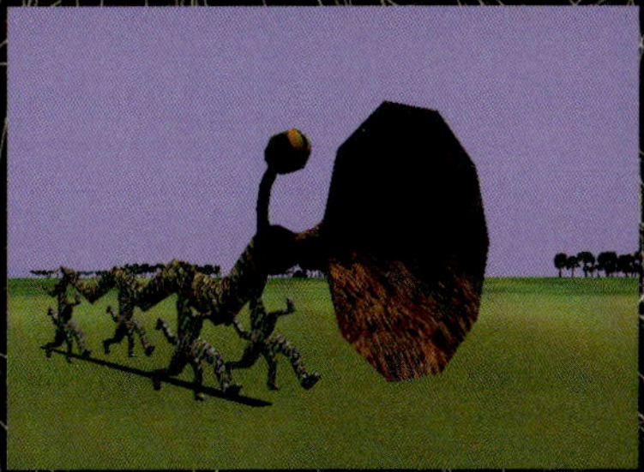

TechnoSphere © Jane Prophet, Gordon Selley and Digital Workshop

Artificial life programs can model complex ecosystems where the 'virtual' creatures behave independently—'living', reproducing and responding to each other and their environment.

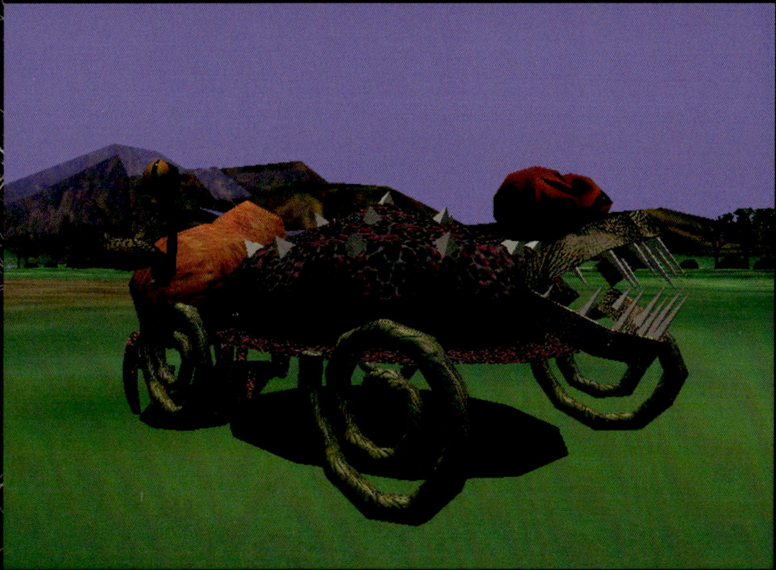

TechnoSphere © Jane Prophet, Gordon Selley and Digital Workshop

The world through their eyes

Sarah Mumford
Head of Education

Only at the National Museum of Photography, Film & Television can you do all these things: find out how Wallace and Gromit came to life, watch films on one of the largest screens in the world, interact with digital images and see live news as it happens. All this is marvellous entertainment, but there is much more to it than just fun.

Photography, film, television—and now digital technologies—are all around us. Media products are created for different reasons and audiences. The film version of a story differs from the book version. Tabloid news is not the same as broadsheet or television news. Underneath the glossy images, good advertising is cleverly composed to get its message across.

Learning about how news photographs, television programmes, films, advertisements and computer games are made is a key to understanding how these media products affect our lives so deeply. The Museum's driving aim is to help visitors take charge of the image-led world, to become more aware and 'media literate' and to enjoy doing it.

'I thought all of it was brilliant. I liked the area with the broadcasting equipment, cameras and models. You can learn things by seeing what goes on in a TV studio and what it would be like working there, doing the jobs. It is also good for young children to see how TV programmes are made.'

Eighteen-year-old male visitor

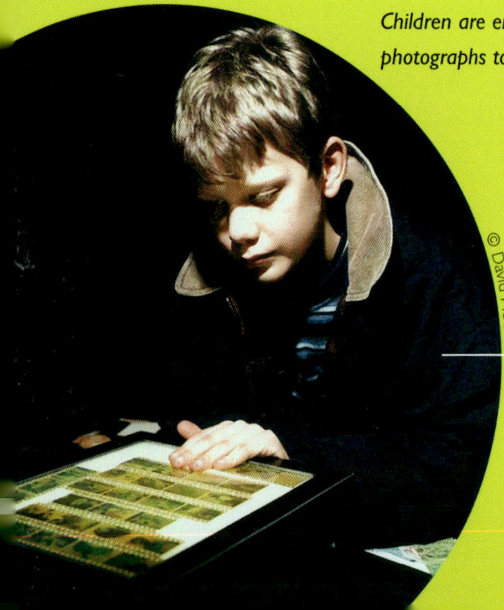

Children are encouraged to look closely at photographs to develop their visual literacy.

© David Moore

'Mirror, mirror on the wall'—**The Magic Factory: Making Light Work.**

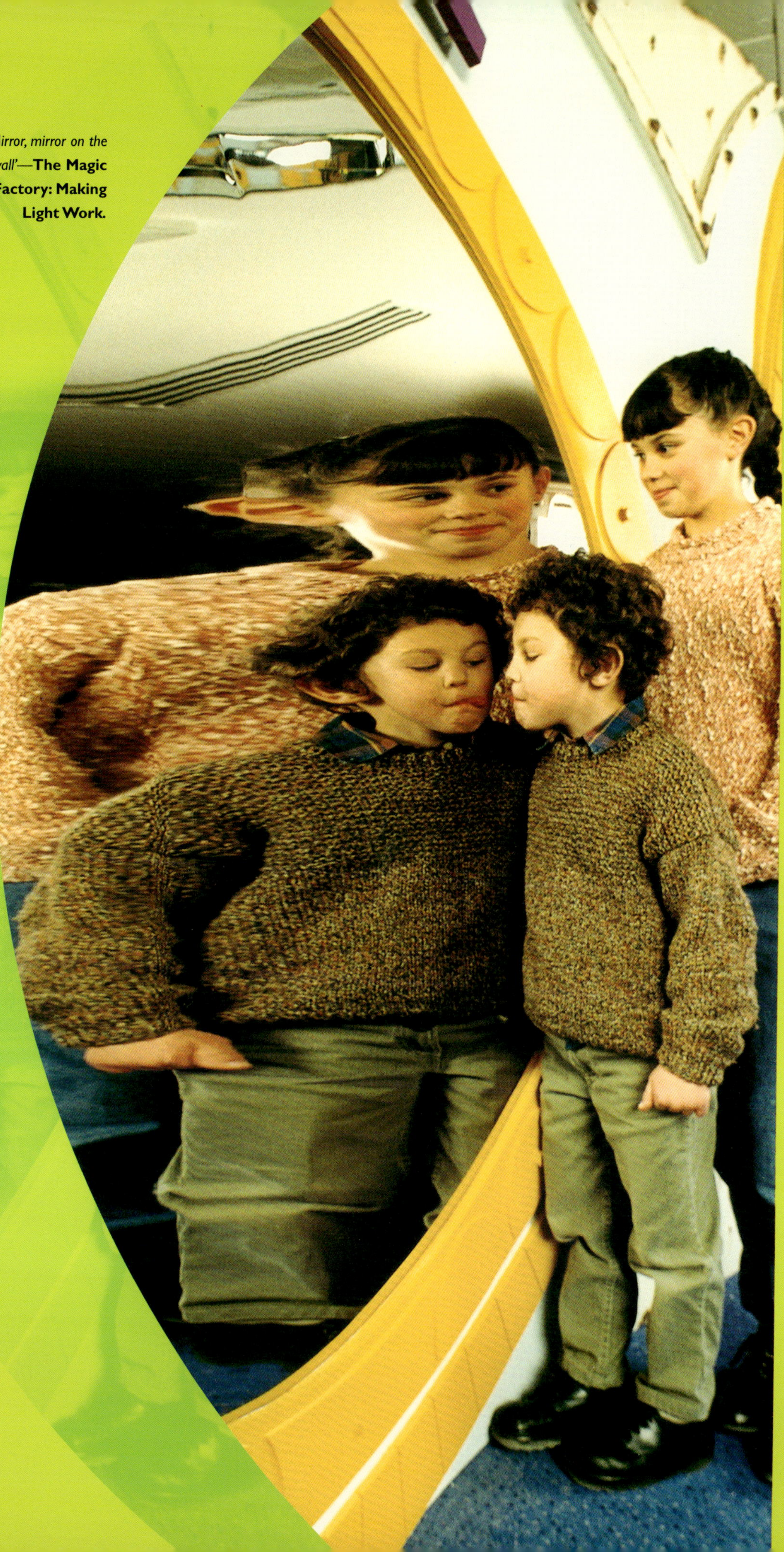

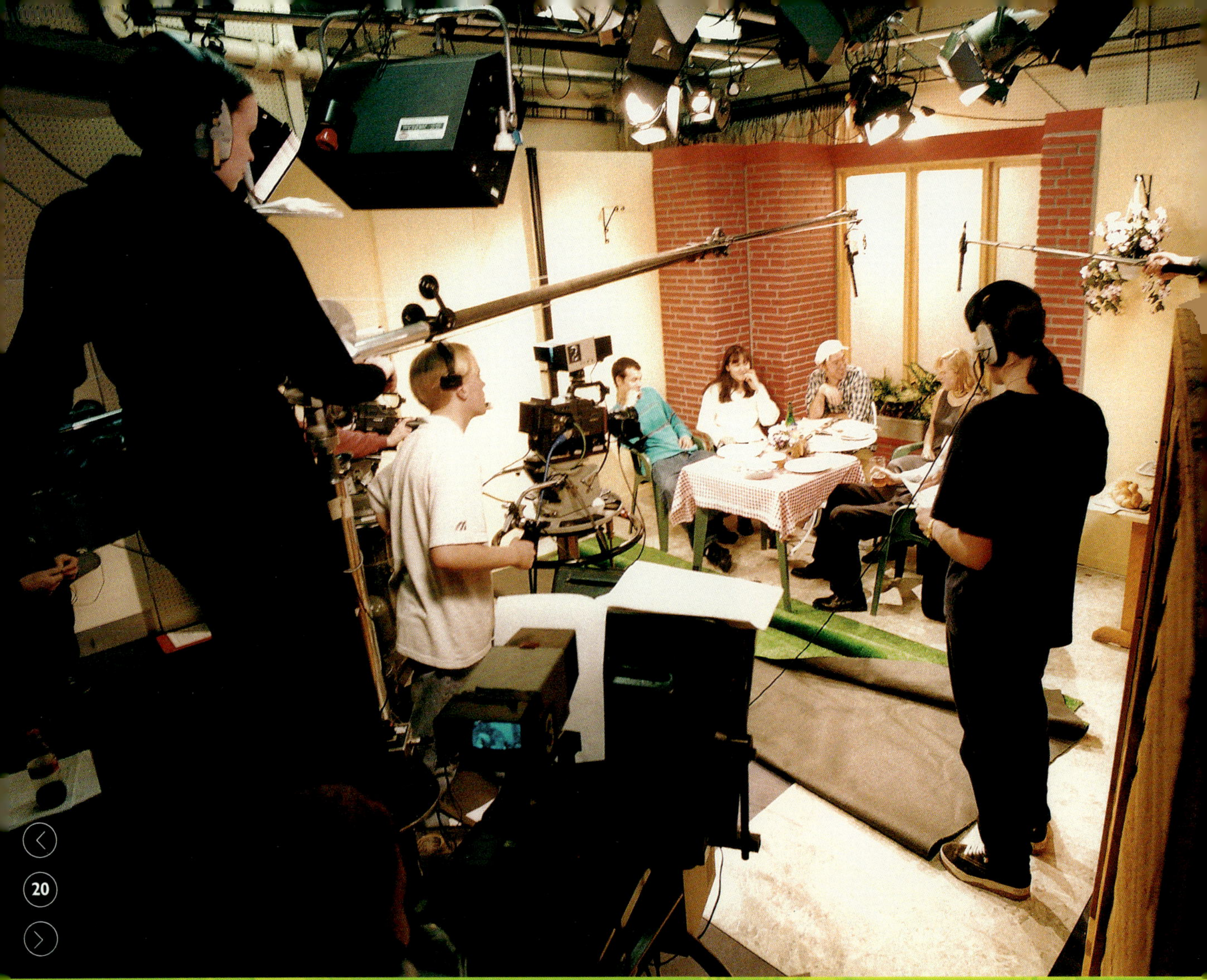

Using real equipment to make a TV programme in the ***Production Studios****.*

Many people want more than simple pre-packaged information. Real knowledge comes from questioning, from looking at a range of options and opinions. Curiosity is often strongest among the young, so the Museum pays particular attention to their needs. A child's interest nurtured from an early stage can often blossom into a life-long passion. However, in this new era of digital communication, education cannot stop after school or college, so the Museum also provides learning experiences for all ages.

We learn most effectively when we actually *do* things, not just watch or read about them. Children are naturally active learners, and many of the Museum's galleries encourage children of all ages to get involved with different aspects of the media.

Learning also takes place by means of the NMPFT's Web pages.

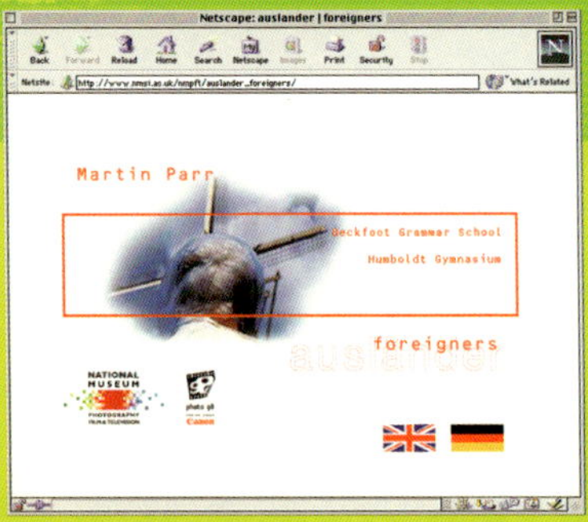

The Magic Factory: Making Light Work gallery, for example, is designed specifically for 7–12- year-olds. Children can explore and discover how light 'works', which helps them to understand how they see the world through their own eyes. They can learn about how 3D images are created and discover some of the basic principles of how cameras capture images. ***The Magic Factory*** is designed specifically to meet the needs of National Curriculum Science, so time spent here is not only great fun, but helps with school work too.

The many exhibitions at the NMPFT help to bring a new understanding of the media to visitors of all ages.

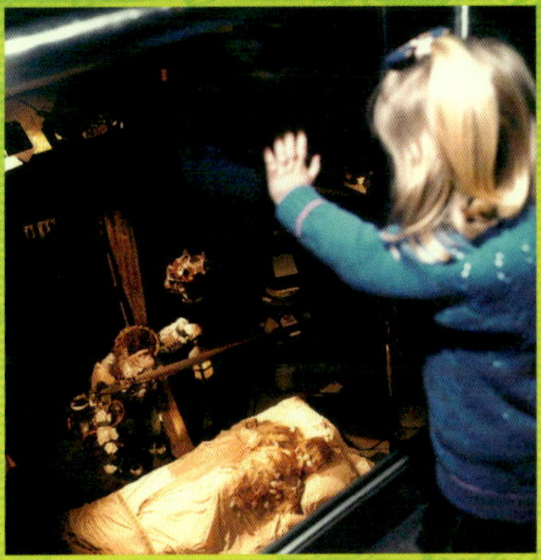

© David Moore

As children grow into teenagers, their media interests change and expand. The IMAX® cinema, with a screen 20 metres wide, offers a taste of spectacular adventures that few young people will ever experience at first hand. Travelling with Africa's wild animals across the Serengeti, exploring the Grand Canyon, or gazing in awe at the haunting beauty of the Earth seen from outer-space—the IMAX experience feels 'so real, you'll think you're there'. Learning behind the scenes about how the IMAX cameras and technology work provides a fascinating contrast to those on-screen adventures.

You can spend your holidays animating in the free drop-in workshops—fun for all!

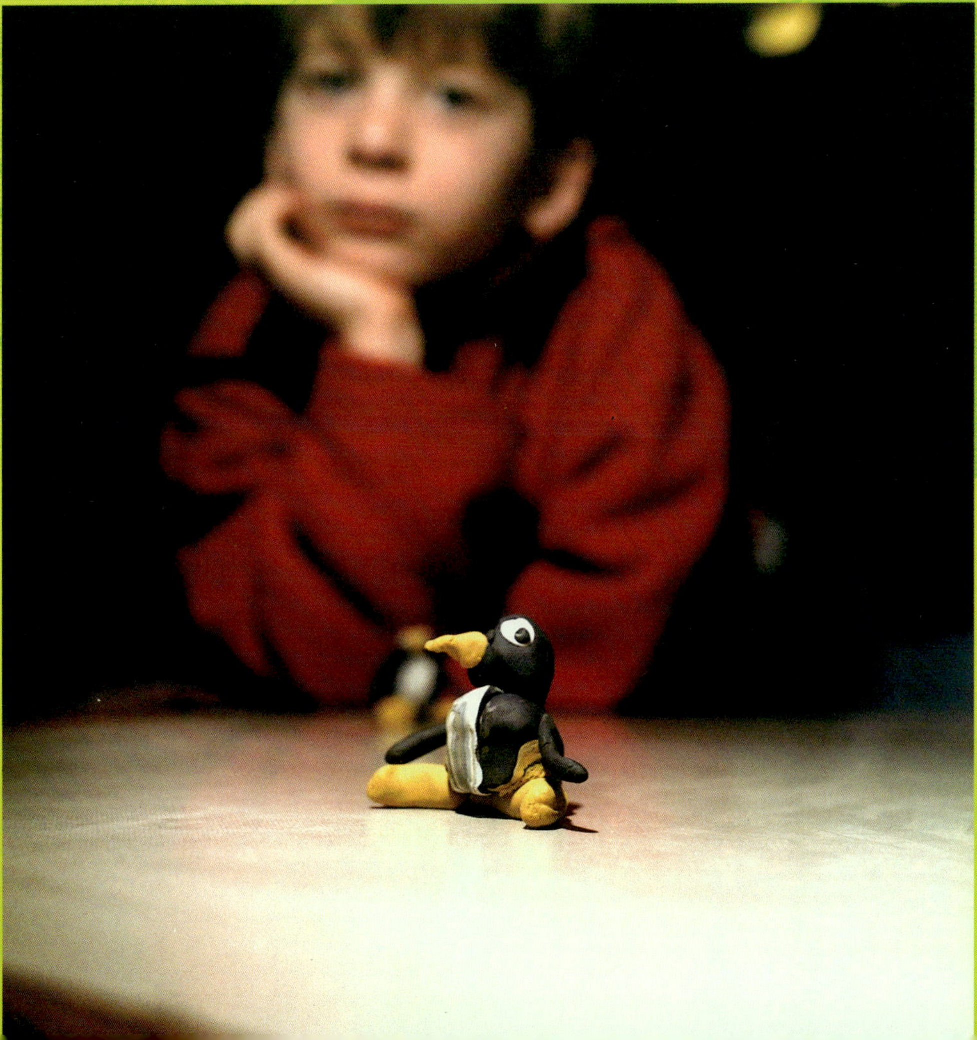

© David Moore

Teenagers are also prime targets for many of today's advertising campaigns, selling anything from cosmetics and clothes to cans of fizzy drink. ***Advertising: The Persuaders' Art*** helps young people understand how these advertisements persuade them to buy certain products and reveals the creative heights and depths to which advertisers will go to win awards—as well as the viewers' money!

Reflecting another aspect of the media, the ***News: Frontlines, Headlines, Deadlines*** gallery tackles images often of a controversial and challenging nature. From salacious pictures taken by the international paparazzi, to harrowing scenes of war and famine, news images have a profound influence on how we see and understand the world. Knowing about the way news is constructed, and being able to identify its use of stereotypes and even propaganda, are essential to forming truly independent opinions in an age when the 'spin-doctors' have so much influence on the media.

'Fantastic and futuristic and hands-on; there are buttons to press, magic carpets to fly on, the news to read ...'
Guardian

During the school holidays the Museum offers hands-on workshops for the whole family. As well as analysing the media, visitors can produce their own animations, take photographs or create their own newspapers. In the Museum's ***Production Studio***, they can use professional equipment to make short television programmes. Operating the cameras, vision mixer and autocue—or performing in their own production, then watching themselves on screen—gives visitors a slice of 'real' action.

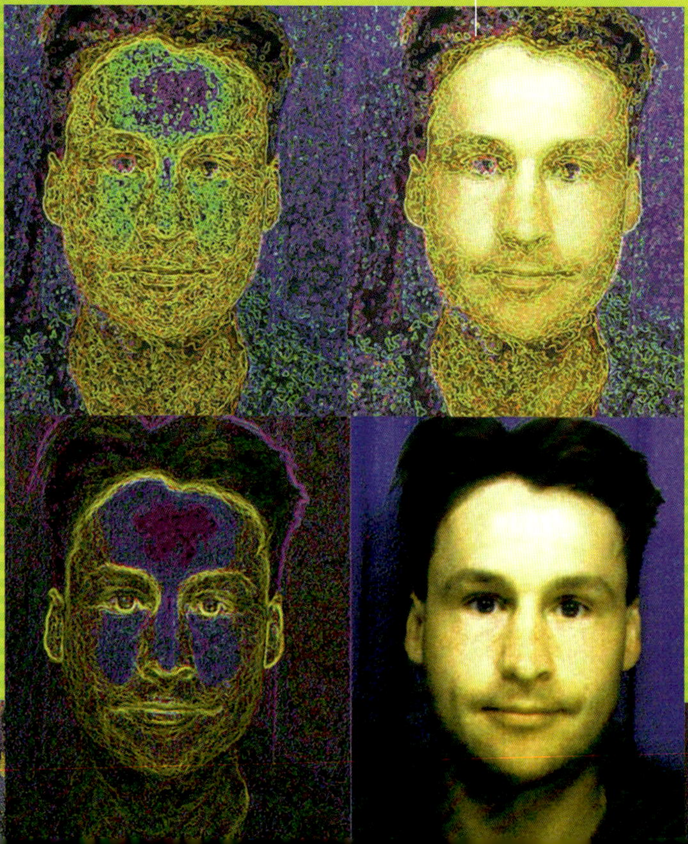

Photograph manipulated by Graham Collier using Adobe Photoshop as part of the BSc Electronic Imaging and Media Communications course, taught jointly by the NMPFT, the University of Bradford, and Bradford College.

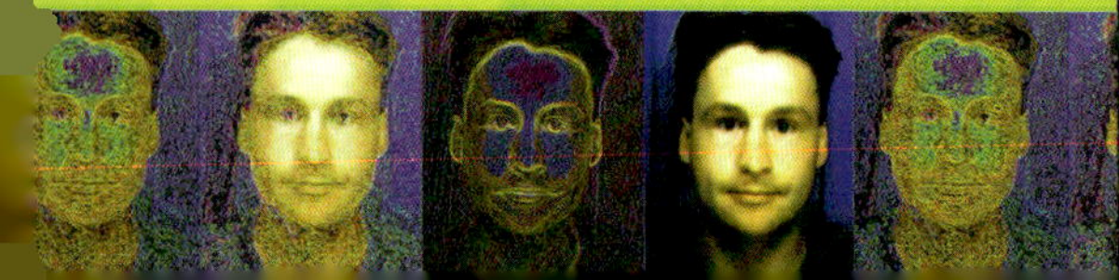

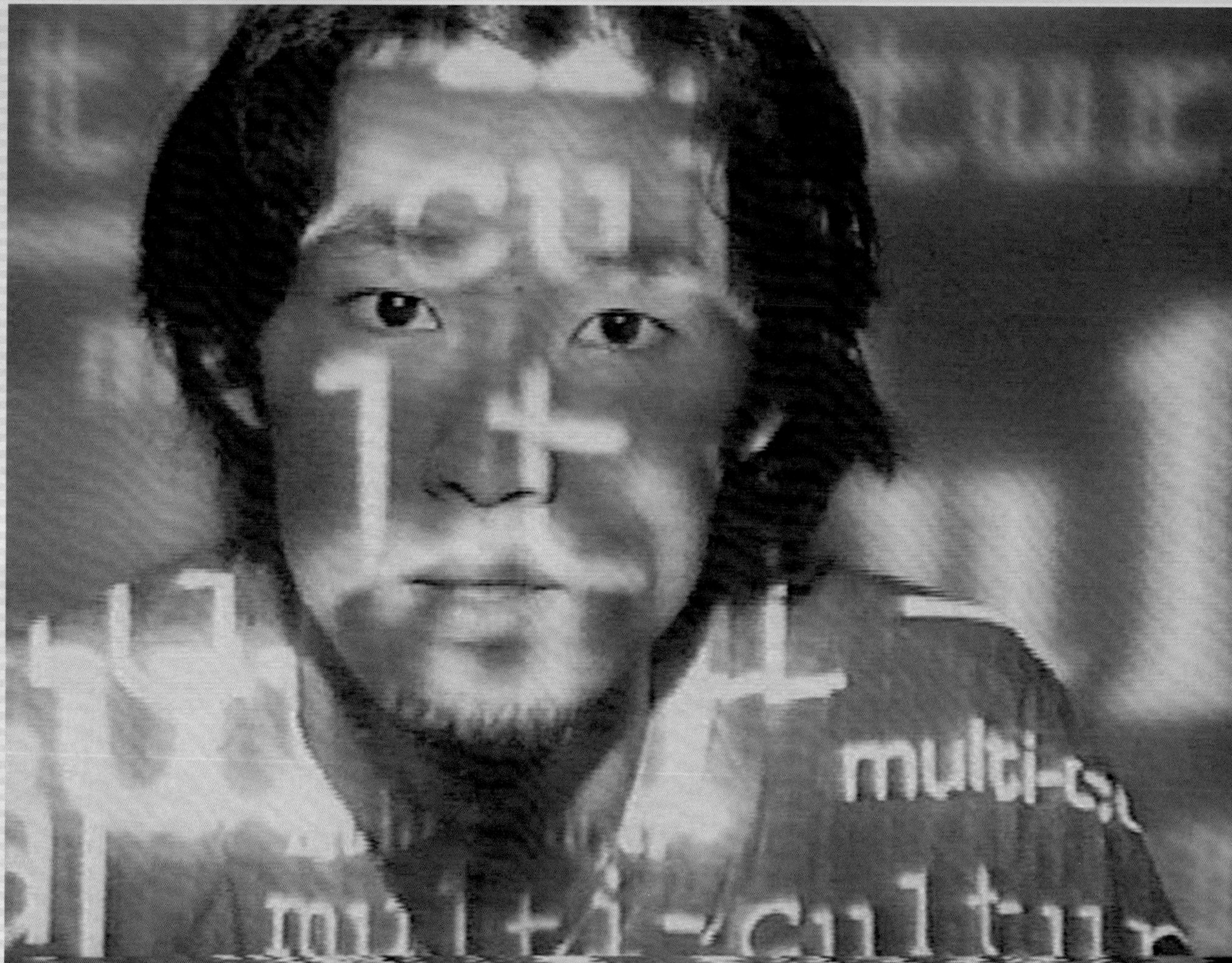

'Feeding the Stereotypes', a third-year project by Richard Hilson carried out as part of the BSc Electronic Imaging and Media Communications course.

The Museum is also an invaluable educational centre for university and college students taking media-related courses. For example, in partnership with the University of Bradford and Bradford College, the Museum delivers a pioneering undergraduate degree course in digital media production and communications. The 300 students a year who use the Museum as a resource for their studies learn how to make television programmes, wrestle with film theory, write programs for CD-ROMs or develop animated computer games.

Whatever their age and experience, visitors to the Museum tend to learn much more than they expected. Many find new or surprising perspectives that change the way they view the media—and often, as a result, how they think about themselves and the world around them. How perceptive of the visitor who, as he was leaving, said cheerfully: 'Now that was a real education—I never realised it could be such pure fun'!

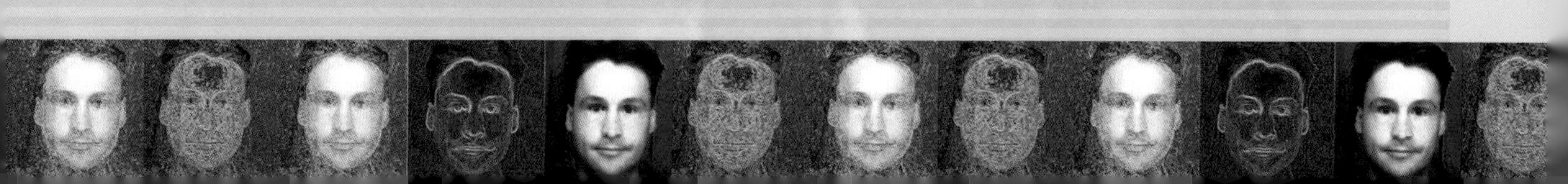

Locomotion:
a public artwork by Ron Haselden

Greg Hobson
Head of Interpretation

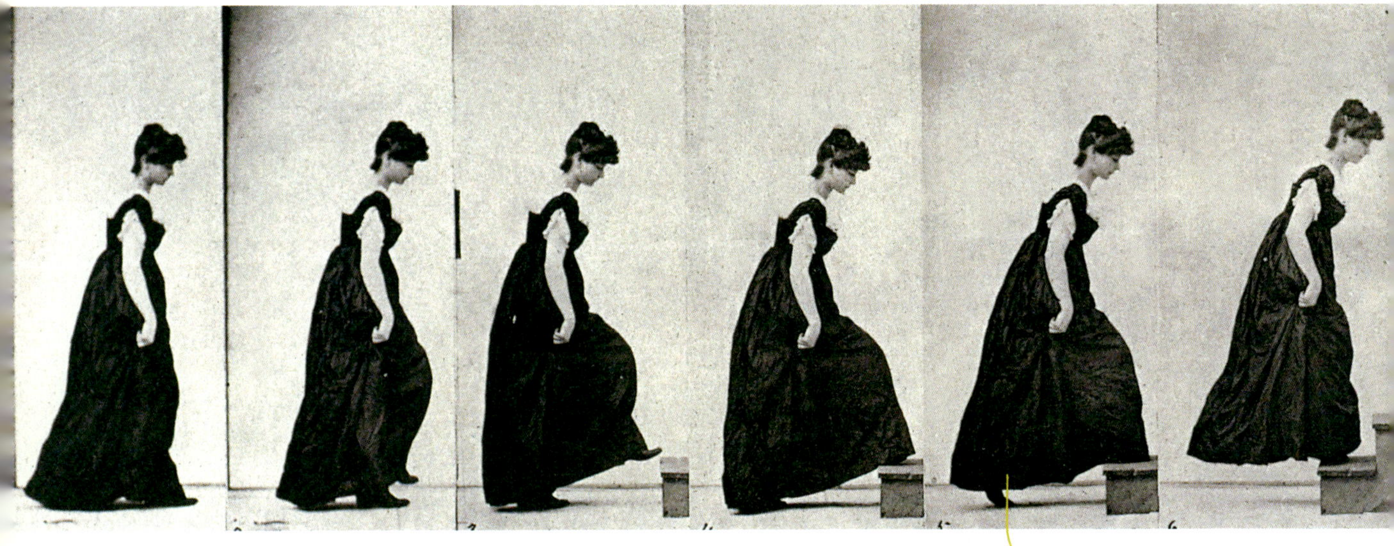

'In my opinion, you cannot say you have thoroughly seen anything until you have got a photograph of it, revealing a lot of points which otherwise would be unnoticed.'
Emile Zola (1840–1902), novelist

When considering where to look for references for his neon sculpture for the rear atrium of the National Museum of Photography, Film & Television, it was no surprise that artist Ron Haselden chose Eadweard Muybridge's remarkable studies of human and animal figures in motion. The photographs, made between 1872 and 1886, caused a sensation when they were originally published and have been an inspiration to artists and scientists ever since, from Degas and Rodin through to the rock band U2! Muybridge's work is as influential and exciting today as it was when first seen.

The somewhat eccentric Muybridge was born in England in 1830. Changing his name from Edward James Muggeridge to Eadweard Muybridge, he moved to the USA in the 1850s. By the 1860s Muybridge had established a reputation as a professional photographer. In 1872 he was contacted by wealthy businessman Leland Stanford to settle a wager. During an argument with fellow horse enthusiasts, Stanford had bet $25,000 on how horses' legs were positioned during a trot. He wanted Muybridge to use his camera to settle the dispute.

'Animal Locomotion', Plate 173

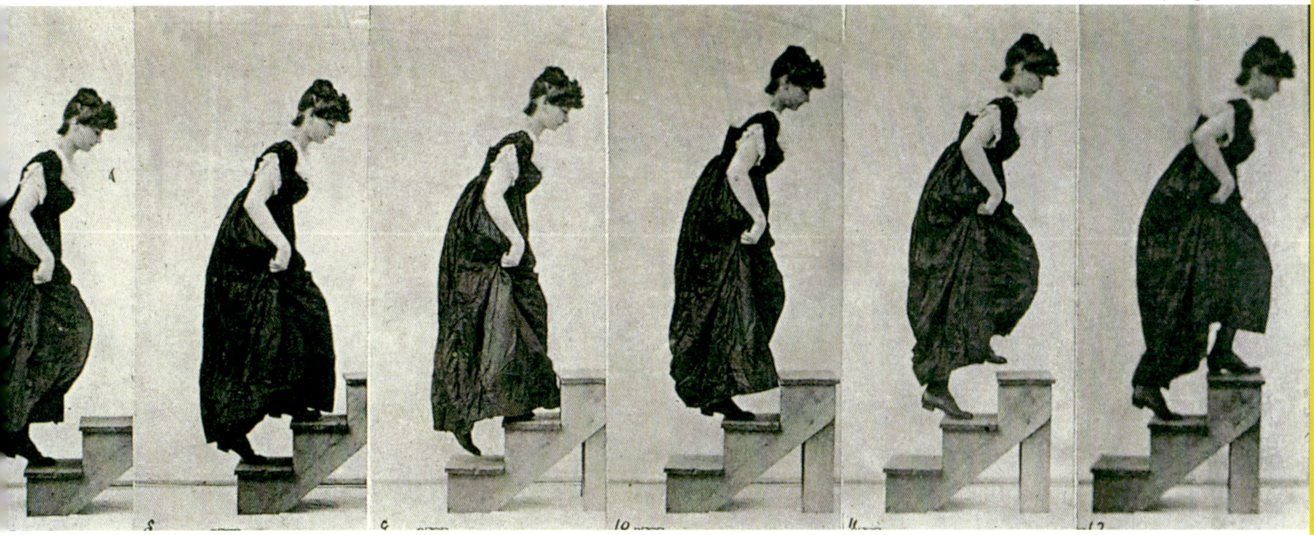

Though Muybridge was able to resolve the wager, the photographs were single images rather than image sequences. Muybridge's life took a turn in another direction when he was accused, tried and subsequently acquitted of the murder of his wife's lover, and he was unable to return to his experiments until 1877. However, by that time he had perfected a shutter movement that was fast enough to capture motion in a more reliable way. Muybridge received funding from Stanford and then from the University of Pennsylvania for his experiments, which enabled him to create an unparalleled dictionary of many thousands of action photographs. Eight hundred of these were selected for publication. By that time Muybridge's interest had extended beyond horses to embrace all manner of living things, including dogs, ostriches and lions. Most intriguing are his photographs of the human form: running, jumping, climbing and dancing men and women, nude and dressed, feature in this vast study. In 1900 Muybridge returned to England, where he lived until his death in 1904.

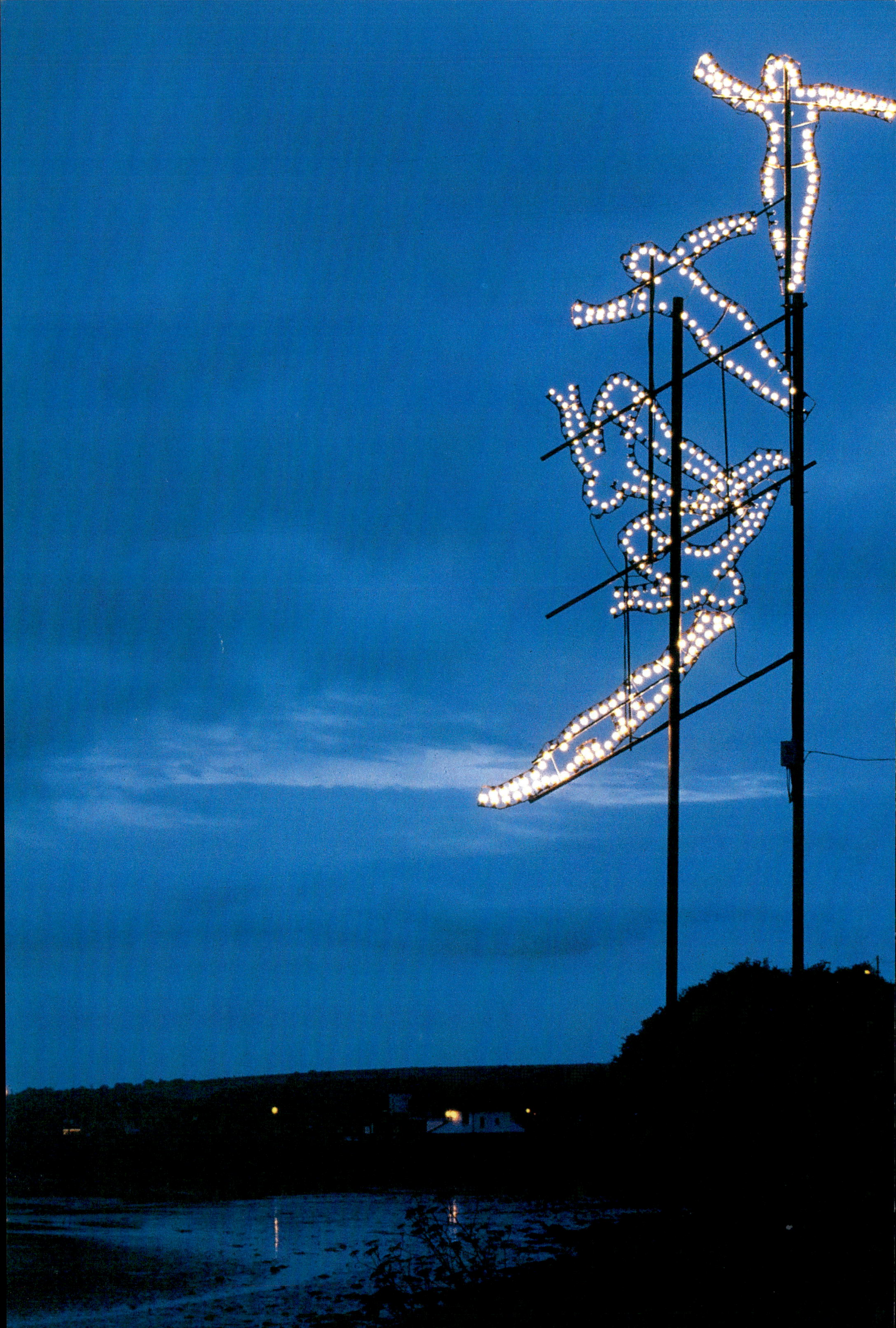

'Diver', Tate, St Ives

For artist Ron Haselden, the choice of Muybridge's photography as the model for his work was a natural one. Haselden wanted to convey movement, yet hint at the romance of the still image. He wanted to evoke elements suggesting the range of media the Museum interprets and he wanted to include interactivity, a key aspect of the Museum experience. The images he chose as the model for his work are both elegant and puzzling: they suggest a kind of surreal theatre, an almost pointless act photographed just for the sake of it. Yet there is a point to it. Muybridge has recorded something that is not normally seen, or is taken for granted, and in doing so has made something extraordinary from the ordinary. Haselden's neon sculpture echoes that transformation. In creating a homage to Muybridge, Haselden celebrates the powerful, enduring nature of the photographic image and its ability to transcend time and medium through its far-reaching influence.

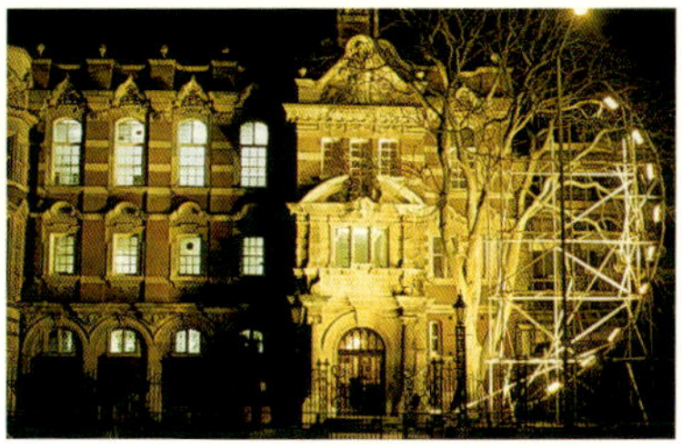

'Golden Crescent', South London Gallery, London

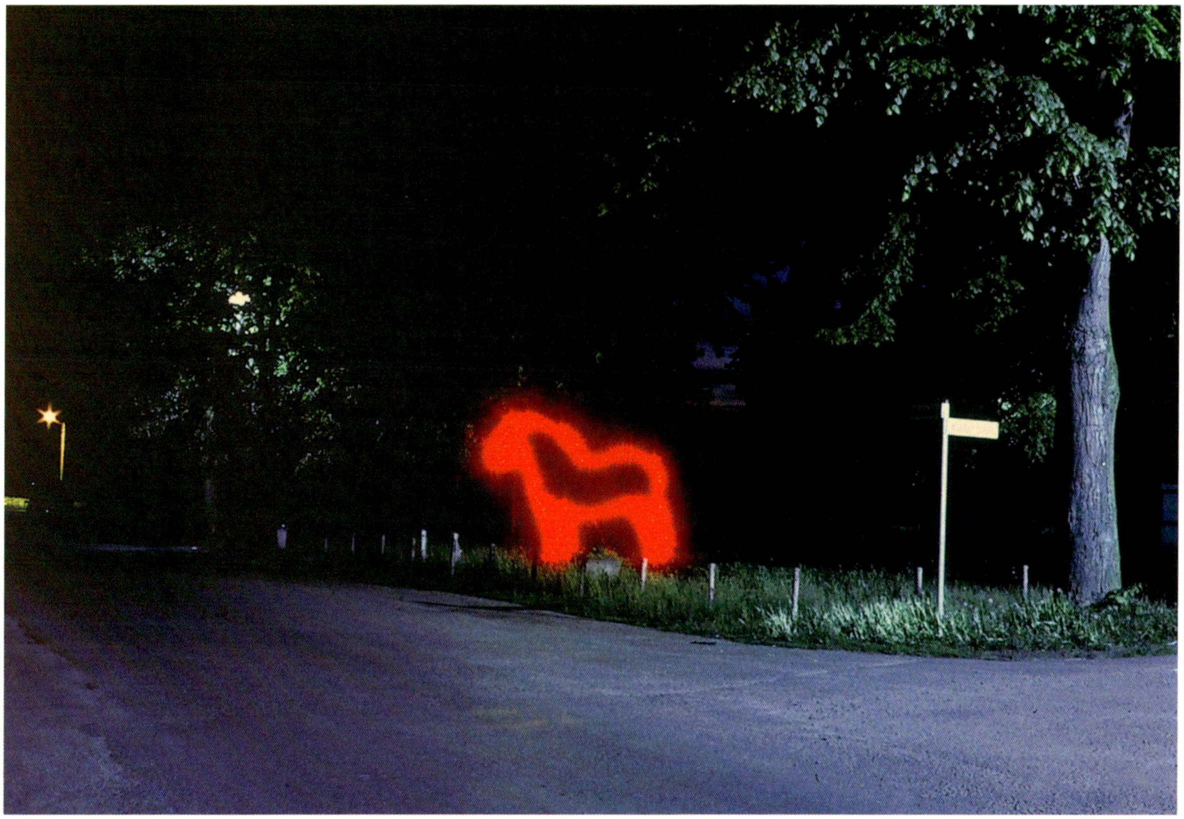

'Drewen Horse', Drewen, Germany

And the winner is . . .
A brief guide to film awards

Bill Lawrence
Head of Cinema

'The Golden Globes are fun. The Oscars are business.'
Warren Beatty, film actor and director

28

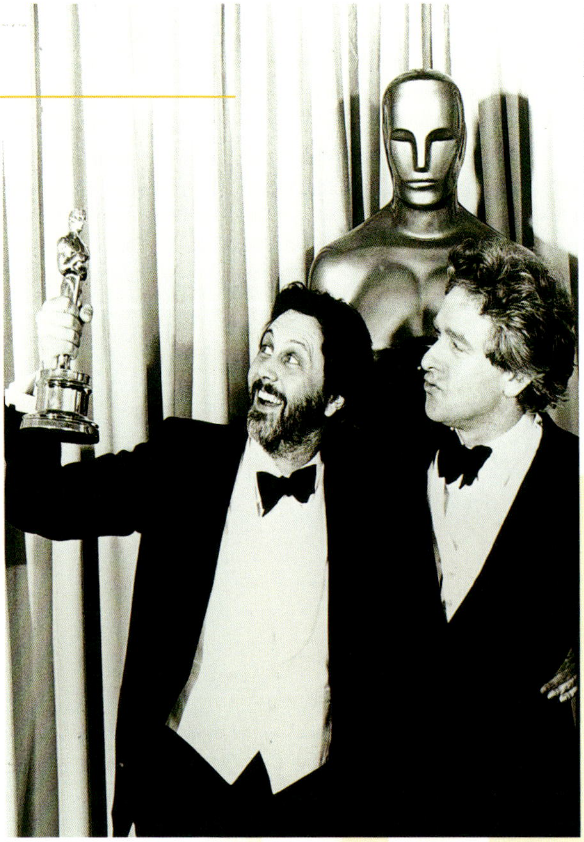

David Puttnam and Hugh Hudson receiving an Academy Award™ for Best Picture of 1981 for Chariots of Fire.

Cinema is about glitz, glamour and success against the odds. The ultimate synthesis of those magical elements is the annual Academy Awards™ ceremony in March, better known as the Oscars.

Each year film studios pour millions of dollars into selling their movies to the members of the Academy of Motion Pictures, Arts and Sciences® in the hope of winning a nomination and the chance to carry off that little golden statuette. Winning an Oscar® is a great honour, but it also gives a worldwide boost to the US film industry.

A film that wins Best Picture award can leap from the 'marginal interest' category to the 'must see', which translates into a wealth of ticket sales. The 1997 winner, *The English Patient*, was virtually dead at US cinemas before winning, but took US$17 million in the two months following the Awards and finished by adding another 35 per cent to its total US box-office sales. The cinema phenomenon *Titanic* was already a major hit when it won 11 Oscars in March 1998, having taken US$490 million in the USA. After the Academy Awards ceremony, however, that figure grew by another 25 per cent. The film was performing strongly overseas as well and by the time it left the big screen *Titanic* had taken over US$1.8 billion worldwide.

'Photography is truth. Cinema is truth twenty-four times a second.'
Jean-Luc Godard, film-maker

This obsession with sales may seem to be a corruption of a ceremony which should be valued purely for its prestige, but in fact the Academy Awards were created by the industry in an attempt to counter political criticism that cinema was perverting the public's morals. The 1920s was not a good time for the public image of Hollywood. The films were making plenty of money at the box-office, but scandals behind the scenes were causing serious concern. The Fatty Arbuckle scandal in 1922 was one such case. After a wild drinking party, which resulted in the death of a young starlet, Arbuckle was charged with manslaughter. He was acquitted after three trials but by then his career was in ruins.

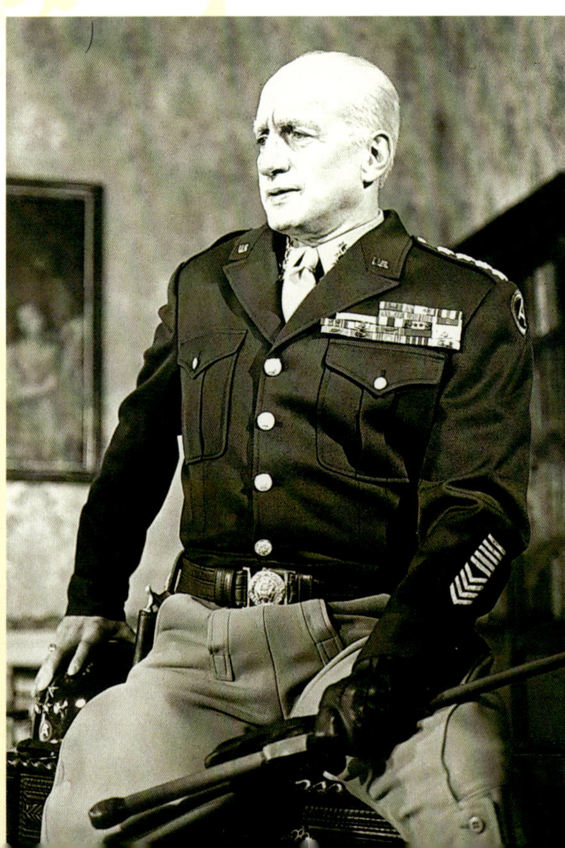

From a script by Francis Ford Coppola, Patton *(1970) won four Academy Awards. It was one of only two films shot in the Dimension 150 process that succeeded Cinerama.*

This sort of scandal led to increased calls for statutory regulation of film. In an attempt to pre-empt government control, the industry introduced the Motion Picture Producers and Distributors Association. With Will H Hays as its first president, the Association set about creating a production code which committed Hollywood to controlling the moral content of its output. In 1927 the industry launched its most ambitious marketing project—the formation of the Academy of Motion Pictures, Arts and Sciences to celebrate the skills and achievements of performers and technicians. The word 'Academy' emphasised the organisation's association with learning and high standards, and its first task was to create a means of honouring those qualities. The Academy Awards were born.

How the award came to be called the Oscar is unclear. Some people claim that Academy librarian Margaret Herrick was responsible. On seeing the statuette for the first time she reportedly said: 'Why, it looks just like my Uncle Oscar.' Others claim that Bette Davis named the award after her first husband. The statuette is 13 inches tall with a 24-carat gold exterior. The composition of its metal interior is a secret, as is its monetary value, and it has been manufactured by the Dodge Trophy Company since 1928. Despite rough handling by many people, including use as a doorstop, the Oscar wears well. Sea air is known to turn it green, but apparently this is easily remedied!

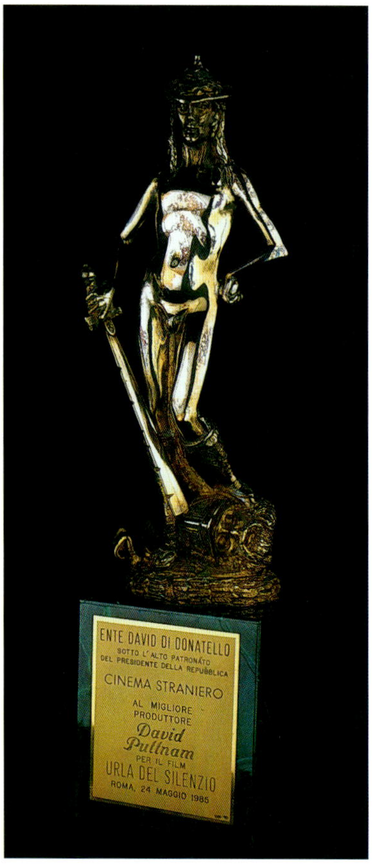

The Italian Academy's award, the David di Donatello, for David Puttnam's The Killing Fields *presented at the ceremony on 24 May 1985. The Donatello is a stunning award, beautifully presented.*

The Palme d'Or. Arguably one of the most prestigious awards, presented to David Puttnam for The Mission *in 1986. The Palme d'Or is presented each year at the Cannes Film Festival by a panel of industry luminaries.*

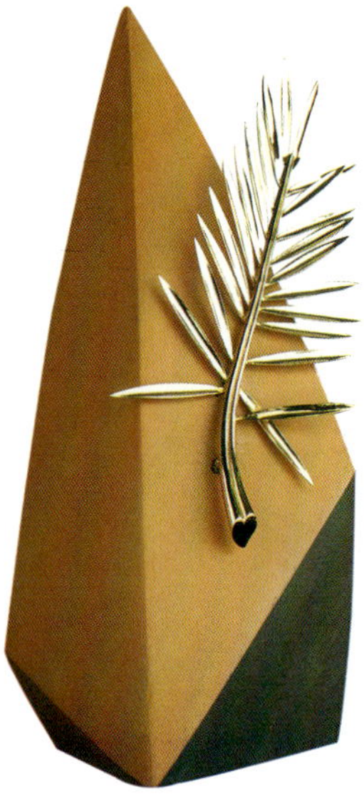

Where to pick up your awards, month by month

January	Golden Globes
February	Golden Bear, Berlin Film Festival
March	Academy Awards (Oscars)
April	BAFTAs
May	Palme d'Or, Cannes Film Festival
June	BAF! Awards, Bradford Animation Festival
July	Grand Prix, Karlovy Vary
August	Amanda Statuettes, Norway
September	Golden Lion, Venice Film Festival
October	Gold Hugo, Chicago Film Festival
November	Golden Alexander, Thessaloniki Film Festival
December	European Film Awards

The winners of the first-ever Academy awards were announced three months before the ceremony. Even before the mass marketing and global television feeds that surround the present-day ceremony, the Academy Awards were taken up quickly by the US public and soon became a key part of the calendar.

During the 1970s there were many controversies surrounding the Oscars. In 1970 George C Scott declined the Award for *Patton*, while Marlon Brando sent a Native American to accept his award and make a speech on behalf of all Native Americans. And in 1974, while Henry Kissinger was negotiating a peaceful settlement to the Vietnam War, the Vietcong sent a congratulatory telegram to the winner of the Best Documentary, *Hearts and Minds,* which was read out at the ceremony.

Fascination with the Oscars is greater than ever and the ceremony is famous for its overstatement and self-congratulatory style. There is little political statement involved nowadays; the greatest controversy is usually about whether one film should have won over another. It has long been recognised by other countries that US movies win the most Oscars, despite Colin Welland's famous remark that 'the British are coming' after winning Best Screenplay for *Chariots of Fire* in 1982.

One interesting feature of film industry awards is their size. In many fields, the size of the award measures its value: in motor racing, for example, trophies seem to grow bigger each time they are awarded. It is a pleasant quirk of the film world that their awards tend to favour aesthetics rather than size. However, to compensate, the industry has created a vast array of awards in almost every country of the world. British films have the chance to win a BAFTA, the French film industry has the Césars, the Spanish industry the Goyas, and the Italians the Donatellos. Every country's industry can feel confident that it has created the best film of year. And if your film isn't recognised at your own country's ceremony, there are festival prizes galore which might see fit to remedy that oversight: the Golden Lions, Golden Leopards, Golden Bears, Golden Palms, Golden Globes, Golden Cameras and Golden Sparrows. Even the worst film can win some glory with the Golden Turkey Award.

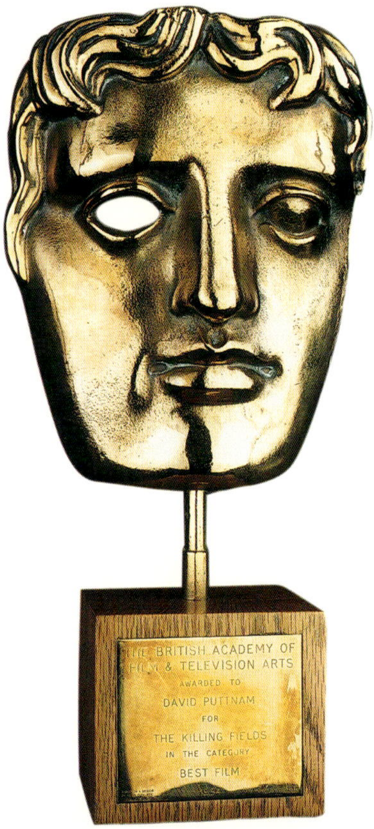

The BAFTA Award, presented by the British Academy of Film and Television Arts. This Award was made to producer David Puttnam for The Killing Fields *(1984) for Best Film. The BAFTA Award is based on a design by Mitzi Cunliffe.*

At the National Museum of Photography, Film & Television the awards culture of the film industry is explored in the ***Profiles*** gallery, through looking at the career of one of Britain's leading film producers, David Puttnam. His many successes include the Oscar for Best Picture for *Chariots of Fire*, the Palme d'Or, various Golden Globes and the David di Donatello. Animator Nick Park is another British Oscar winner, carrying off three of the coveted statuettes for his Wallace and Gromit series and *Creature Comforts*. The Museum's gallery ***Animation: Brought to Life*** takes the visitor through the history of animation, from early experiments in moving images to the work of the great artists of the medium. It also shows how Britain has won its status as a world leader in the animation industry.

Shaken, not stirred

A less celebrated Academy Award is the Irving G Thalberg Memorial Award. Thalberg was arguably Hollywood's most brilliant producer. The award is made to producers who have made an outstanding contribution to the film industry. In 1982 Albert R Broccoli was presented with the award, despite working outside Hollywood.

Born in New York City, 'Cubby' Broccoli learnt his trade as assistant director with Twentieth Century Fox. In the early 1950s he headed for Britain and formed a partnership with Irving Allen, founding Warwick Pictures.

During this time he produced a series of memorable British films, from *Paratrooper* (1953) to *The Trials of Oscar Wilde* (1960). In the 1960s the public mood was captured by the magnificent children's film *Chitty Chitty Bang Bang*, re-released in the 1990s.

However, it was by teaming up with Harry Saltzman and obtaining the rights to Ian Fleming's *James Bond* novels that Broccoli's name became established in the history of cinema. With a low-budget production, *Dr No* (1961), he launched a series of films that remain highly popular. Broccoli was able to develop the James Bond franchise so quickly that by the fourth film in the series, *You Only Live Twice* (1967), the main set cost more than the entire budget of *Dr No*.

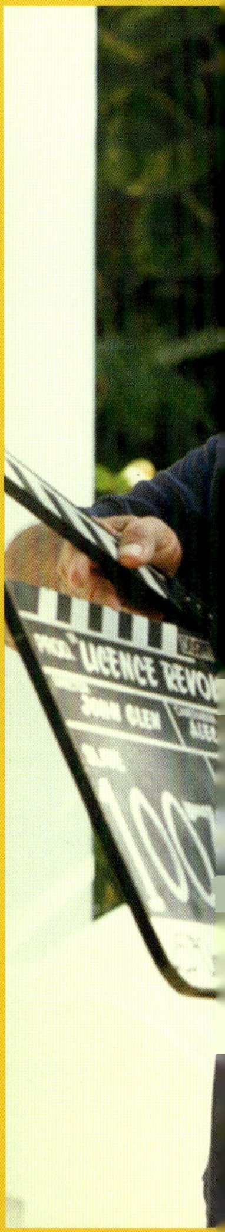

'Cubby' Broccoli, producer of the James Bond films since the beginning of the series, opens the shooting of a sequence for Licensed to Kill.

Not to be outdone, the Museum has its own awards ceremony: the BAF! Awards. Introduced in 1994 to celebrate the work of animators the BAF!s are presented each year at the Bradford Animation Festival and comprise four professional categories, one amateur category and one children's category. Past winners of the professional prizes include Barry Purves for *Screenplay*, Piet Kroon for *TRANSIT* and Candy Guard for *Pond Life*.

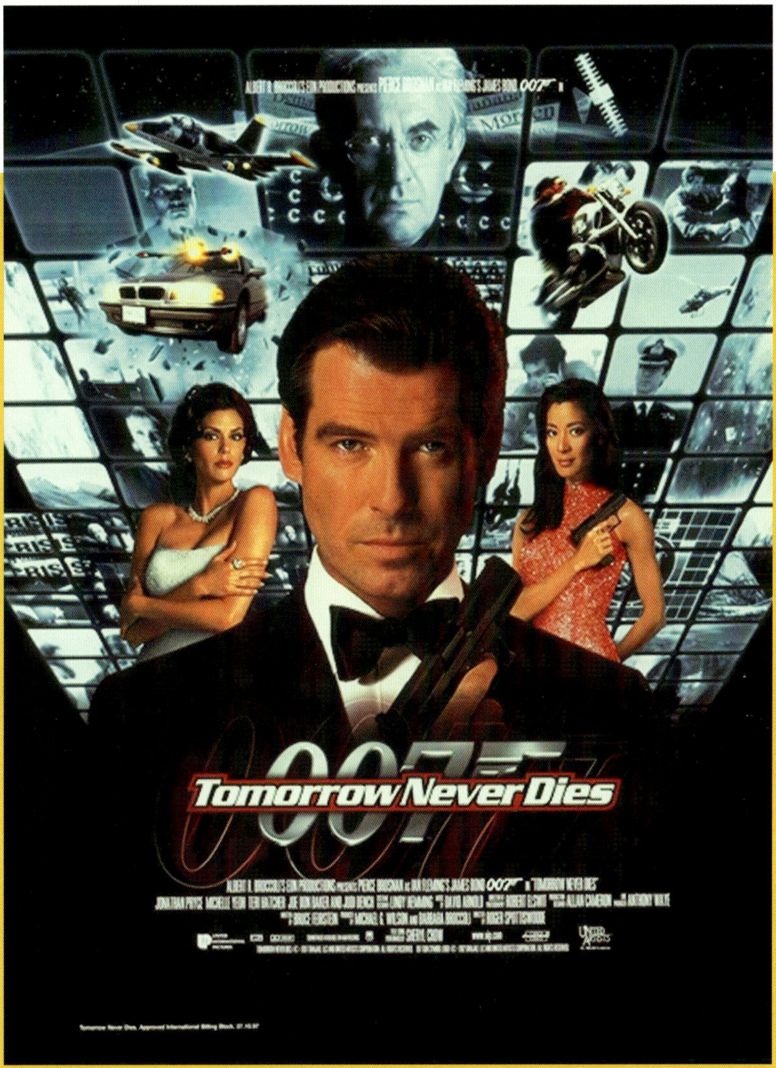

Tomorrow Never Dies *is the eighteenth James Bond film in the most successful film series of all time.*

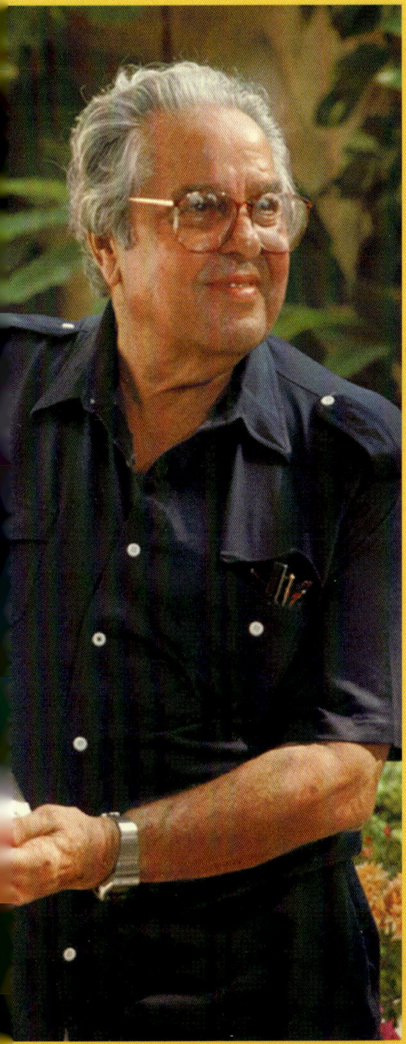

The Face in the Desert

Portraits and stories from the *Daily Herald* Archive, a public artwork by Joachim Schmid

Greg Hobson
Head of Interpretation

The National Museum of Photography, Film & Television's Photography Collection holds a hidden jewel: an archive containing over one million photographs taken between the early 1900s and 1969, covering every major newsworthy event during that time. The archive is that of the *Daily Herald*, once the world's best-selling daily newspaper and a pioneer of the innovative use of photographs in news journalism.

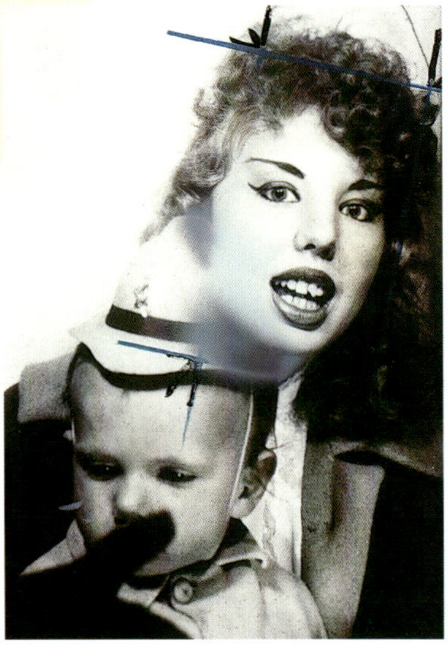

From 'The Face in the Desert' (Daily Herald *Archive)*

The *Daily Herald* began life as a weekly strike sheet for the London printing unions in January 1911. It quickly grew in popularity and in 1912 became a daily. In 1929 the paper was financed by Odhams Press and a combination of wily marketing and popular reporting led in 1933 to the *Daily Herald* becoming the world's top-selling newspaper with sales of over two million each day. Sadly, fierce competition forced the paper into relaunching as the *Sun* in 1964. After an initial increase in circulation, sales declined and in 1969 the *Sun* was sold to Rupert Murdoch's News International organisation and the *Daily Herald* came to an end.

The photographs that appeared in the newspaper have been carefully stored, each filed with their related stories appended to the reverse of the image. The images have come from a variety of sources: in addition to highly-skilled staff photographers, the *Daily Herald* also sourced many pictures from the Press Association, picture agencies and other photographers, and all found their way into the archive. The archive is a complex and fascinating collection of photographs, containing subject matter as disparate as state funerals, sporting events, armed conflict and even alleged encounters with aliens. A combination of haphazard filing and sometimes bizarre subject matter means that there is always something new and unexpected to discover. Interpreting the collection is an exciting prospect but, with approximately 1.3 million photographs, where do we begin?

The Museum's permanent gallery displays and its programme of special exhibitions have always drawn on the vast resource of the *Daily Herald* Archive, using the material to investigate and enhance the thematic exploration of photography, film and television. However, the challenge is to find new ways of showcasing the diversity and richness of the material.

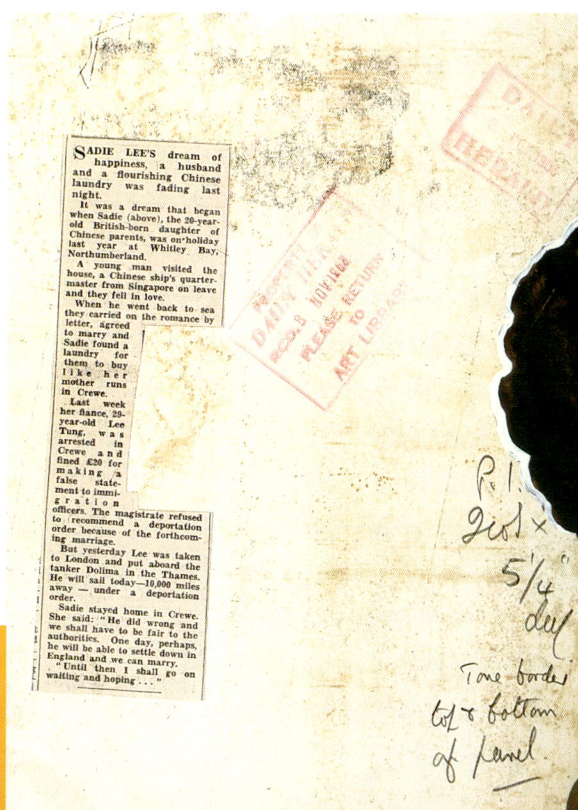

SADIE LEE'S dream of happiness, a husband and a flourishing Chinese laundry was fading last night.

It was a dream that began when Sadie (above), the 20-year-old British-born daughter of Chinese parents, was on holiday last year at Whitley Bay, Northumberland.

A young man visited the house, a Chinese ship's quartermaster from Singapore on leave and they fell in love.

When he went back to sea they carried on the romance by letter, agreed to marry and Sadie found a laundry for them to buy like her mother runs in Crewe.

Last week her fiance, 29-year-old Lee Tung, was arrested in Crewe and fined £20 for making a false statement to immigration officers. The magistrate refused to recommend a deportation order because of the forthcoming marriage.

But yesterday Lee was taken to London and put aboard the tanker Dolima in the Thames. He will sail today—10,000 miles away — under a deportation order.

Sadie stayed home in Crewe. She said: "He did wrong and we shall have to be fair to the authorities. One day, perhaps, he will be able to settle down in England and we can marry.

"Until then I shall go on waiting and hoping . . ."

From 'The Face in the Desert' (Daily Herald *Archive)*

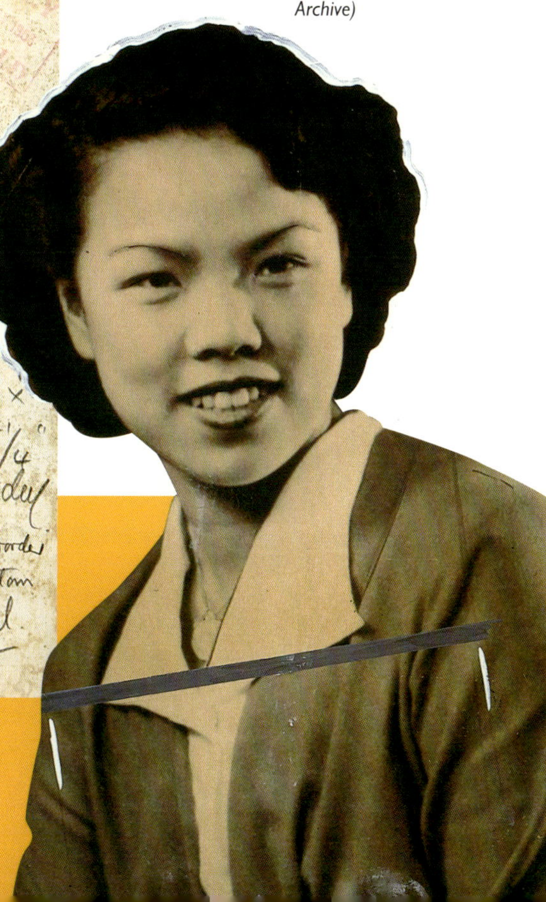

From 'The Face in the Desert' (Daily Herald *Archive)*

In 1996 the Museum developed a proposal for a public artwork which would suggest a unique environment in which to explore photographs from the *Daily Herald* Archive. The environment—the then-dilapidated subway running between the Museum and Bradford city centre—offered new ways of engaging with photography outside the confines of the gallery, or the controlled environment of the Museum's archive. Today artworks are placed in a variety of public places, from bus stops to hospitals to billboards. The Museum hopes that by placing works of art in public places, more people will access the archive, and in turn the work will extend its scope and impact by reaching a wider and more diverse audience. For many people, making a visit to a gallery or museum is an unfamiliar experience. The practice and policy of placing works in public places attempts to redress the balance. The transformation of the subway into a gallery environment was undertaken in that same spirit and for the same reasons.

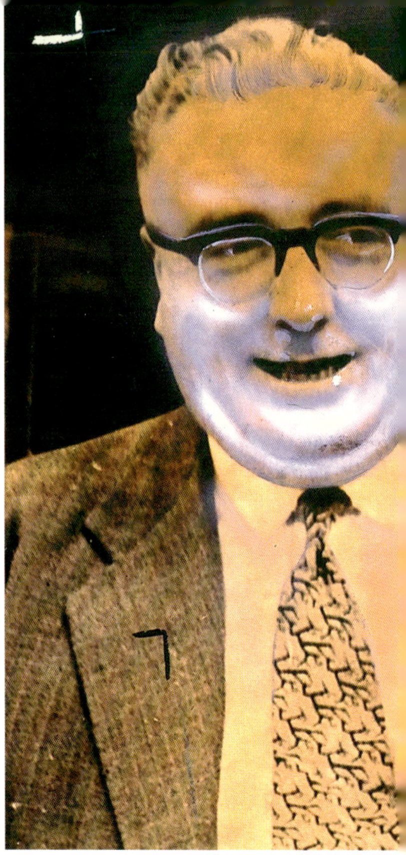

From 'The Face in the Desert' (Daily Herald *Archive)*

Working in partnership with the photography festival Photo 98 and the City of Bradford Metropolitan District Council, finances were secured for the redevelopment of the subway and the commissioning of an artist to work on the project.

The next challenge was to find someone who could provide a considered yet new take on the archive, someone who would seek out or recontextualise material that may previously have been overlooked. German artist Joachim Schmid was a perfect choice. Schmid works solely with photographs that he finds, or that already exist in archives, asserting that 'basically everything in the world has now been photographed in every possible way'. His skill lies in seeking out juxtapositions between photographs that give them new meaning, at the same time as questioning the role of the photographic image in defining the past.

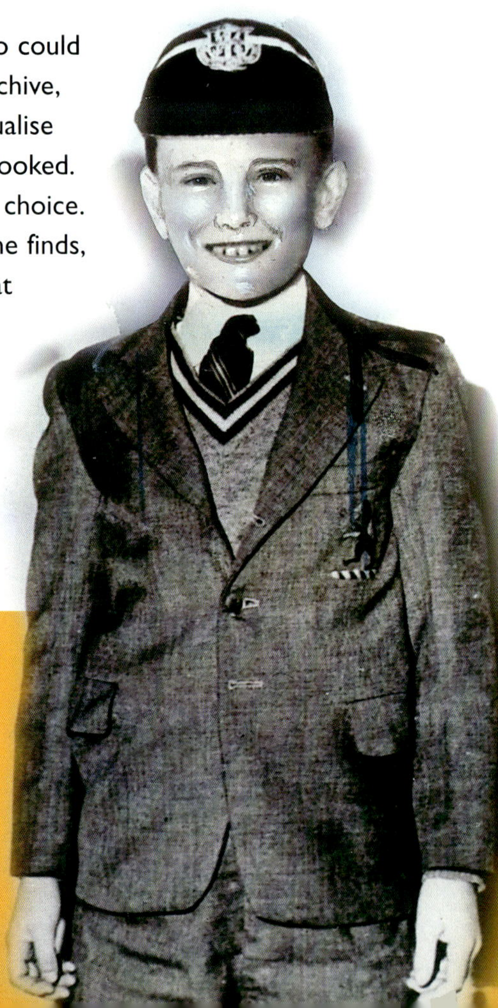

From 'The Face in the Desert' (Daily Herald *Archive)*

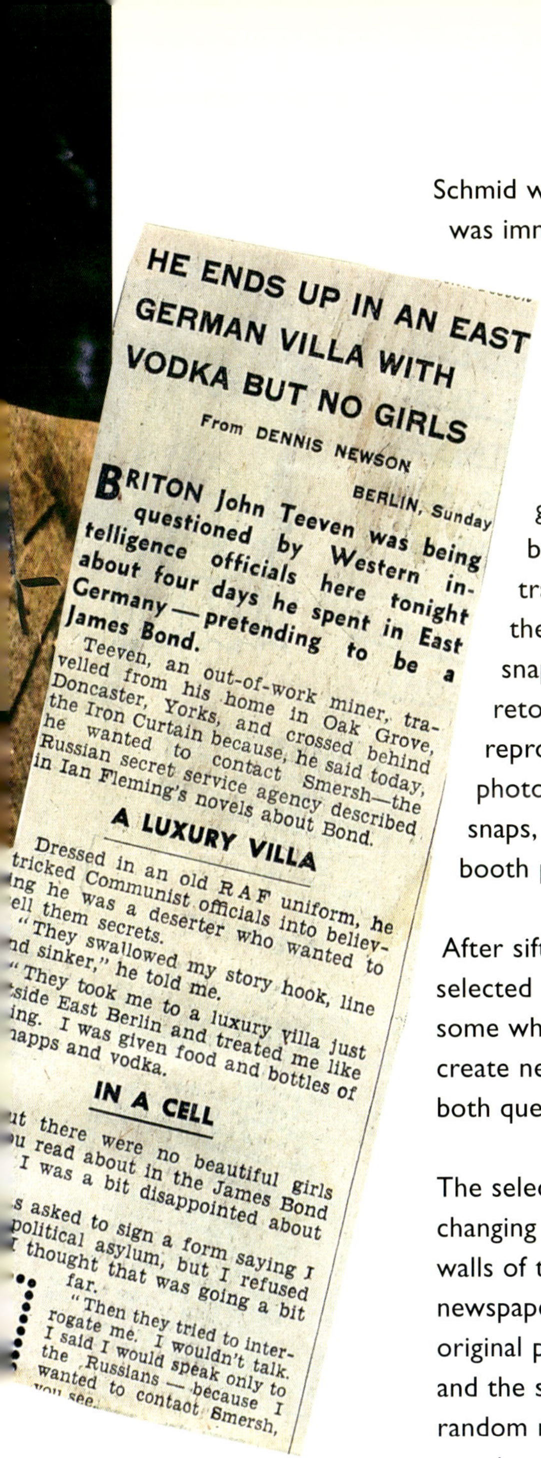

HE ENDS UP IN AN EAST GERMAN VILLA WITH VODKA BUT NO GIRLS

From DENNIS NEWSON

BERLIN, Sunday

BRITON John Teeven was being questioned by Western intelligence officials here tonight about four days he spent in East Germany—pretending to be a James Bond.

Teeven, an out-of-work miner, travelled from his home in Oak Grove, Doncaster, Yorks, and crossed behind the Iron Curtain because, he said today, he wanted to contact Smersh—the Russian secret service agency described in Ian Fleming's novels about Bond.

A LUXURY VILLA

Dressed in an old RAF uniform, he tricked Communist officials into believ-ing he was a deserter who wanted to ell them secrets.

"They swallowed my story hook, line nd sinker," he told me.

"They took me to a luxury villa just side East Berlin and treated me like ing. I was given food and bottles of napps and vodka.

IN A CELL

ut there were no beautiful girls u read about in the James Bond I was a bit disappointed about

s asked to sign a form saying I political asylum, but I refused thought that was going a bit far.

"Then they tried to interrogate me. I wouldn't talk. I said I would speak only to the Russians—because I wanted to contact Smersh, you see...

From 'The Face in the Desert' (Daily Herald *Archive)*

Schmid was given a free hand in selecting from the archive. He was immediately drawn to the enormous section titled 'People, Miscellaneous'. Consisting of more than 200 filing drawers of photographs, the section contains portraits of people who, prior to their involvement in an event that thrust them into the media, were relatively anonymous. From the man who travelled to East Germany impersonating James Bond to the young girl who survived being shot in the heart, the stories behind the pictures are bizarre, comic and sometimes tragic: all are compellingly eccentric. The photographs themselves are also intriguing. Often copied from family snapshots or formal portraits, they have been heavily retouched to make them suitable for newspaper reproduction. Loved ones have been painted out of wedding photographs, whole families have been chalked out of holiday snaps, and features have been painted into blurry photo-booth portraits, suspending the subjects in an eerie isolation.

After sifting through thousands of photographs, Schmid finally selected 24 portraits and 24 stories, some of which relate and some which do not, using them to weave new narratives and to create new fictions from news stories whose provenance is both questionable and insupportable.

The selection of portraits is now on display, presented in a changing series of 12 which are randomly projected on the walls of the newly refurbished subway. Supported by a newspaper-style catalogue of both the stories and pictures, the original photographs have come full circle. Both the installation and the supplement act as a comment on the sometimes-random nature of news, the function of the archive and the transient nature of the truth of a photograph. Consigned to drawers where they could have remained for ever, the subjects of these long-forgotten news stories are now destined for another 15 minutes of fame or notoriety.

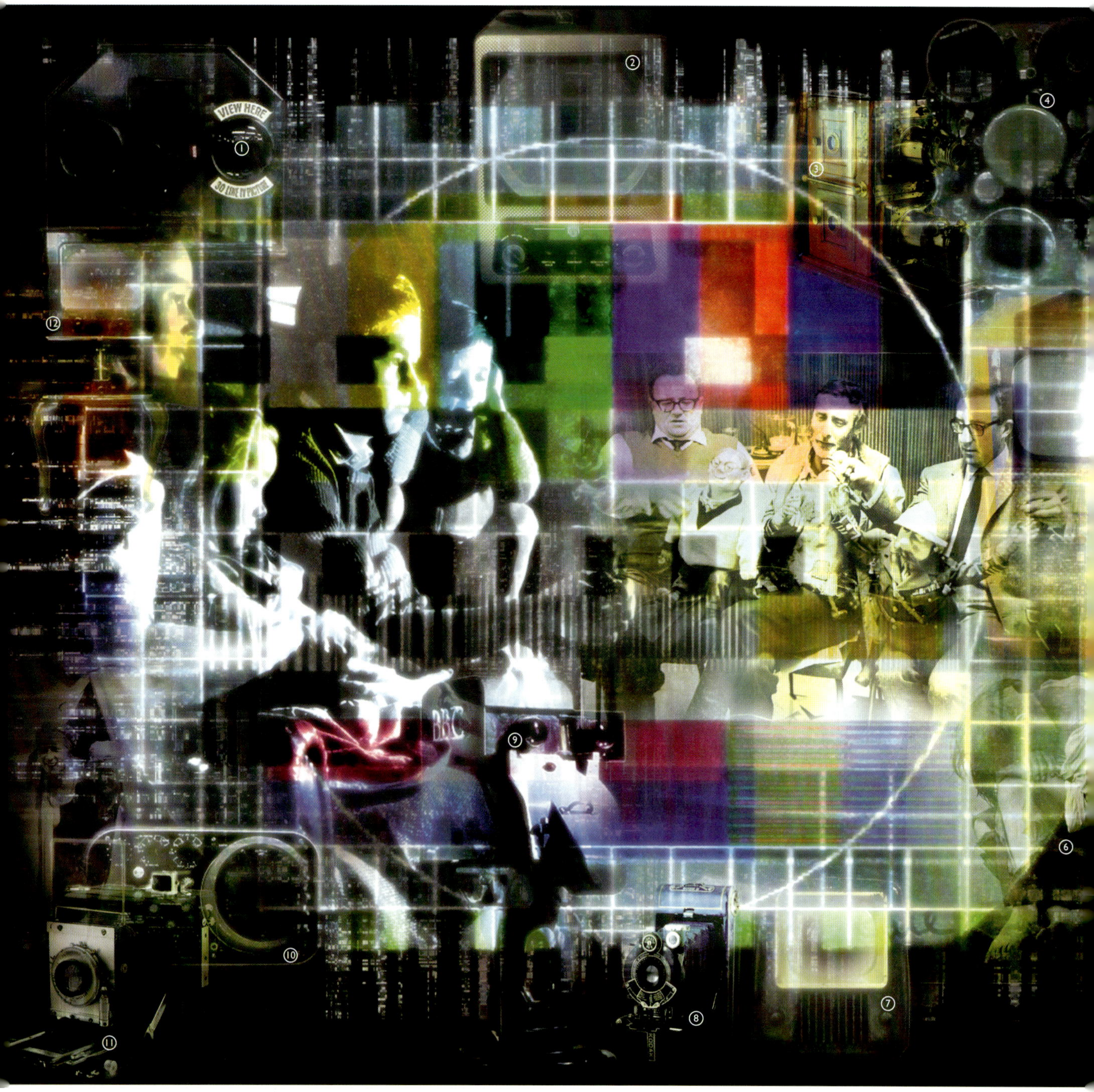

1 Baird Televisor Model C, c. 1933
2 EKCO TMB272 television receiver, 1955
3 Riley Monarch Ethopticon bi-unial magic lantern, c. 1880
4 EMI 203 television camera, 1960s
5 'Julia Jackson', by Julia Margaret Cameron, 1867
6 'A night on the streets of London' by O.G. Rejlander, c. 1857
7 GEC BT 2147 television, 1949–50
8 Vanity Kodak camera, 1928–33
9 EMI Emitron television camera, 1936
10 Marconi Mark III waveform monitor, 1954
11 Speed graphic camera, c. 1950
12 McMichael Model 512 television receiver, 1950s

Every collection tells a story

Paul Goodman
Registrar

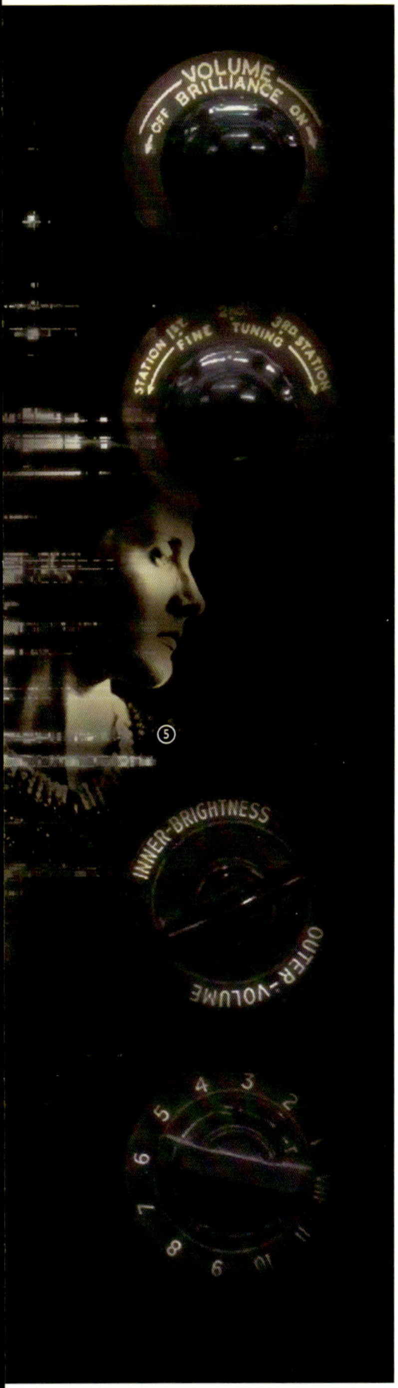

© The Works

Imagine digging for precious objects and unearthing a treasure trove. In 1996 a collector based in the most westerly province of Canada, British Columbia, offered the National Museum of Photography, Film & Television his collection of historic television broadcast equipment. The Museum decided to pursue the offer and engaged a team of specialist contractors to collect and ship the material—an apparently straightforward task. Unfortunately on arrival the shippers found that the equipment was stored under the floorboards of the owner's house—a fact he had conveniently omitted to mention during his negotiations with the Museum. What's more, all the carpets, household fixtures and furniture were still in place. The shippers had to remove the furniture from the room, lift the floorboards to gain access, then ferret around in a void of two feet to access the equipment. And, once the equipment had been successfully extracted and packed, they had to replace everything exactly as it had been before. An Aladdin's cave awaited the Museum, however, containing a complete Marconi Mark II television camera (only the second known surviving example in the world), along with an extremely rare American RCA TK30A camera (even earlier than the Marconi) which was the first reliable US broadcast television camera ever made.

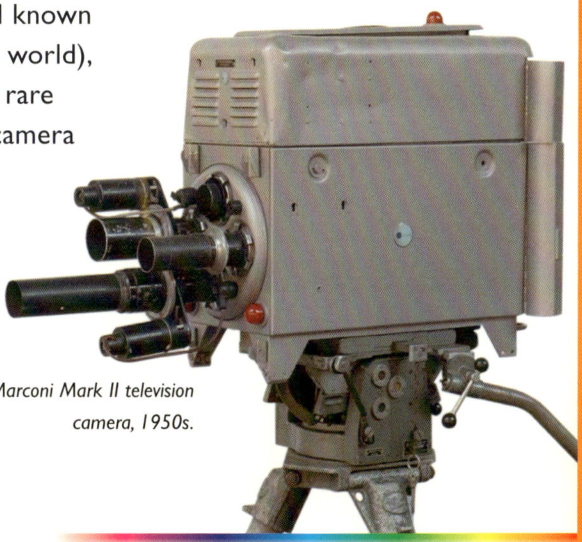

Marconi Mark II television camera, 1950s.

This story shows the lengths to which the Museum will go to expand and continually improve its already world-class holdings. As a result, the Museum's collections are constantly growing: sometimes objects are donated as gifts, at other times the Museum borrows or buys them from individuals or other institutions. In the past, Museum staff have removed and replaced door frames to collect objects from houses, attics and cellars, and even rescued historic gems from rubbish tips. A blend of knowledge and serendipity has played its part in the growth of the Museum's collections, and material has been acquired from all over the world, from Bradford, West Yorkshire, to Bradford, Ontario.

'The camera relieves us of the burden of memory.'
John Berger (b.1926), art critic and author

Every one of these objects tells a story, be it a tale of ingenuity and innovation, espionage and intrigue, triumph over the odds, truth and charlatanism, eccentricity and diversity, or humour.

The unusual, high-quality Compass miniature camera, 1937. It could be used with 24 x 36 mm glass plates or a roll-film back. An estimated 5000 were manufactured before the Second World War.

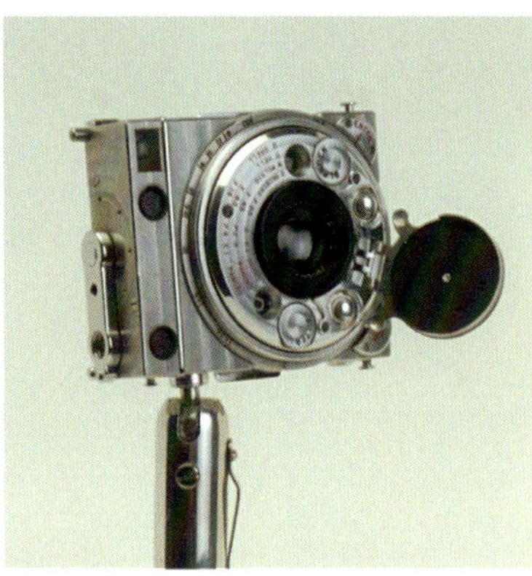

A Polyrama Panoptique, made in the 1820s. The thin paper transparencies were printed on both sides with different scenes. The viewer moved the shutter to light a transparency from the front or the back, producing different images.

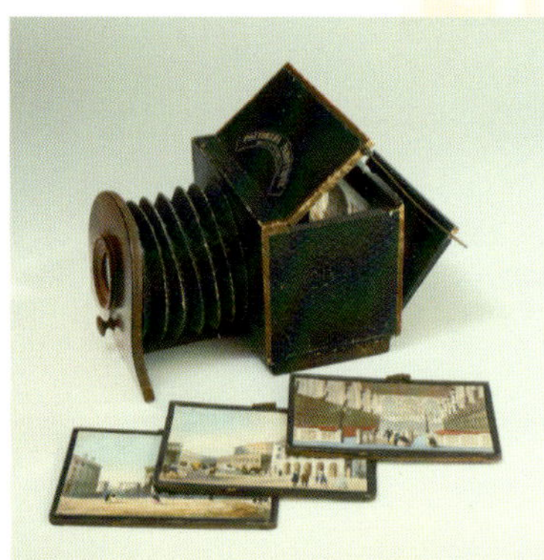

The quarter-plate 'Midg' folding camera which in 1917 was used by two Bradford schoolgirls, Elsie Wright and Frances Griffiths, to photograph the famous 'Cottingley Fairies'.

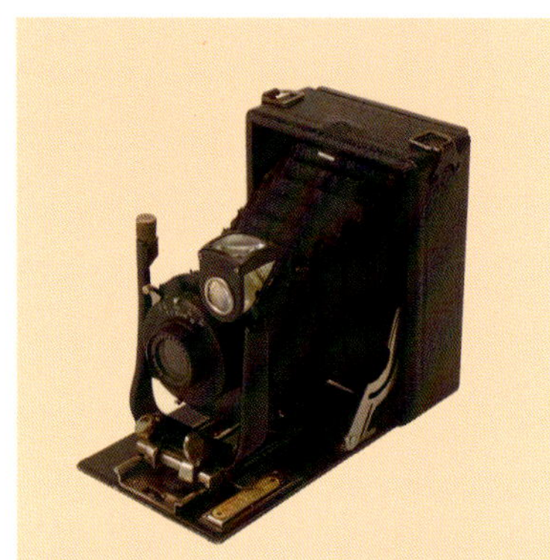

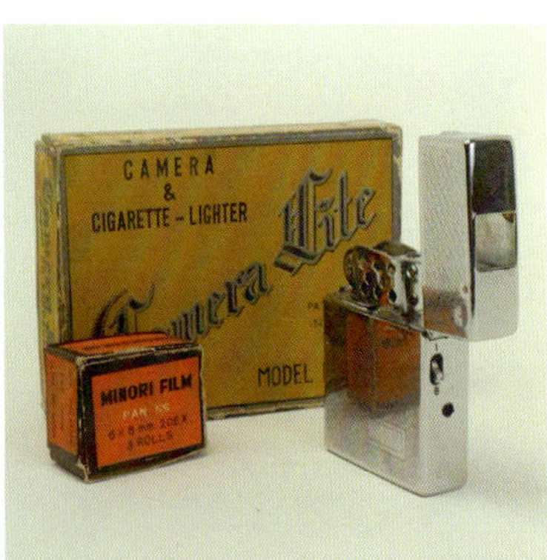

The 1955 Camera Lite, Model B, is a sub-miniature cine camera combined with a cigarette lighter. It took specially-manufactured 8 mm wide film in small magazines.

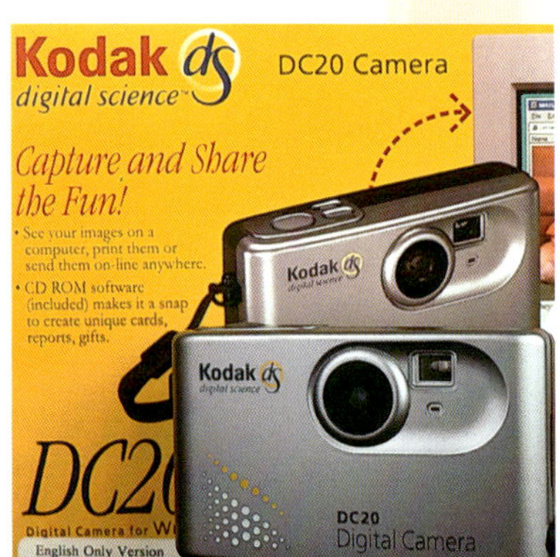

Kodak Digital Science DC20 digital imaging camera with publicity ephemera, 1996. It was the first digital camera aimed specifically at the 'snapshot' market.

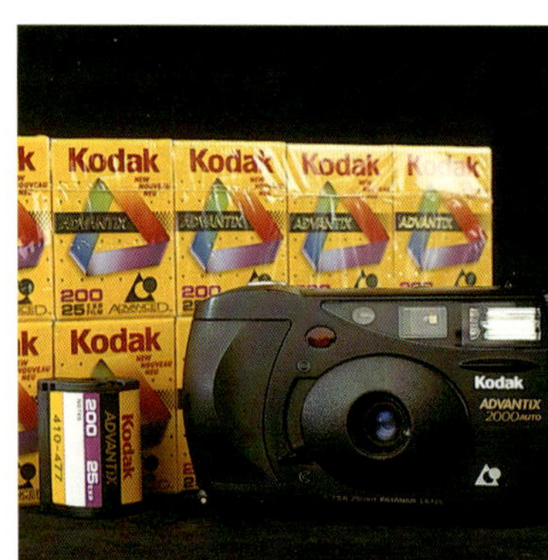

Kodak Advantix 2000 Auto advanced photographic system (APS) camera with boxes of film, 1996.

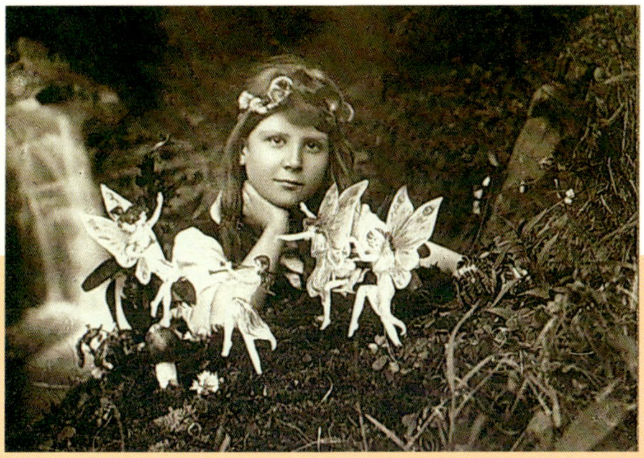

'Alice and the fairies' (Frances Griffiths was 'Alice'), taken in July 1917 with the 'Midg' camera which belonged to Elsie's father.

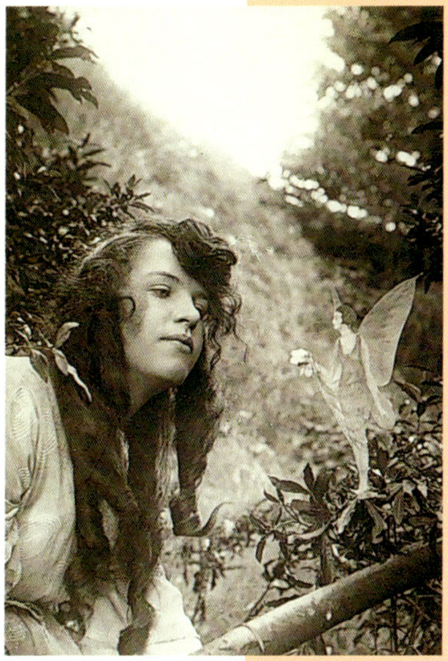

'Fairy offering flowers to Iris' (Elsie Wright was 'Iris'), taken in August 1920 with the 'Cameo' camera.

The Cottingley Fairies

In the summer of 1917, 15-year-old Elsie Wright and her 10-year-old cousin, Frances Griffiths, claimed to have taken photographs of fairies not far from Elsie's home at Cottingley, near Bradford. Although initially greeted with disbelief, the girls' 'discovery' came to the attention of Edward Gardner, a researcher into the paranormal. He gave each of the girls a 'Cameo' plate camera to replace the 'Midg' camera with which they had taken the first photographs. The girls produced more fairy photographs, and these were noticed by Sir Arthur Conan Doyle, who published them in Strand magazine and later wrote a book entitled *The Coming of the Fairies*.

The photographs attracted worldwide attention and intense debate as to their authenticity. They have continued to capture the public's imagination; indeed, there have been two feature films based on the story: *Photographing Fairies* (1997) and *Fairy Tale—A True Story* (1998). It was not until 1983 that Elsie Wright finally admitted that the photographs had been a hoax.

In 1998, the cameras used to take the photographs, along with contact prints plus a quantity of manuscript and other material, were going to be put up for auction—but the Museum could not afford to buy them. However, *Amateur Photographer* suggested that a public appeal be launched for money to purchase the material. Public subscription and financial support from companies such as Canon, Jessops and Olympus raised enough to meet the asking price. In June 1998, amongst a blaze of publicity, in front of an enthusiastic and proud Bradford public, the cameras were formally handed over by *Amateur Photographer* to the Museum.

Greasepaint and gore

During the 1960s and 1970s, Hammer horror films were hugely popular. Actors such as Christopher Lee and Peter Cushing starred in films about vampires, monsters and other ghouls. These films, now regarded by film critics and film-goers as masterpieces of gothic horror, were produced on shoestring budgets, and what helped to make them enormously successful was the work of two exceptional make-up artists, Phil Leakey (1908–92) and Roy Ashton (1909–95).

Ashton and Leakey's pioneering use of prosthetics (false body parts) to transform an actor's appearance became absolutely pivotal. Their work truly represents the essence of Hammer films and was instrumental in making Hammer one of the most significant production companies in British film history.

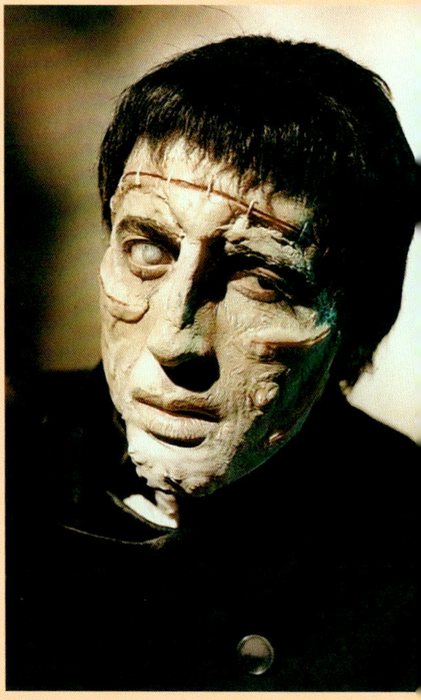

Christopher Lee as Frankenstein's monster in The Curse of Frankenstein *(1957).*

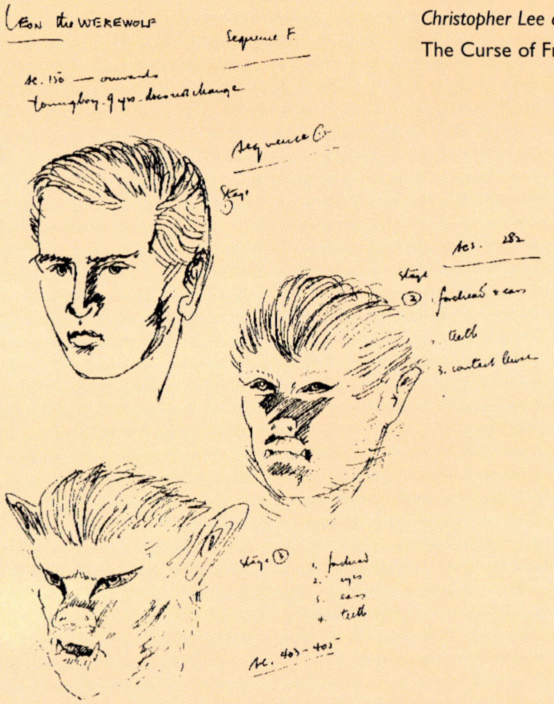

Roy Ashton's sketches illustrating lighting and make-up for The Curse of the Werewolf *(1961).*

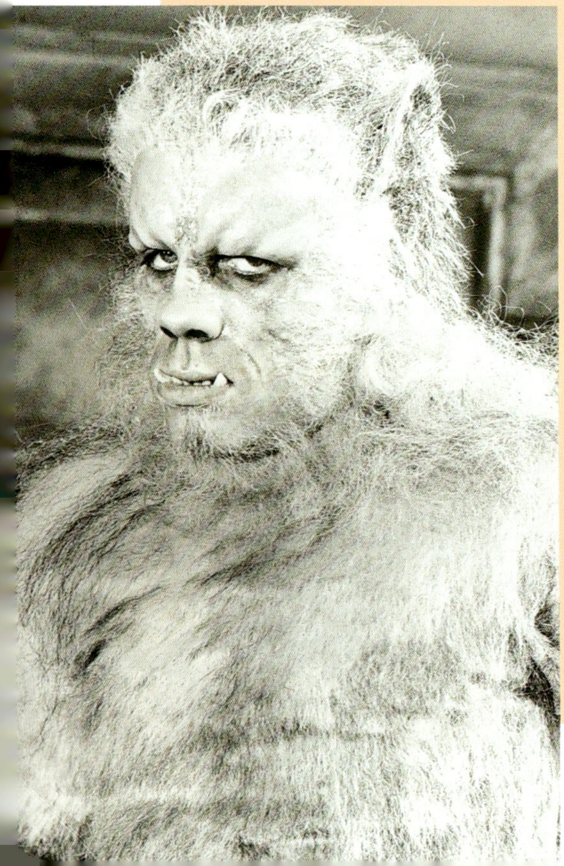

Oliver Reed in The Curse of the Werewolf *(1961).*

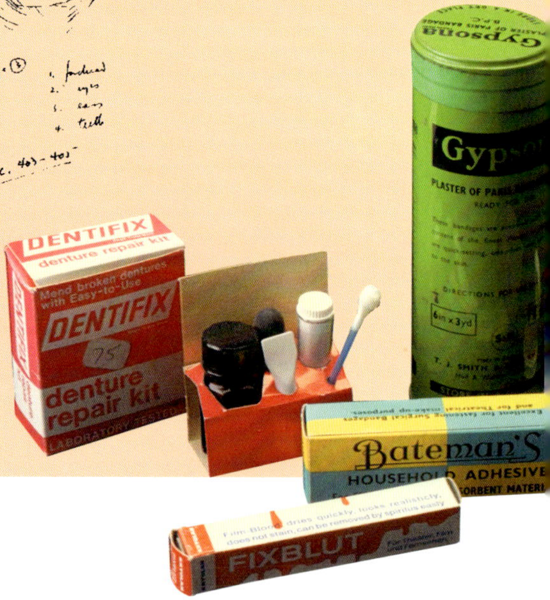

Selection of household products used by Phil Leakey and Roy Ashton to create horror make-up for Hammer films during the 1960s and 1970s.

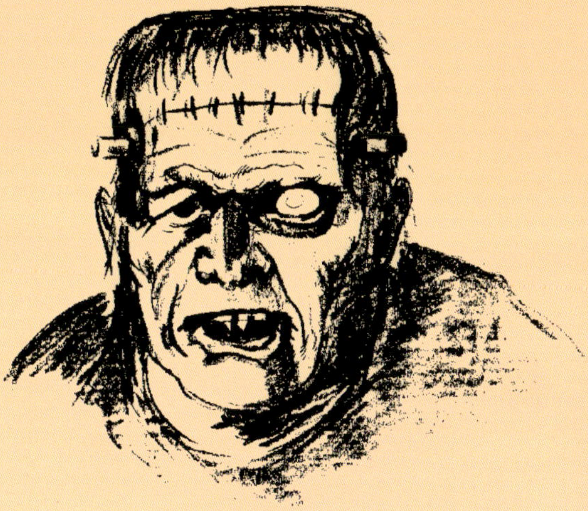

Charcoal study of the monster for The Evil of Frankenstein *(1964).*

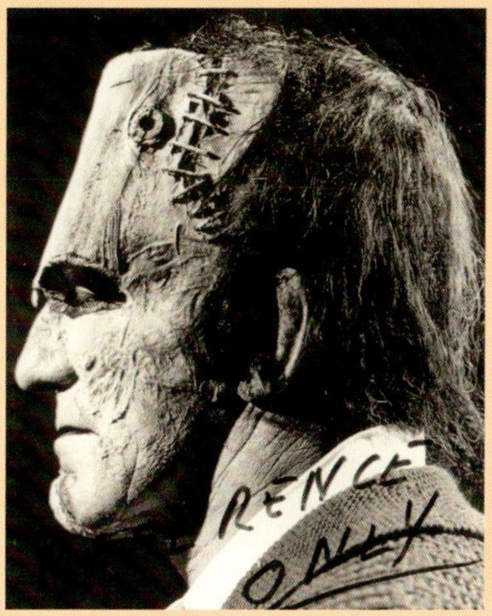

Kiwi Kingston in The Evil of Frankenstein *(1964).*

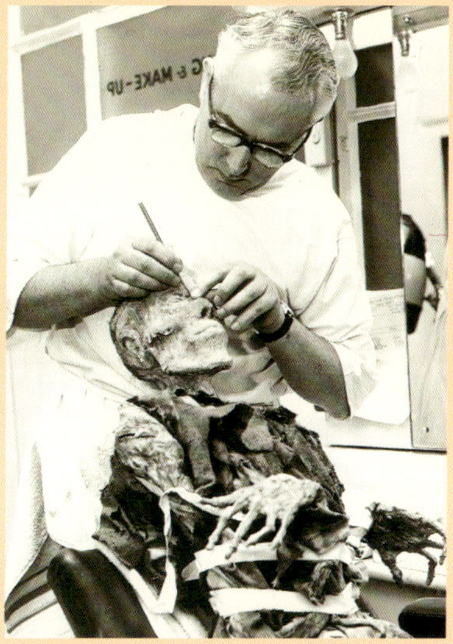

Roy Ashton at work on a creature for Paranoiac *(1963)*

Leakey and Ashton achieved memorable special effects by combining specialist and everyday products with an enormous amount of ingenuity. Their ground-breaking work—widely acknowledged within the horror movie field—inspired a later generation of special-effects technicians, including Rick Baker, responsible for creating the amazing physical transformations in *An American Werewolf in London.*

With the aid of a Heritage Lottery Fund grant, the Museum acquired this unique collection, unrivalled anywhere else in the world, left by two of the industry's outstanding craftsmen. The Phil Leakey and Roy Ashton collection comprises over 500 artefacts, ranging from concept sketches and notes, models and continuity photographs through to many of the prosthetics themselves. It includes the bloody fangs worn by Christopher Lee in *Dracula* and the contact lenses created for the monster in *The Curse of Frankenstein.* The collection offers a fascinating insight into how pioneering special effects were developed.

Hammer films have become cult classics—an important part of Britain's film culture. This collection of Leakey and Ashton's artefacts, sketches and notes will help us understand how they achieved their creations and add to our knowledge of film production in Britain.

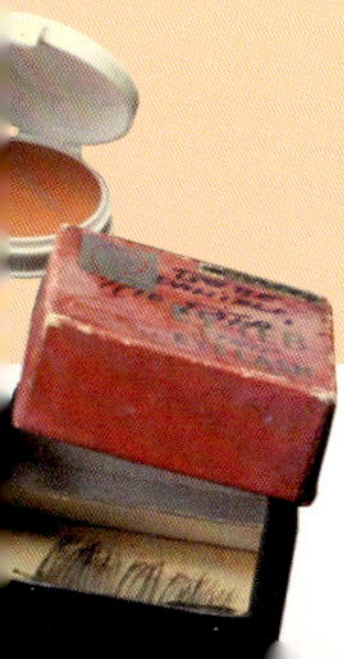

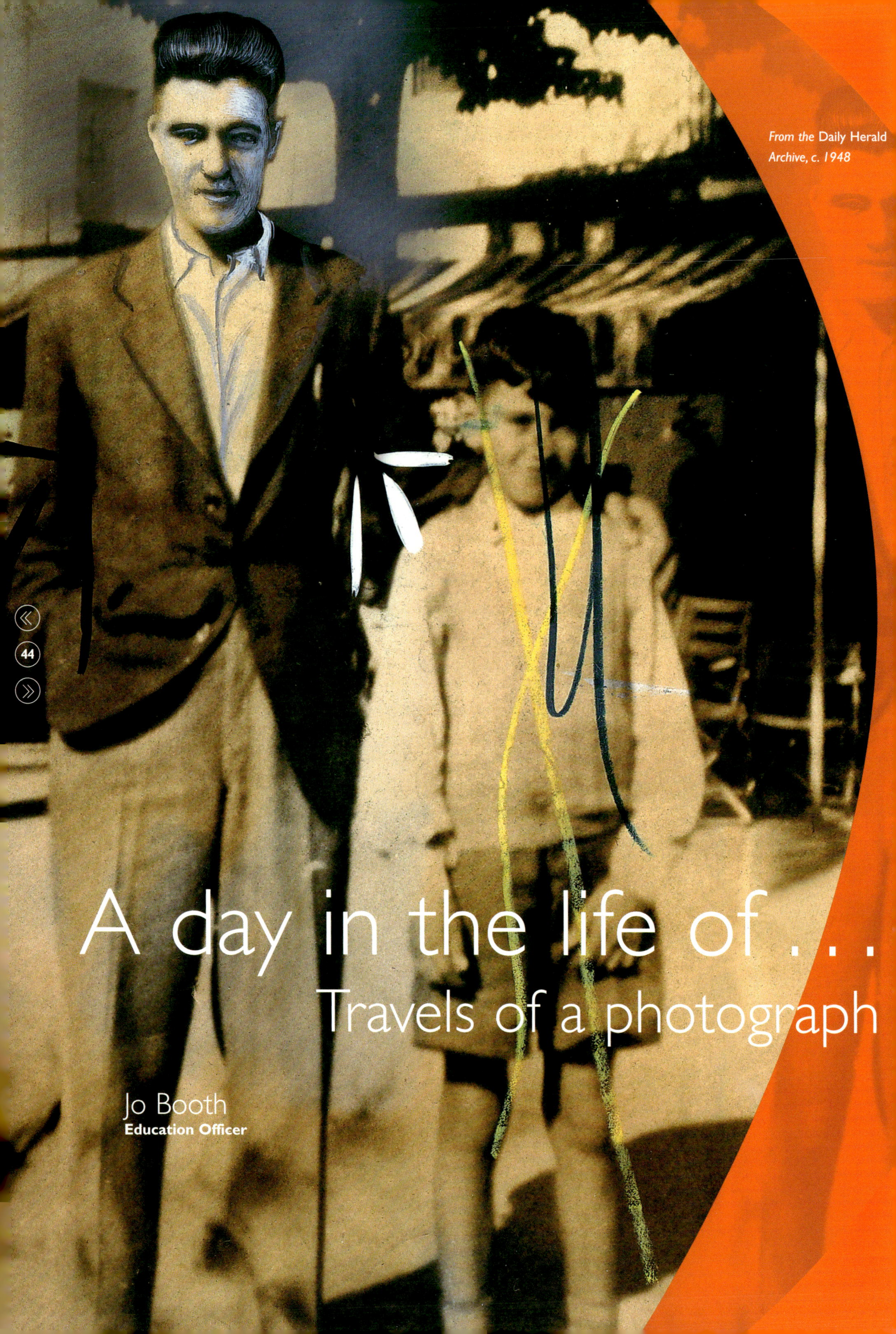

From the Daily Herald *Archive, c. 1948*

A day in the life of . . .

Travels of a photograph

Jo Booth
Education Officer

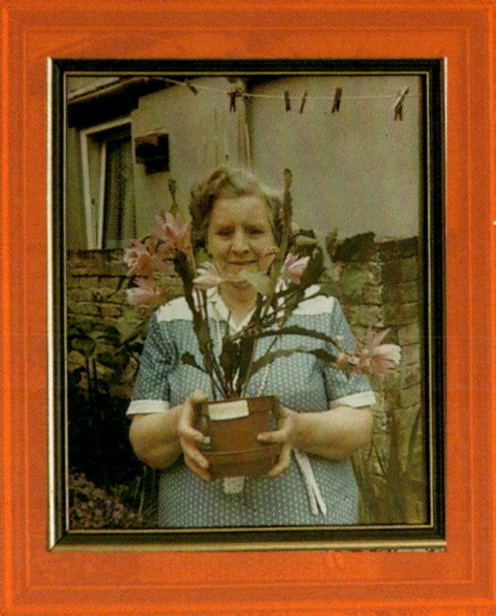

Photograph by Charlie Snelling, re-photographed by Julian Germain. From the series entitled 'For Every Minute You Are Angry You Lose 60 Seconds of Happiness', 1992.

'To fix fleeting images is not only impossible, as has been demonstrated by very serious experiments in Germany, it is a sacrilege.'
German press, 1830s

Imagine the scene. A photograph is taken for personal reasons—to remember a person, a day out or a party perhaps. The photograph itself is unremarkable—similar to thousands of others in family albums all over the world. Suddenly, out of the blue, the person in the photograph is involved in an unexpected event. The event might be tragic, surprising or just simply bizarre—perhaps the person has defied death, or won a million.

The event has a profound effect on the person's family, who in turn, are approached by a daily newspaper with a huge circulation. The newspaper is interested in running the story as a feature. It requests that the family supplies a photograph of the person, and they oblige. Their snap is re-photographed by newspaper staff and the original is returned. The new print is treated like all newspaper photographs: the person's facial features are emphasised with chalky paints and special pencils, which slightly change the shape of the eyes and lips. All excess information, background mostly, is cropped away.

Some aspect of this person's life has gone public, and the once-private snap is seen by millions. To the family, the photograph looks unfamiliar: the face is different, somehow. It is odd to see the photograph in this new context, surrounded by pictures by professional photographers, and reproduced on newsprint.

Family album photograph, 1965

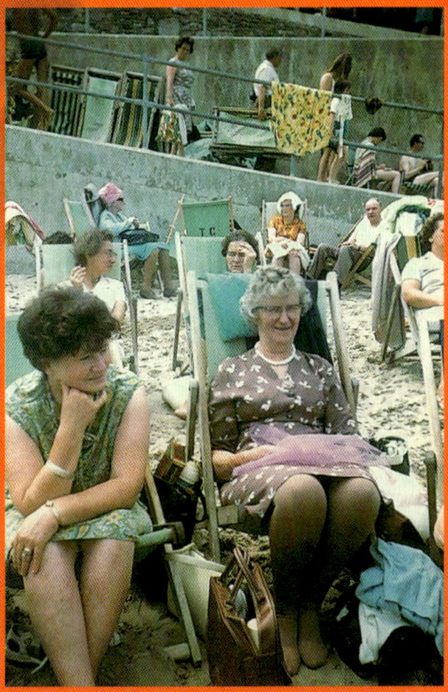

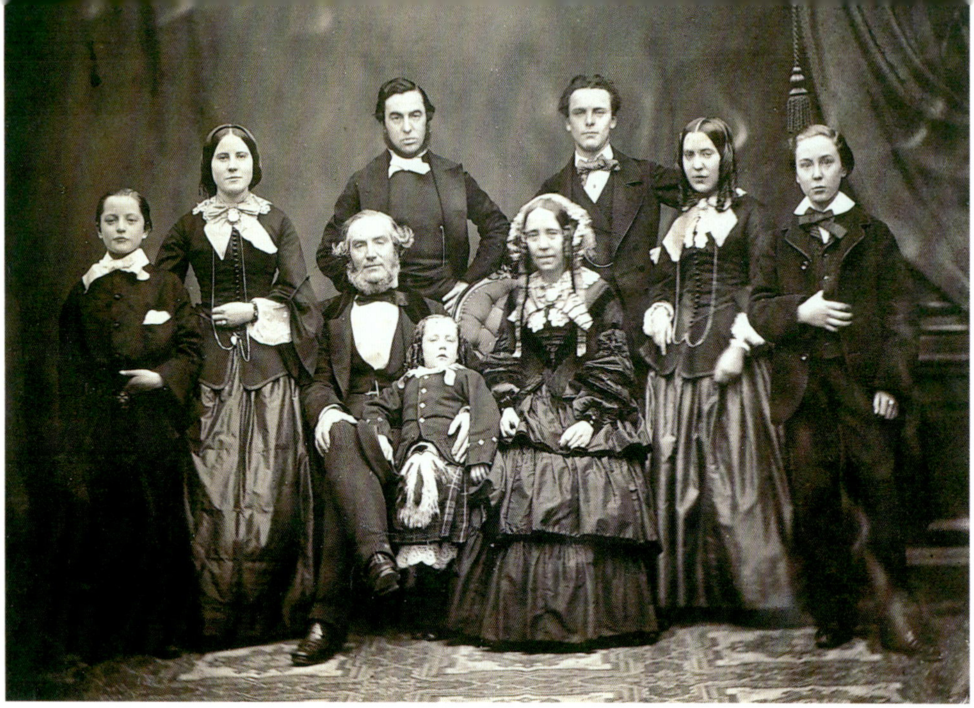

Victorian group portrait of a family, c. 1860.

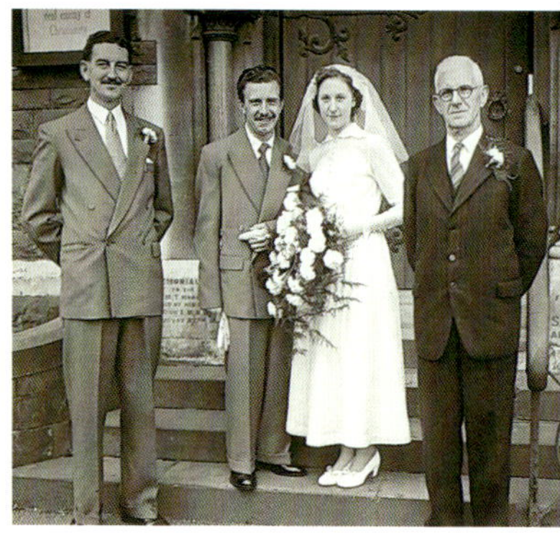

Family album photograph, 1950

A few days later the photograph is placed in the newspaper's archive. The archive is vast. Photographs are filed according to subject, in four-drawer filing cabinets and small metal boxes. It smells of photographic chemicals. Details of the story are attached to the back of the print, and it is placed in a brown card file (already full of photographs), and returned to its cabinet.

Years pass. Eventually the paper is taken over by another publishing house and relaunched under a new name. The demise of the paper means that its archive becomes redundant. It is eventually donated to a National Museum dedicated to photography, film and television, which undertakes to look after it and preserve it for the nation.

Our photograph remains in its box. From being an ordinary snapshot, it has changed into an image used by a newspaper and circulated to millions, and then into an item of national significance. As such it is stored in a controlled environment with round-the-clock security. It rests in its file, seen by nobody except the occasional researcher and the museum curators. Then, the museum receives grants to redevelop its site, facilities and galleries. A special exhibition is planned which profiles material from the museum's collections and, in particular, its mainly informal photographs of families.

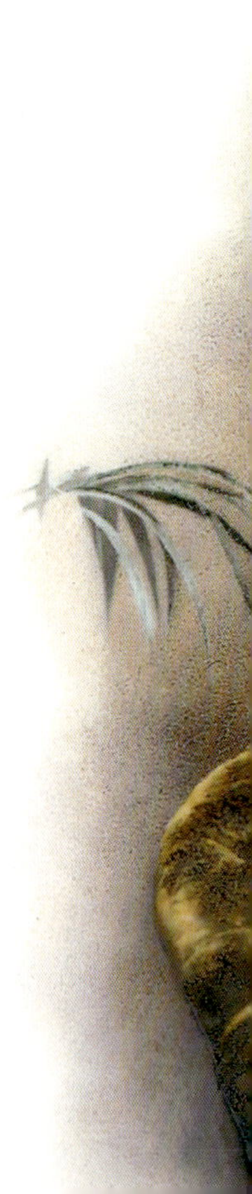

Opaltype of a child, hand-coloured, c. 1900.

'Most things in life are moments of pleasure and a lifetime of embarrassment; photography is a moment of embarrassment and a lifetime of pleasure.'

Tony Benn (b.1925), British politician

Two hundred photographs are selected by a curator and our photograph is among them. Some works in the selection are by pioneers of photography—special, precious, valuable. Others have been taken by Kodak staff photographers to advertise the company's products. Then there are the everyday ones. The curator wishes to include these because these are the ones that most of us recognise—snapshots by people of individuals and places they love. She hunts in the archive for them—they are spread around in different contexts because some are recent and others are over a hundred years old. Some are nearly as old as photography itself. All are fragments of human lives and experiences.

Our photograph is framed as an artwork and hung in the gallery along with the others. The gallery environment seems to change the photographs—they look different now. Perhaps it's because they are on public display in a large national institution.

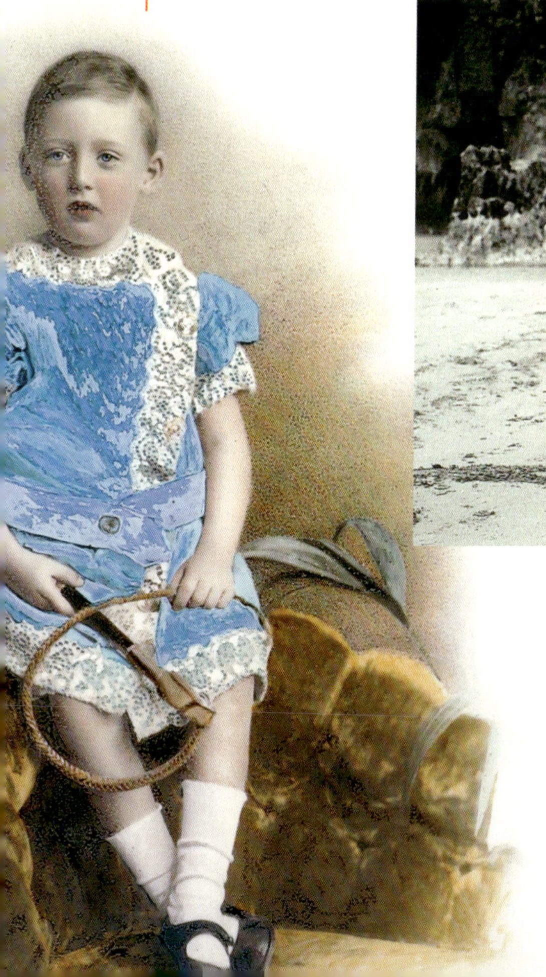

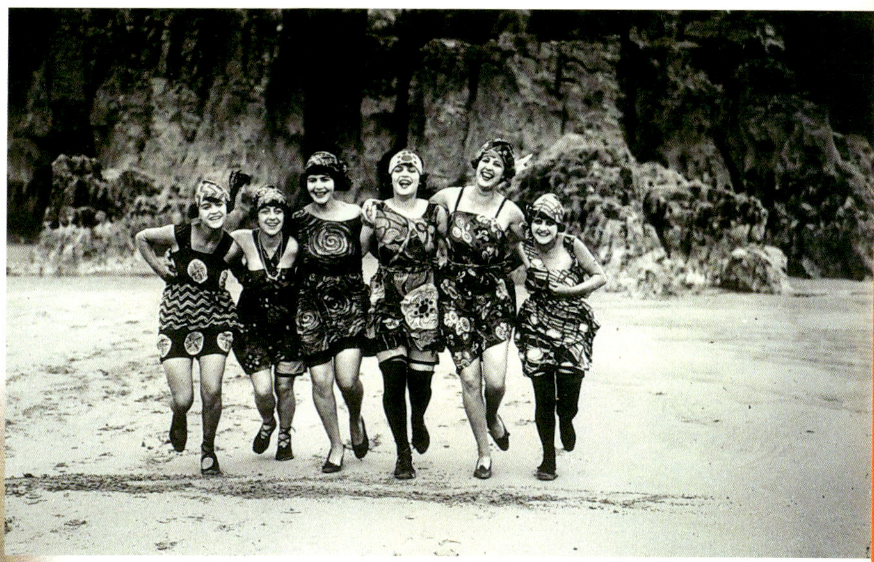

From the Kodak Collection, c. 1925

Although the museum has not collected family photographs as a distinct category, the curator finds them everywhere in the collection—in the newspaper archive which has been kept for its cultural, economic and social importance, in the huge beautifully bound Victorian albums kept for their historical significance, in the material that documents the arrival of colour photography, in the contemporary collection of work by art photographers.

The exhibition is maintained by museum staff, and education notes are provided for students, lecturers, teachers and children who are encouraged to consider and discuss photography—its diversity, its universal language. The museum and the curator are interested in the way that the photograph can at once be both historical and aesthetic, personal and public.

Family album photograph, 1994

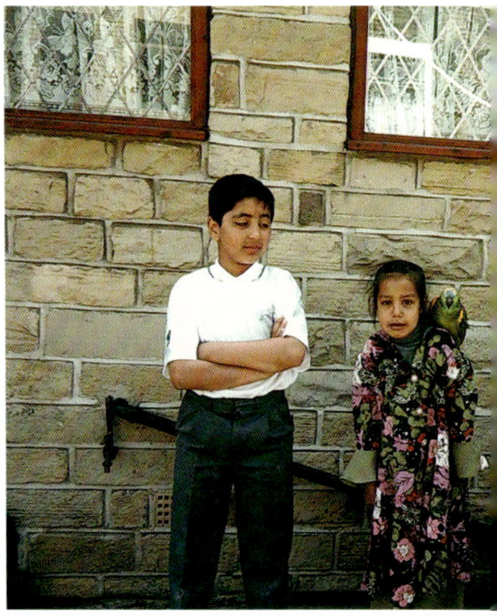

From the Kodak Collection, c. 1935

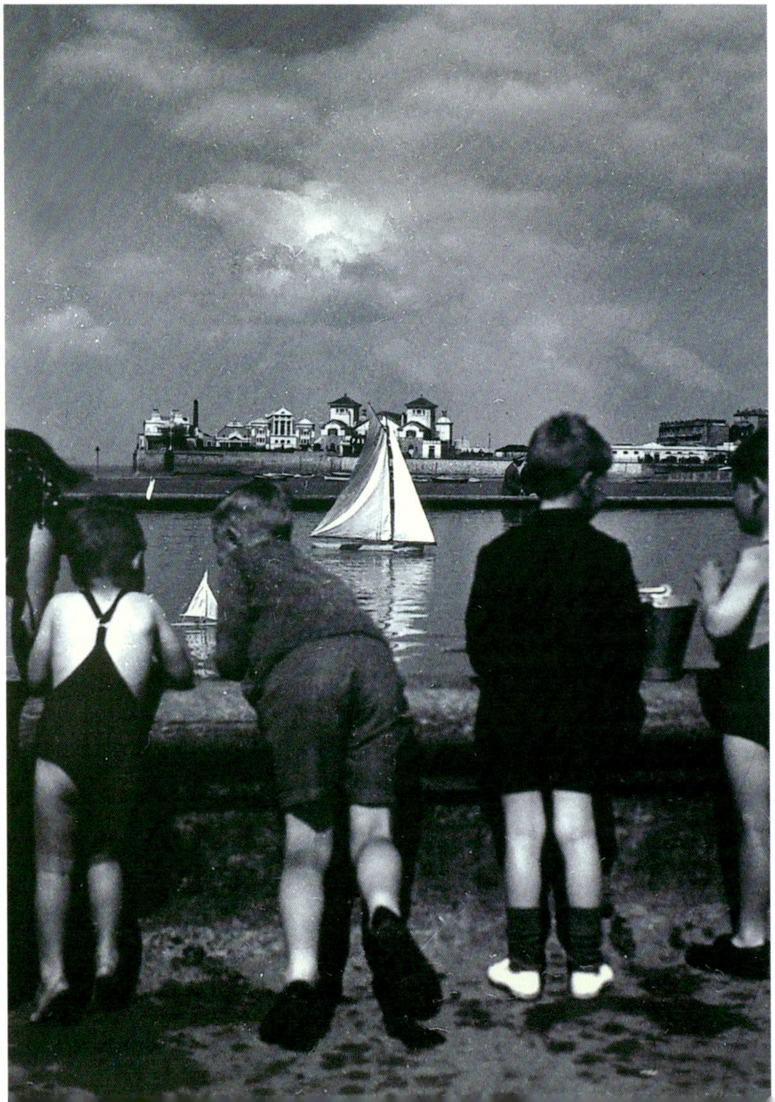

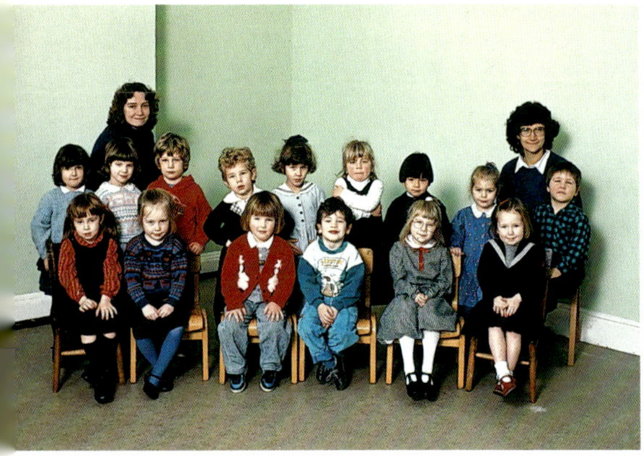

Family album photograph, 1989

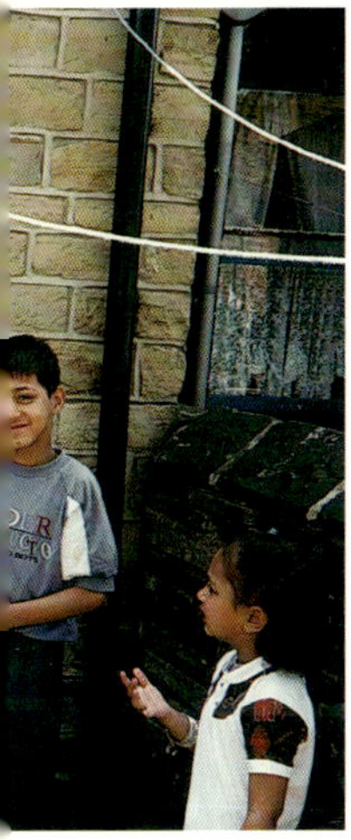

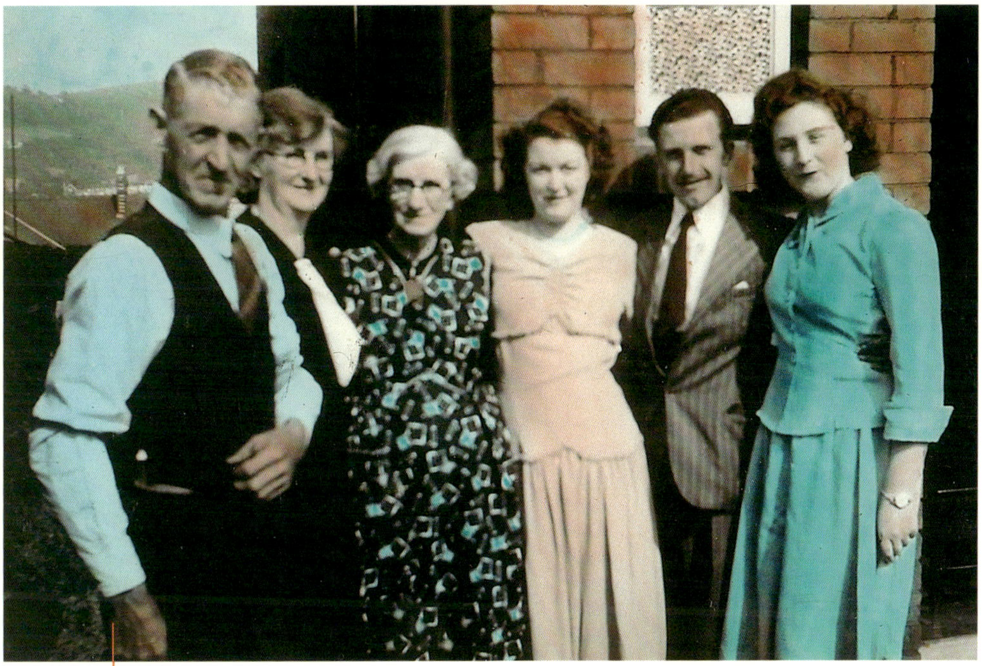

Family album photograph, hand-coloured, c. 1950

'The International Tribune, no less, dubbed it "The world's most popular institution devoted to photography" . . .Expansion isn't a luxury, it's a copper-bottomed necessity. Whatever it takes . . . it is a genuine national treasure.'

Practical Photography

The museum's Press Office sends details of the exhibition to the regional, national and specialist press. The written press releases are accompanied by copies of one of the photographs in the exhibition—ours. Newspaper staff arrive, photograph the exhibition and the new museum, then return to their offices with pictures and a story. New press prints make their way into other newspaper archives. Our photograph and that ordinary person (whose identity has now been obliterated) are back in the news.

After three months, the exhibition is taken down. The photographs are put away in their metal cabinets and drawers. Our print returns to its box.

The original photograph has stayed with the family since it was returned to them by newspaper staff. The person died a long time ago, and his story has been forgotten. His grandchildren own the picture now, along with the yellowing clipping from the newspaper. They keep the photograph in the same tin that their parents used. Lots of other pictures are kept in that tin, pictures of their grandparents and their parents as children, a glass negative, and a little lock of baby hair, kept since the 1930s.

The Kodak Girl

Colin Harding
Kodak Curator and Curator of Photographic Technology

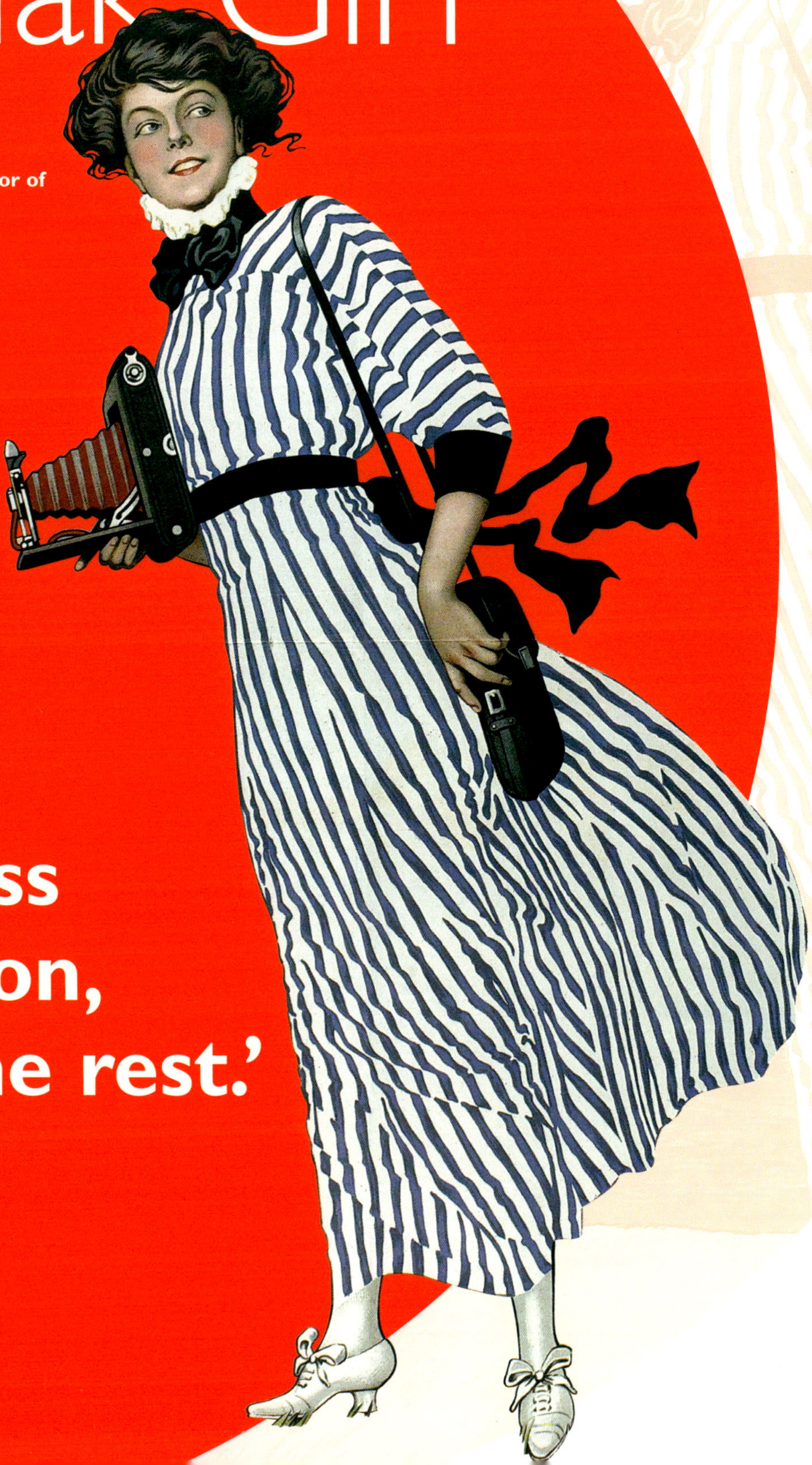

‘You press the button, we do the rest.’
George Eastman

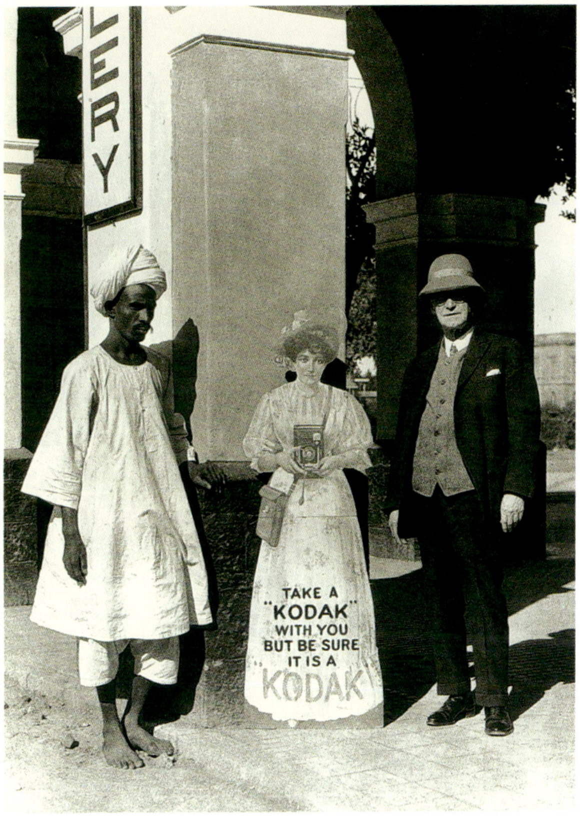

In 1928, on his second African safari trip, George Eastman met a Kodak Girl outside a shop in Nairobi.

She is delicate and sweet;
She is pretty and petite;
Her hair is either fluffy or in curl;
And a man with any taste
Would go far to clasp her waist;
While her dainty ankles make
your senses whirl.

When I see her calm and bland
With a Kodak in her hand
Prepared to take a snap-shot,
sun or rain,
My eyes have snapped her face
In its witchery and grace
And have printed it in colors on
my brain.

How I hope that in her glee
She has had a shot at me
With the Kodak which she
carries in her hand
For I know my photograph
In her eyes will loving laugh
When she puts it on the mantle
in a stand.

William E S Fales, 1902

In the mid-1880s George Eastman, the founder of Kodak, observed that 'a picture of a pretty girl sells more than a tree or house'. At the time, images of women were already being used to sell a wide range of goods and products. Eastman, with his keen awareness of the power and importance of advertising, was quick to grasp the selling potential of a pretty face. When the first Kodak camera appeared in 1888 some of the earliest advertisements showed it being used by women.

By November 1892, in a letter written by Eastman, the young woman with a camera had acquired a name: the 'Kodak Girl'. Little could Eastman have realised that she was destined to become one of the most successful and long-lasting of all advertising icons—the personification of popular photography in the public imagination. Wearing the latest fashions she appeared in a range of American magazine advertisements, drawn by eminent artists such as Frederic Remington. By the turn of the century such was her popularity that the Kodak Girl became immortalised in both music and verse. A number of poems were inspired by the 'rose-crowned "Lady Dainty" of the ads' and William T Cramer even composed a march and two-step entitled 'The Kodak Girl', dedicated to the Eastman Kodak Company.

In Britain, too, Kodak Limited had used images of young women with cameras in its advertising campaigns from the early 1890s. It was not until 1910, however, that a striking new element was added: drawn by the leading poster artist, John Hassell, this Kodak Girl was shown wearing a long striped dress. She wasn't the product of the artist's imagination but was based on a posed photograph of a live model. The photographer was Cavendish Morton, a well-known photographer, actor and author of a book on the art of theatrical make-up; the model was his wife Mary. Unfortunately, we do not know whether the photographer, the model or Kodak Limited should take the credit for the inspired decision to use a striped dress.

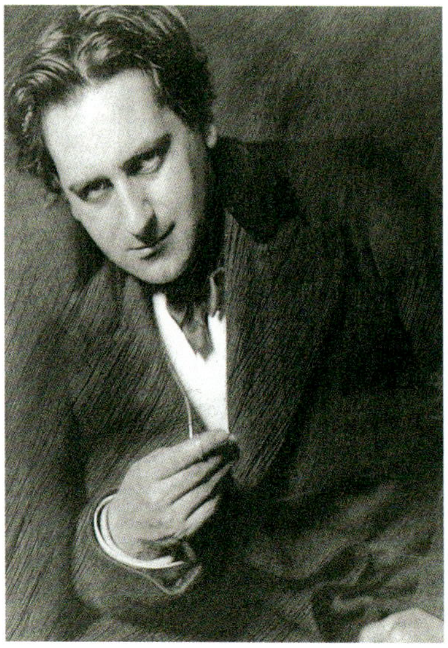

Cavendish Morton (1874–1939), author, actor, photographer and originator of the Kodak Girl.

On 22 April 1910 the Kodak Girl in her striped dress made her public debut in a full-page advertisement on the front page of the *Daily Mail*:

> This elfish figure—created by a distinguished artist—is an attempt to symbolise the spirit of Kodakery. It is a phantasy, not a portrait: an artistic conception, drawn with a touch of Parisian abandon. Live with the freshness of mountain air and the sparkle of the sunshine, the figure typifies the Kodak Girl—alert and keen, vivacious and jolly.

The first public appearance of the Kodak Girl in her characteristic striped dress in a full-page advertisement on the front page of the Daily Mail*, 22 April 1910.*

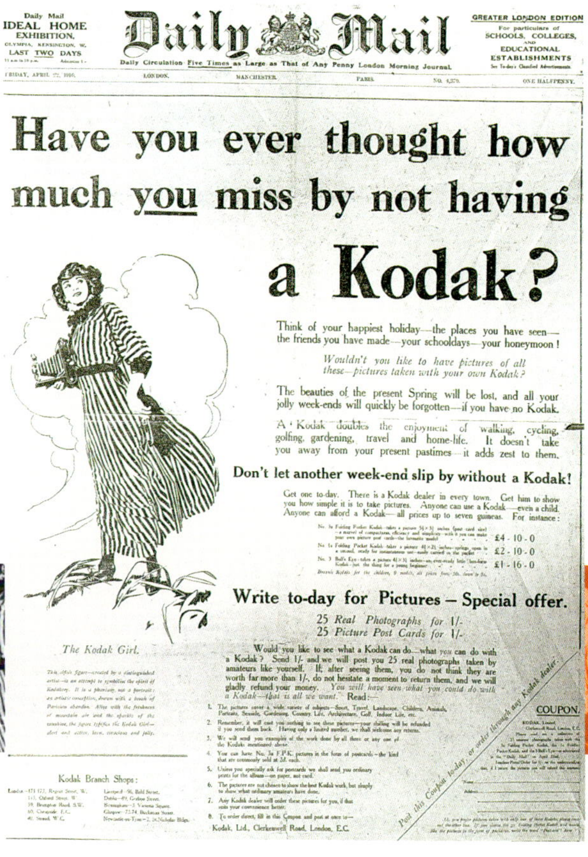

Daily Mail IDEAL HOME EXHIBITION, OLYMPIA, KENSINGTON, W. LAST TWO DAYS

Daily Mail

Daily Circulation Five Times as Large as That of Any Penny London Morning Journal.

GREATER LONDON EDITION
For particulars of SCHOOLS, COLLEGES, AND EDUCATIONAL ESTABLISHMENTS

LONDON. MANCHESTER. PARIS. ONE HALFPENNY.

Have you ever thought how much you miss by not having a Kodak?

Think of your happiest holiday—the places you have seen—the friends you have made—your schooldays—your honeymoon!

Wouldn't you like to have pictures of all these—pictures taken with your own Kodak?

The beauties of the present Spring will be lost, and all your jolly week-ends will quickly be forgotten—if you have no Kodak.

A Kodak doubles the enjoyment of walking, cycling, golfing, gardening, travel and home-life. It doesn't take you away from your present pastimes—it adds zest to them.

Don't let another week-end slip by without a Kodak!

Get one to-day. There is a Kodak dealer in every town. Get him to show you how simple it is to take pictures. Anyone can use a Kodak—even a child. Anyone can afford a Kodak—all prices up to seven guineas. For instance:

£4 - 10 - 0
£2 - 10 - 0
£1 - 16 - 0

Write to-day for Pictures – Special offer.

25 Real Photographs for 1/-
25 Picture Post Cards for 1/-

Would you like to see what a Kodak can do—what *you* can do with a Kodak? Send 1/- and we will post you 25 real photographs taken by amateurs like yourself. If, after seeing them, you do not think they are worth far more than 1/-, do not hesitate a moment to return them, and we will gladly refund your money. *You will have seen what you could do with a Kodak—that is all we want.* Read:—

Kodak, Ltd., Clerkenwell Road, London, E.C.

The Kodak Girl.

Kodak Branch Shops:

Post this Coupon to-day, or order through any Kodak dealer.

COUPON.

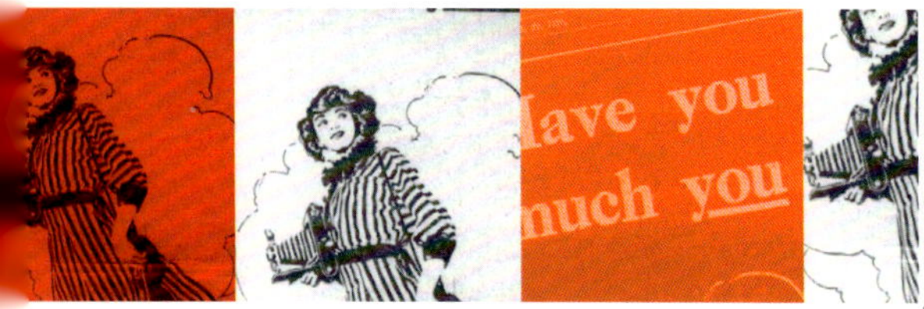

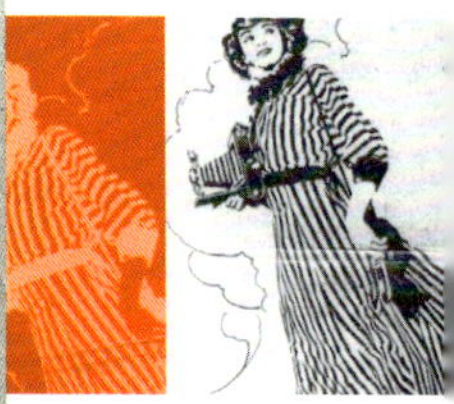

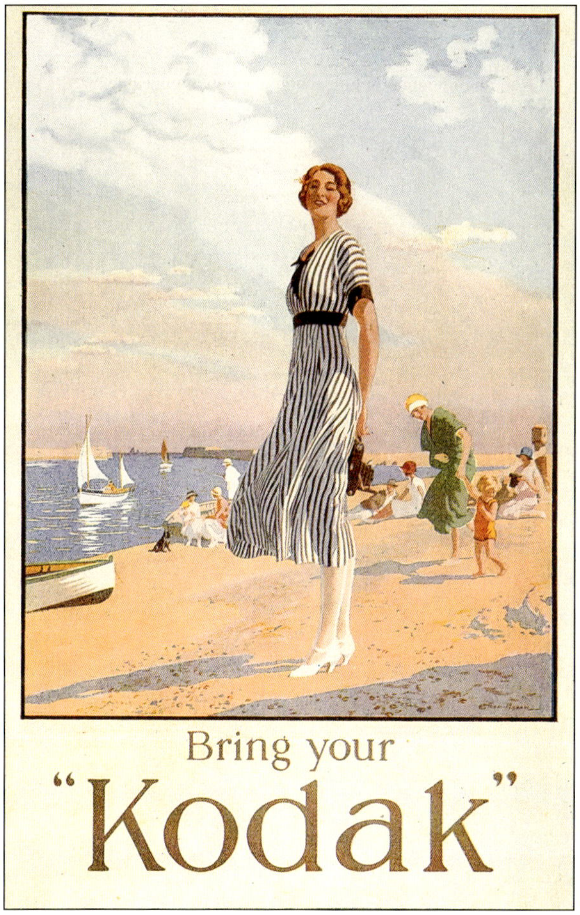

'Several decent young men, I hear, are forming a Vigilance Association for the purpose of thrashing the cads with cameras who go about at seaside places taking snapshots at ladies emerging from the deep. I wish the new society stout cudgels and much success.'

The Weekly Times and Echo, 1893

Early 1920s poster with a simple message, featuring a confident, independent Kodak Girl in a seaside setting.

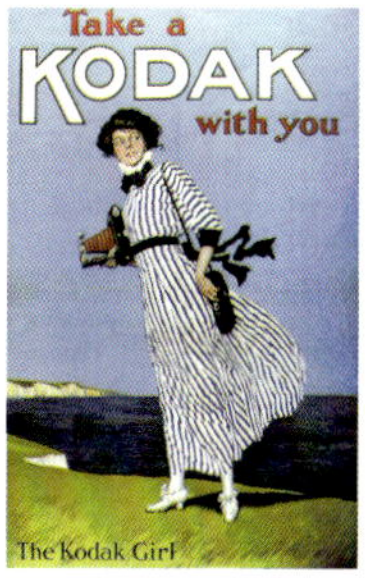

Immediately capturing the public's affection, the Kodak Girl in her characteristic stripes became the embodiment of snapshot photography. The central motif in all Kodak advertising campaigns, she appeared on posters, in shop displays and in magazine and newspaper advertisements. She was created by some of the leading artists and illustrators of the day, including Claude Shepperson, Dudley Harvey, Horace Rich and, most prolifically, Fred Pegram. The epitome of modern, confident, independent womanhood she found herself portrayed in a variety or settings—domestic, seaside, town and countryside—both at home and abroad. Whatever her location, her messages were always simple and direct: 'Save your happy memories with a Kodak'; 'Tell the story of your happy days—with a Kodak'; 'No holiday is complete without a Kodak'; 'All outdoors invites your Kodak.'

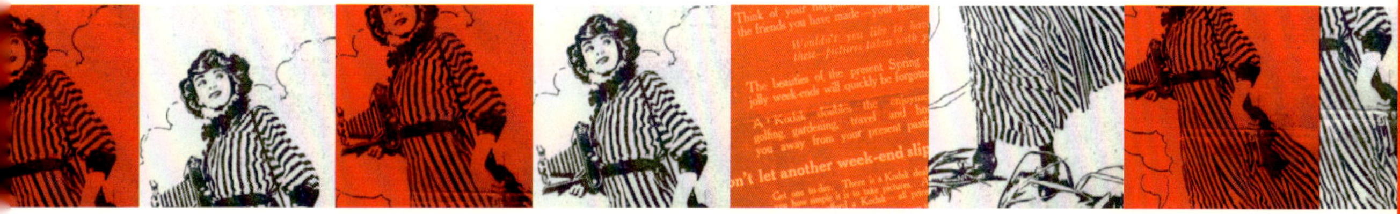

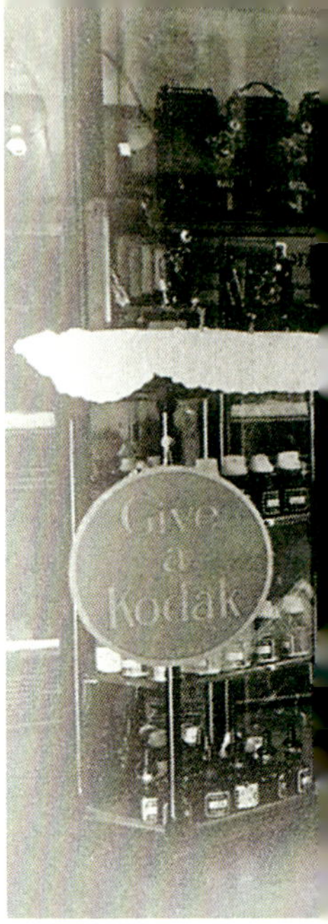

As the decades passed, the Kodak Girl, forever young, kept pace with the changing fashions of the day. The long hemlines of the first Kodak Girls were gradually raised to reveal a pair of shapely calves, and by the late 1920s she had become a flapper with knee-length skirt and cloche hat. By the 1950s her dress had become even more abbreviated, eventually being replaced by a swimming costume. Throughout all these changes in fashion, however, one factor remained constant: whatever the Kodak Girl wore, it was always striped.

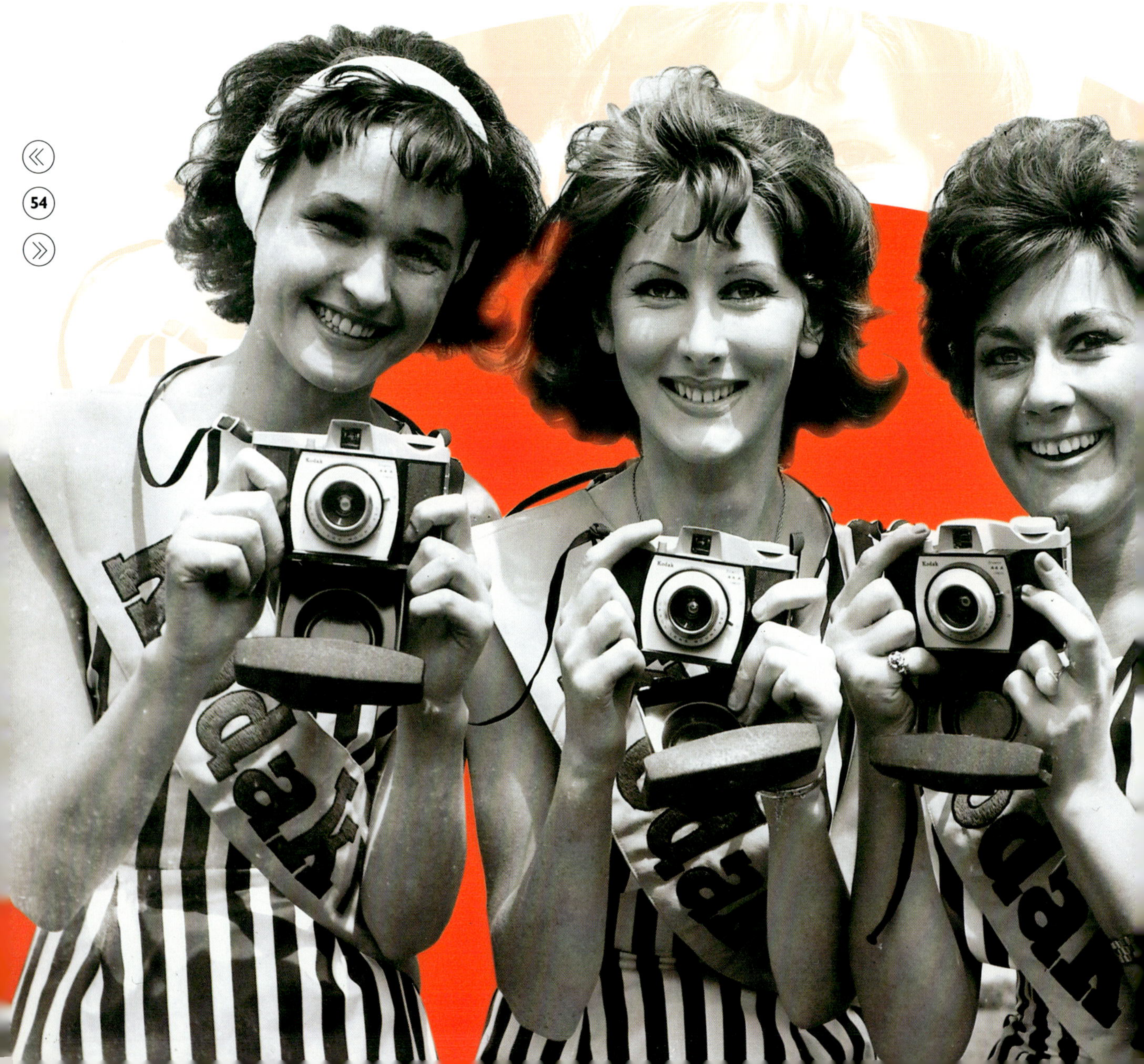

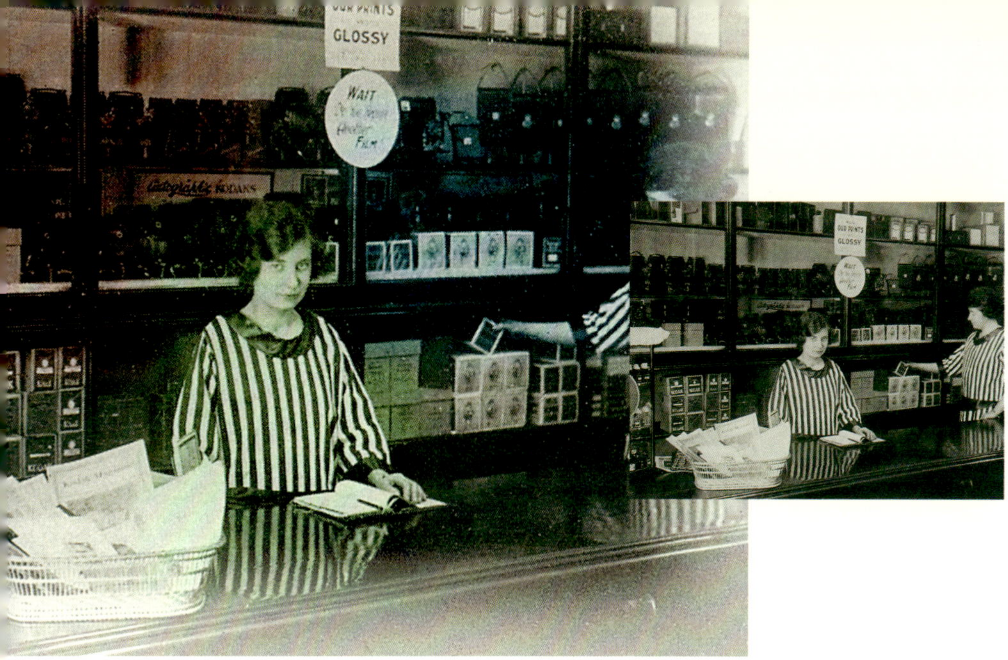

Staff at Messrs Nash, Kenyon & Co. Ltd, Southport, 1924, dressed in their Kodak Girl outfits.

Kodak Girls were not confined to posters or life-sized cardboard cutouts. Flesh-and-blood Kodak Girls were a common sight at fêtes, processions and carnivals throughout the 1920s and 1930s and no fancy-dress competition was complete without a Kodak Girl entrant. Many photographic shops began to dress their female staff in striped dresses; Kodak even supplied the blue-and-white-striped cotton fabric. And for those dealers who did not want to go to the trouble of having dresses made up, Kodak supplied ready-to-wear outfits. All the dealer had to do was provide the height and waist measurements of his staff. During the 1950s and 1960s a team of Kodak Girls toured Britain's seaside resorts, reminding holiday-makers that 'no holiday is complete without a Kodak'. Described as 'walking advertisements' they were tasked to spread the gospel of popular photography.

With the coming of the 1970s the Kodak Girl was approaching the end of her career. Even though images of young women were still used in Kodak advertising, there was no longer a role for the Kodak Girl. She had served the cause of popular photography well for over 60 years and who could deny her right to a peaceful retirement? But watch this space: is the new millennium the time for the Kodak Girl to make a comeback—in a new and ultra-hip incarnation, of course?

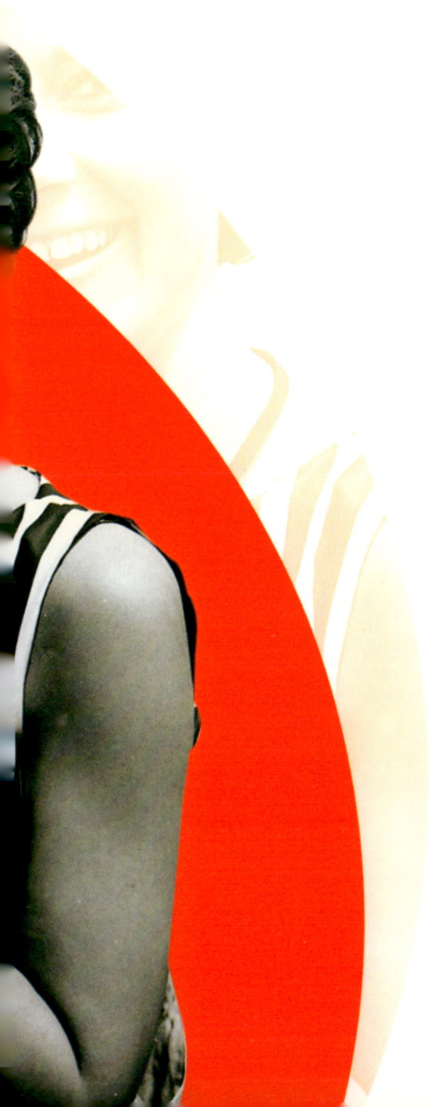

A happy group of Kodak Girls with their Brownie 44A cameras, c.1963. During the 1950s and 1960s Kodak Limited employed teams of Kodak Girls to tour Britain's seaside resorts.

Why does Mickey Mouse wear white gloves?

Mary Murphy
Head of Collections

Why is an antique camera, or a photograph of someone unknown, important enough to be in a museum? On their own, such objects may be intriguing, beautiful or poignant. What really gives them life and meaning, though, is the story of who used the camera or took the photograph; what their intentions were and what techniques they used; what the photograph was about and what impact the image created on others. It is these rich stories behind the evolution of photography, film and television that the Museum tells in its permanent galleries and touring exhibitions. The twentieth century is the first to be defined through pictures, both still and moving, so these stories also reflect the wider human experience.

The Museum's role is to explore and preserve, as well as tell these stories. It looks after one of the world's most important and diverse collections of images, equipment and contextual material. The Collection includes such irreplaceable objects as the earliest surviving negative from 1835, made by photography's inventor, William Henry Fox Talbot; John Logie Baird's earliest surviving television equipment, together with the world's first recorded television pictures from 1927. There are some three million photographs: from rare examples of the work of leading photographers, to the *Daily Herald* Archive, an astonishing photographic legacy of the twentieth century. The Collection is constantly growing, both as new historic material comes to light, and as the media respond to developments such as the digital revolution.

FIND

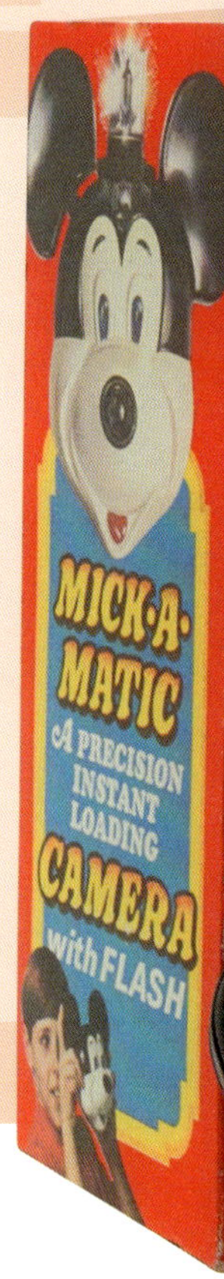

The Oscar for Best Picture awarded to David Puttnam for Chariots of Fire*, 1981.*

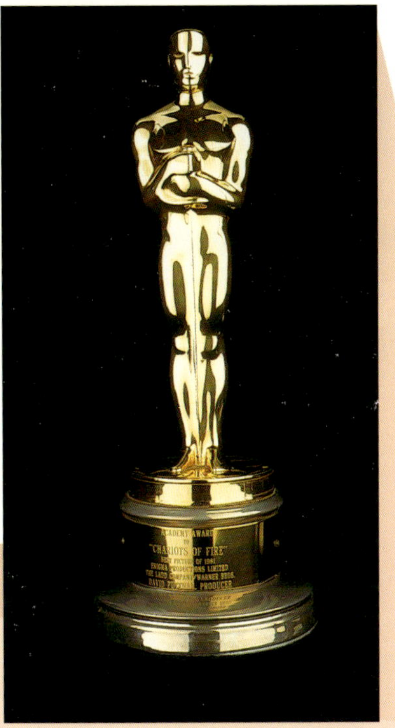

Only a fraction of this enormous Collection can be put on show at any one time. Yet one of the Museum's fundamental aims is to provide the best possible access to these national treasures for all visitors. So the new Museum includes a dedicated ***Research Centre***, housing the vast majority of the Collection.

One of the main aims of the ***Research Centre*** is to store all parts of the Collection in the correct way to preserve it for as long as possible. All objects tend to deteriorate over time, but photographs and other ephemeral material can be particularly fragile and sensitive to climate. Light levels, which can be very damaging, are strictly controlled. Some photographs are even kept in boxes marked 'do not open'! Temperature and humidity are also carefully monitored.

'If you gave him a good script, actors and technicians, Mickey Mouse could direct a movie.'
Nicholas Hytner, director of *The Madness of King George* and *The Crucible*

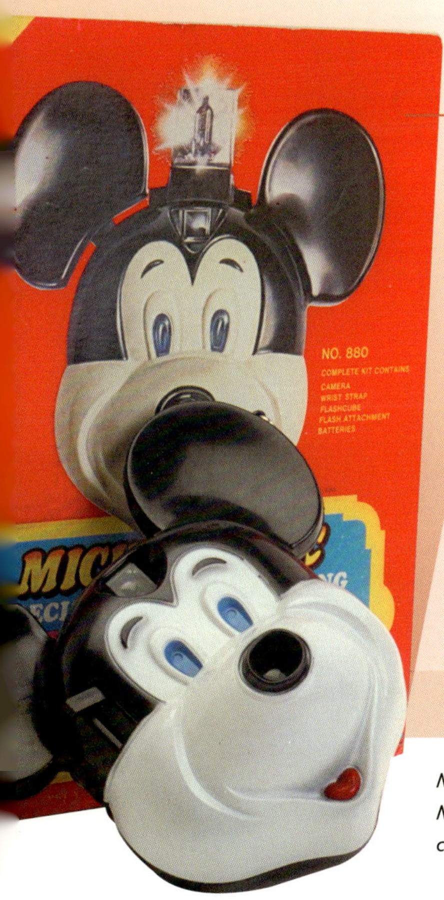

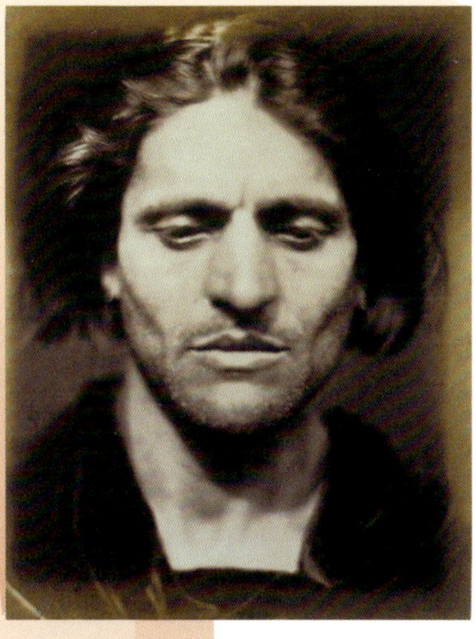

'Iago', an albumen print made in 1867 by Julia Margaret Cameron.

Mick-a-matic camera, made in 1970 in the USA. Mickey Mouse's head contains a 126 camera for children, with the lens in Mickey's nose.

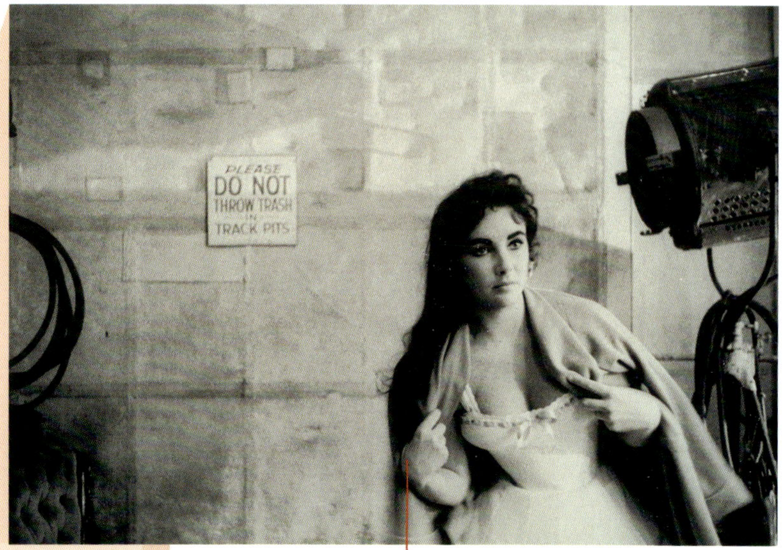

Elizabeth Taylor photographed by the acclaimed US photographer Bob Willoughby on the set of the 1956 film Raintree County.

'To collect photographs is to collect the world.'
Susan Sontag (b.1933), author, photographer and film-maker

The ***Research Centre*** is laid out to give easy access to the many types of object. There are separate rooms and storage systems for different parts of the Collection. Many of the smaller items of equipment, where security could be a problem, are stored in specially designed 'visible display' cabinets with clear Perspex fronts. On the other hand, it may not be desirable for larger objects to be housed in cases, since they may not be easy to move for research or conservation purposes. The Gandolfi and Print Viewing Rooms have special facilities for studying photographs, film, printed material such as packaging, books and posters, as well as smaller items from the technology collections.

Nothing can replace the excitement of seeing 'the real thing'. However, before viewing the originals, many visitors need a way to explore what is available and to help identify items of interest. 'The Investigator' has been developed for just this purpose. This computer-based information catalogue provides easy touch-screen access to high-quality digitised still and moving images of objects from the Collection.

Visiting curators and researchers come from as far afield as the USA, Japan and Australia. They might be here for just a short while, or for several months working on an exhibition or publication. Objects are constantly in demand for loans to museums around the world, or for use on film sets and television programmes. Camera collectors, film and television enthusiasts frequently come to the Museum to view particularly rare trade literature or even packaging.

The ***Research Centre*** is not only designed for specialist researchers. Anyone—whether a school group, student or academic, camera enthusiast, amateur film society or an individual with a passion for the work of a particular photographer—can make an appointment to use the ***Research Centre***. There are also frequent lectures and behind-the-scenes tours led by curators.

Thousands of people a year who cannot visit the Museum ring or e-mail the Museum's Enquiry Service with such demanding and intriguing questions as: 'What was the film speed of 16 mm film in 1934?'. One question which confounded not just us, but Disney too, was: 'Why does Mickey Mouse wear white gloves?' If you know the answer, please tell us!

Hughie Green, host of the TV talent contest, Opportunity Knocks, *which ran between 1956 and 1978.*

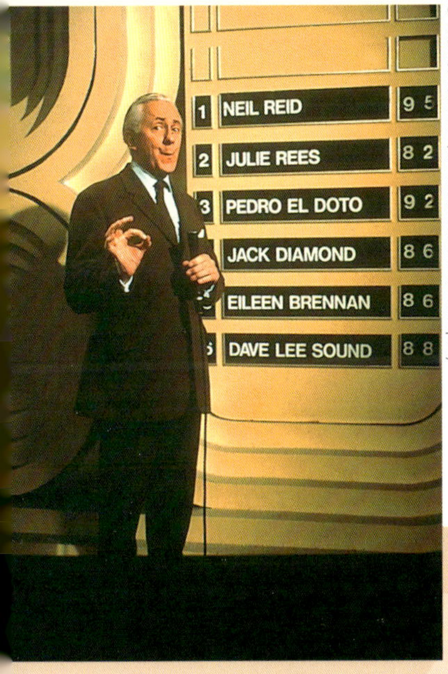

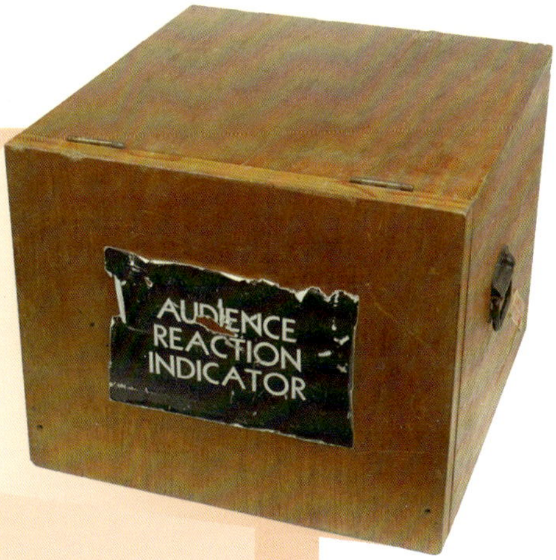

The 'clapometer' used on Hughie Green's Opportunity Knocks *to register the studio audience's approval of performers on the show.*

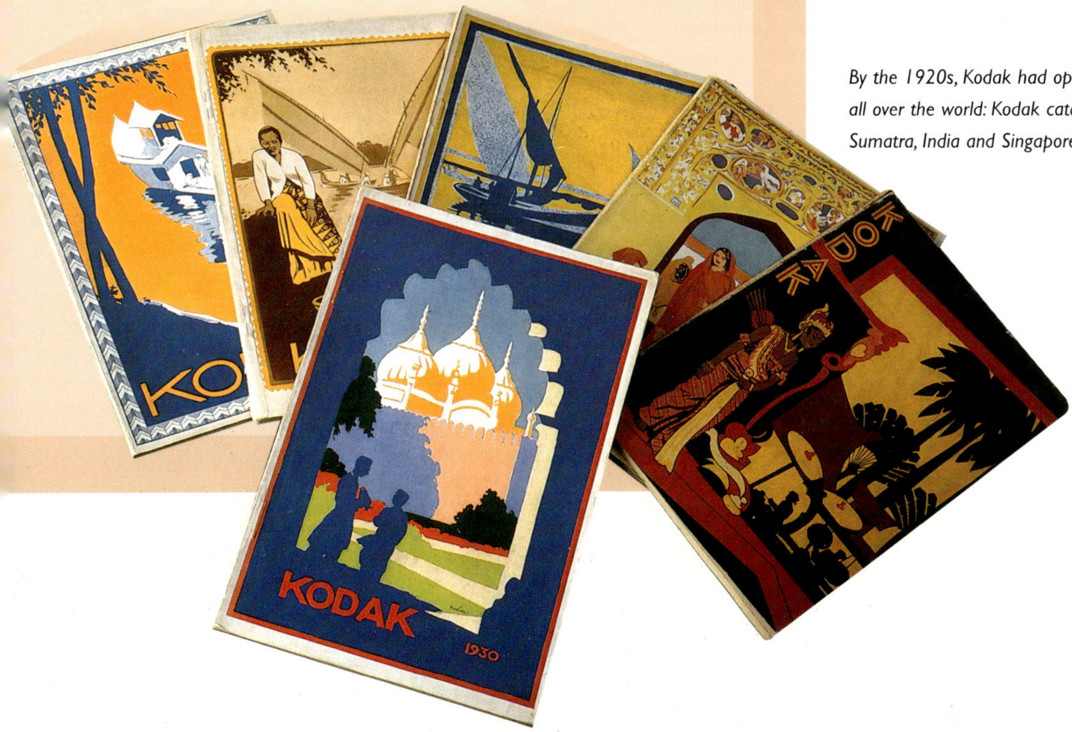

By the 1920s, Kodak had opened branches all over the world: Kodak catalogues for Java, Sumatra, India and Singapore, 1927–31.

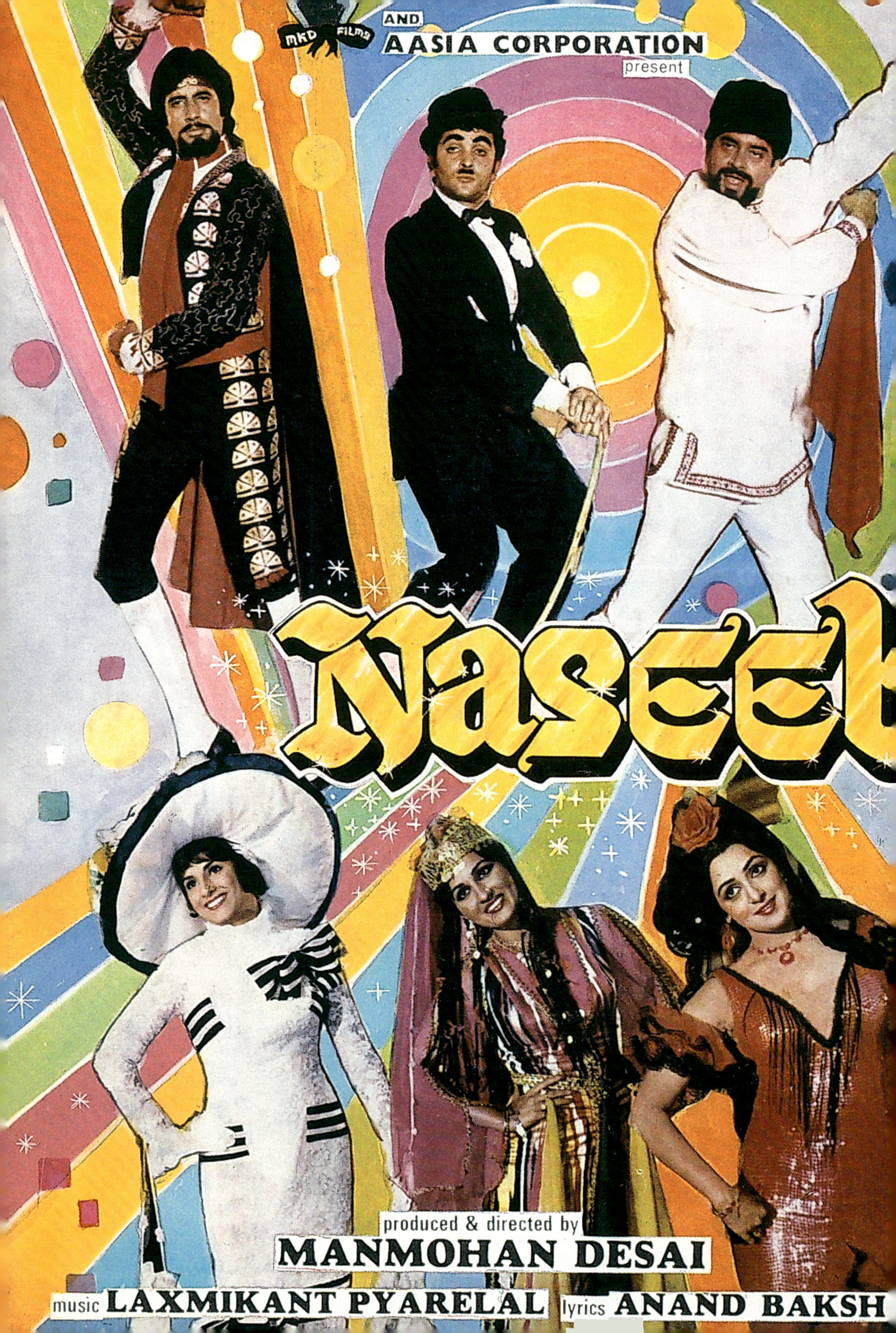
MKD FILMS
AND
AASIA CORPORATION
present
Naseeb
produced & directed by
MANMOHAN DESAI
music LAXMIKANT PYARELAL
lyrics ANAND BAKSHI

Bollywood: a film phenomenon

Irfan Ajeeb
Film Programmer

The magical partnership of Desai and Bachchan experienced another success at the box office with Naseeb *(1981), a much-anticipated, extravagantly plotted film. The director creates an impressive cast that includes Rishi Kapoor and Shatrughan Sinha, as well as the Big B. Female superstar Hema Malini was cast alongside Amitabh in this story about greed and deception.*

In the 1950s the Asian Film Society held screenings of Indian films at the old Scala Cinema in London. It was a huge event and the cinema was always full to capacity. People came from all over England and made a day of it. Hundreds of people who hadn't seen each other for months, sometimes years, bumped into each other at the Scala and stayed on to chat. A visit to the Scala was the highlight of the week, and a great way for Asian families to socialise.

In Bradford in the 1960s and 1970s going to the cinema was the major social event for Asian families. Outside London, Bradford was the most popular destination, and there were half-a-dozen or so cinemas dedicated purely to Bollywood films located around the city. Sadly, those cinemas no longer exist: the arrival of videos on the market in the late 1970s kept people at home and left the cinema auditoriums empty. However, in the 1990s the public got tired of hiring poor-quality tapes from the local video shop, and cinemas came back in a big way, with Bollywood starting to show its true potential. But what is Bollywood? How did this phenomenon start, and why does it fascinate so many people—black and white?

'The Museum is a cineaste's paradise.'
Harpers & Queen

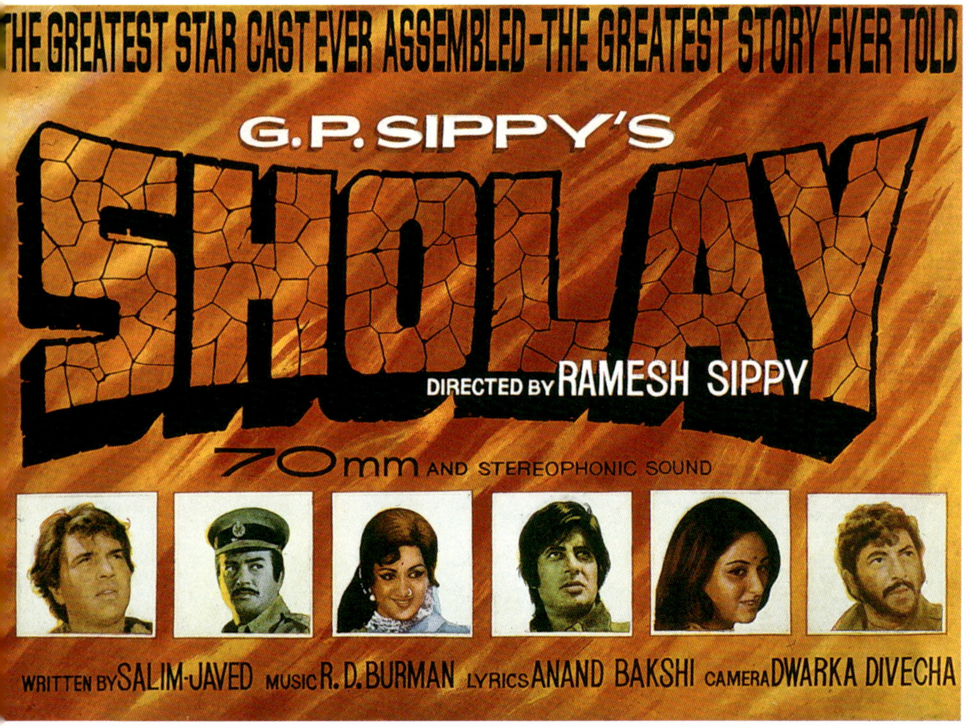

Sholay (1975) is by far the most successful Bollywood movie ever made. The young and talented film director, Ramesh Sippy, helped by the amazing script created by the legendary Salim-Javed, delivered this massively popular spaghetti Western that created the 'Angry Young Man'. Amitabh was paired with another action hero, Dharmendra, in this wonderful tale of action, romance, comedy and emotion.

Bollywood is based in Bombay, India, hence the name. The largest film industry in the world, it churns out over 400 movies a year, making its counterpart in California look like a cottage industry. Arguably, one man was responsible for steering Bollywood on to the international stage: Amitabh Bachchan, known to many as the Big B, or the Angry Young Man, and one of the most influential figures in the history of Bollywood. *Sholay*, a spaghetti Western, was the vehicle which first grabbed the world's attention and brought the Big B into the spotlight. (*Sholay* was also the debut of legendary villain Gabbar Singh, portrayed by the late Amjad Khan, an influential figure in his own right.) Other Amitabh classics include films such as *Zanjeer, Muqaddar Ka Sikandar, Deewar* and *Shakti*, which saw Amitabh rise to fame as the Angry Young Man, an individual at odds with the society around him.

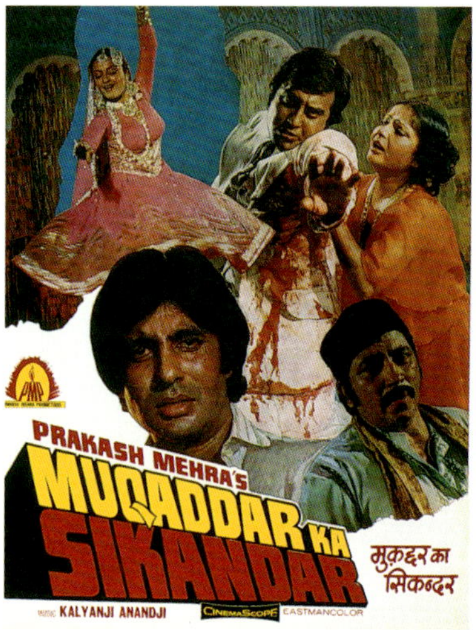

In Muqaddar Ka Sikandar *(1978) a tale of love and sacrifice directed by the legendary Prakash Mehra, superstar Amitabh Bachchan is cast alongside Vinod Khanna. The year 1978 was good for the actor, with a string of box-office blockbusters such as* Don *and* Kasme Vaade*, establishing him as a Bollywood phenomenon.*

After a period of poor-quality films in the 1980s, when the industry was struggling to match the standard set in the previous decade, the craze for Bollywood was ignited again in the early 1990s with the release of an eagerly anticipated family saga called *Hum Aapke Hain Kaun? (What Are We to You?)* which saw newcomer Salman Khan make a serious bid to claim the Big B's pole position.

The queues outside the cinema hall were extraordinary. Peopled with young men in ragamuffin clothes eyeing up teenage girls dressed in shimmering chiffon saris or the tapering trousers of *shalwaar-kameez* beneath their winter coats, with old women shivering in the cold, their Kashmiri shawls drawn tightly around their shoulders, and with young couples whose impatient children had the scent of popcorn in their nostrils, this particular film brought a longed-for new dimension to the Bollywood film industry. Out went the 'action man' and in came the 'lover boy' as the industry looked back to the 1960s when Bollywood superstars like Dilip Kumar and Shammi Kapoor dominated with their clean-cut boy-next-door image.

It was in 1993, with the arrival on the scene of the triple Khans—Salman, Aamir and Shahrukh—that the Big B's reign in Bollywood was threatened. Movies such as *Maine Pyar Kiya, Dil Hai Ke Maanta Nahin* and *Baazigar* established the three Khans as

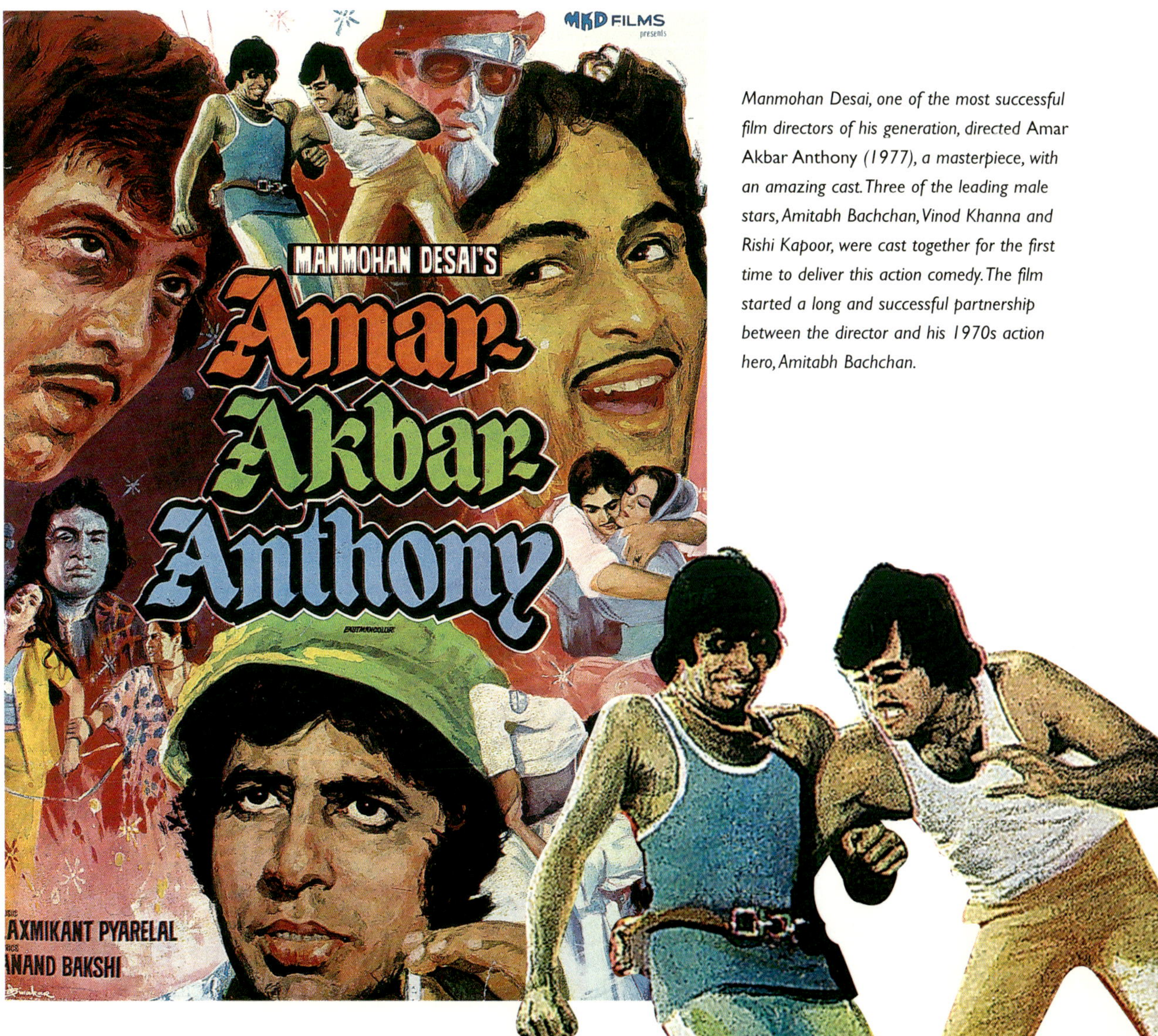

Manmohan Desai, one of the most successful film directors of his generation, directed Amar Akbar Anthony *(1977), a masterpiece, with an amazing cast. Three of the leading male stars, Amitabh Bachchan, Vinod Khanna and Rishi Kapoor, were cast together for the first time to deliver this action comedy. The film started a long and successful partnership between the director and his 1970s action hero, Amitabh Bachchan.*

major box-office material. Of the three, Shahrukh Khan has become the next Bollywood superstar, pioneering a daring new angle in the industry with three of his early movies, *Baazigar, Darr* and *Anjaam*, which became box-office hits. Realising that the Bollywood audience was losing enthusiasm for action films, he introduced a love story with a new dimension: for the first time the leading male was playing the role of a villain, a manipulative psychotic killer. The public accepted him and, in 1998, with a long line of love-story blockbusters under his belt, Shahrukh attained the same level of popularity that the Big B experienced in the 1970s and 1980s. Hits such as *Dil Se*—the first Hindi film ever to enter the UK top ten charts—and *Kuch Kuch Hota Hai*—which went one better than *Dil Se* and broke into the top five films in Britain—established Shahrukh as the front-runner to take Bollywood into the new millennium.

The National Museum of Photography, Film & Television plays a key role in promoting Asian cinema in Britain. Its Bite the Mango Film Festival, dedicated to African and Asian cinema, has established itself as the leading European–Asian film festival in

Shammi Kapoor's most popular film, Junglee *(1961), had this Bollywood good guy paired with 1960s dream girl Saira Banu in a light-hearted love story. Kapoor went on to become famous in the 1960s with hits such as* Kashmir Ki Kali *and* Teesri Manzil.

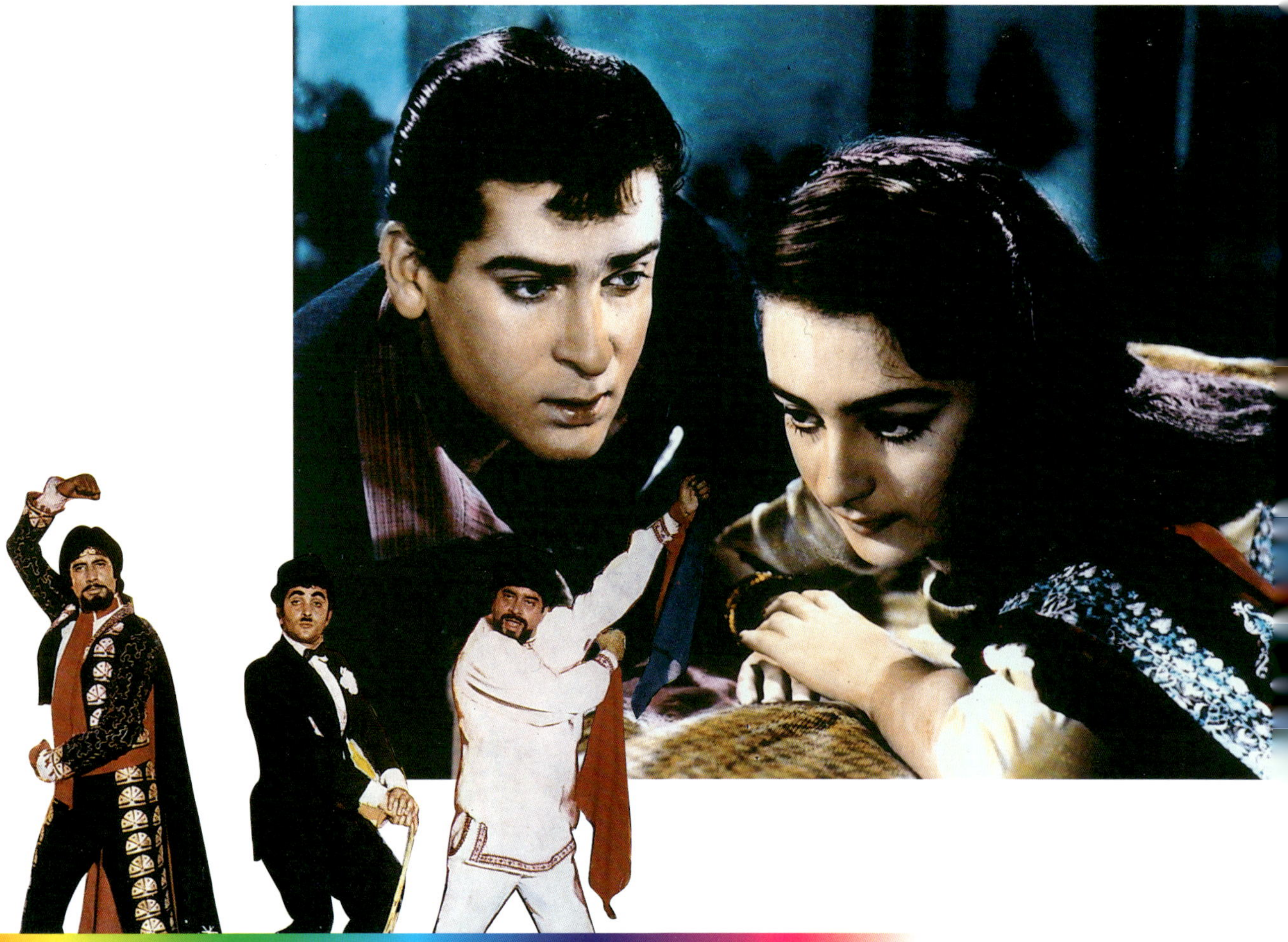

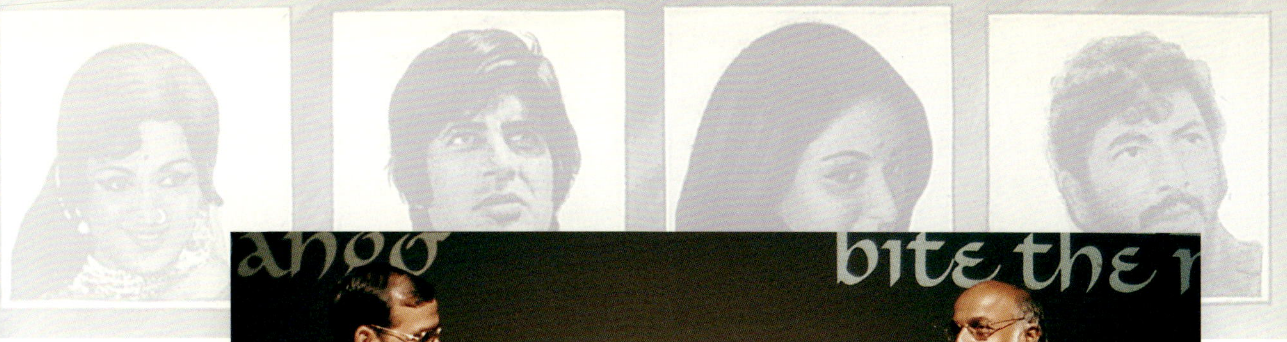

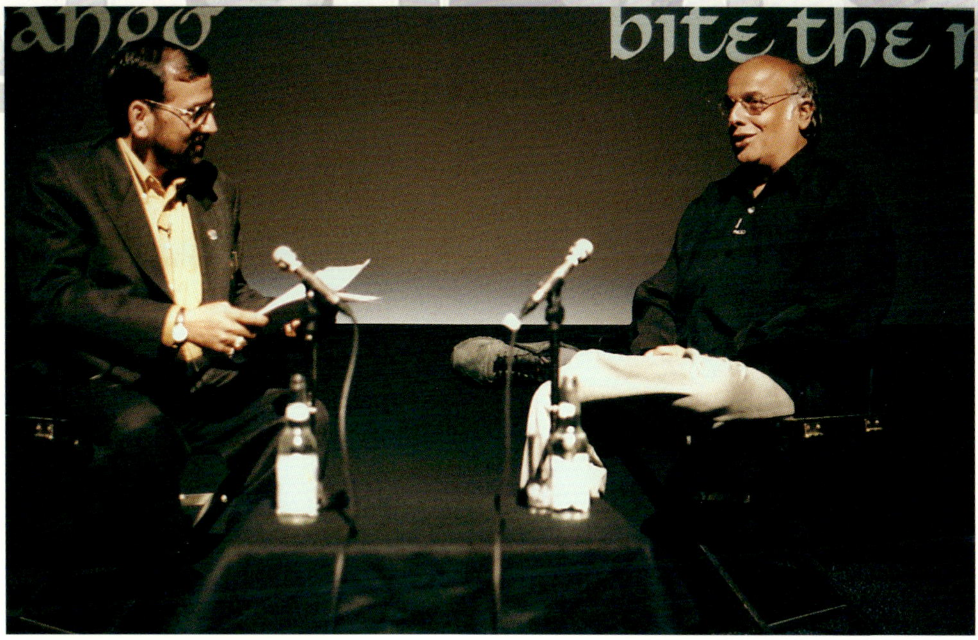

Opening the Bite the Mango Film Festival in 1998 was Bollywood director Mahesh Bhatt with a screening of his film Duplicate, *starring Bollywood superstar Shahrukh Khan. Bhatt is seen talking to film historian Lalit Mohan Joshi about his previous films, such as the controversial* Arth *and recent* Duplicate.

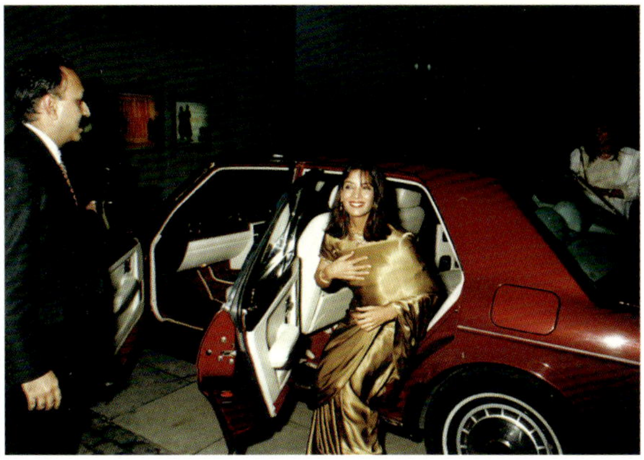

One of the most influential actresses in Bollywood, Shabana Azmi, attended the Bite the Mango Film Festival in 1997 for a premiere of the controversial film Mrityudand, *where she was cast alongside superstar Madhuri Dixit. Shabana has starred in classics such as Mahesh Bhatt's* Arth, *Desai's* Amar Akbar Anthony *and even Hollywood hits such as* City of Joy *with Patrick Swayze.*

the world, attracting appearances by major stars from India and Pakistan. Past guests include Shyam Benegal, Shabana Azmi, Subhash Ghai, Mahesh Bhatt, Zeba Bakhtiar and Samina Peerzada—all major stars from the worlds of Bollywood and Lollywood—the Pakistani film industry based in Lahore.

It will be interesting to see the cultural development of Pakistani and Indian cinema, as Bollywood already boasts a more powerful range of women stars and directors than even Hollywood. For example, Shabana Azmi plays a key role in Indian politics, and Zeba Bakhtiar produces her own films. The baton is already firmly in the hands of the next generation, with Pooja Bhatt leading the way for a new era of women directors and producers. The future of south Asian cinema is changing dramatically, and we eagerly anticipate the results.

TV: telling and selling stories

Sarah Mumford
Head of Education
and
Ian Potter
Curator, *TV Heaven*

The first advertisement to be shown on British television was in 1955, a black-and-white one-minute commercial for Gibbs SR toothpaste. It showed an image of a healthy-looking, attractive young woman brushing her teeth with the product, and the voiceover praised the product's fresh taste and stressed its medical virtues. A big event back in 1955, but nothing out of the ordinary for today's television viewer.

A comparison of that first advertisement with those we see today reveals some striking differences. Most obviously, the advertisements of today are much more sophisticated. They are filmed in colour and use slick, digital, computer-generated graphics that flash past our eyes at a rapid rate. Their tone is more informal and less direct, they don't used repetition as often, and they are at least half the length of that very first advertisement.

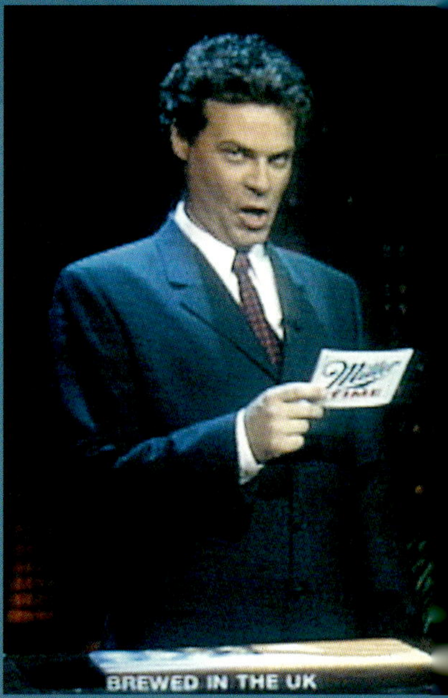

Advertisers often copy other television formats, such as game shows, to make products more appealing.

All images supplied 'courtesy of D&AD' have previously been represented in the British Design & Art Direction Annual.

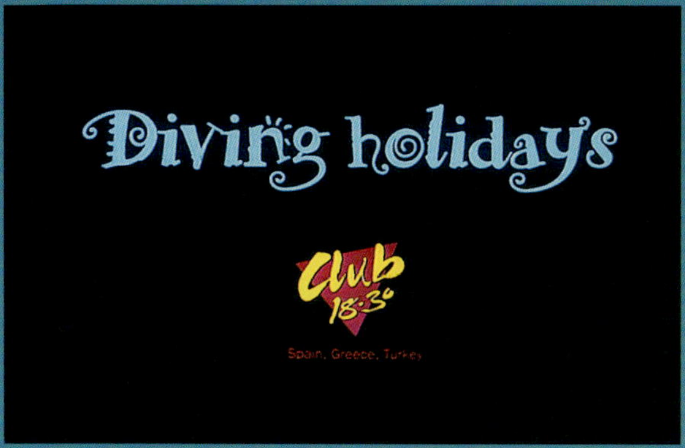

Saatchi & Saatchi for Club 18–30, image courtesy of D&AD

Saatchi & Saatchi used subtle humour to sell Club 18–30 holidays.

GGT Advertising for Scottish Courage, image courtesy of D&AD

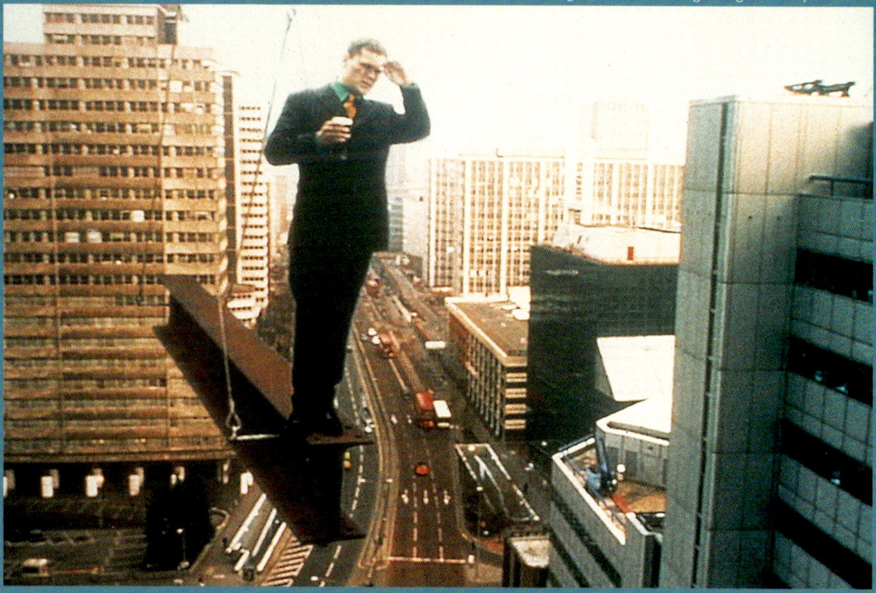

Digital technology is used in adverts to make the impossible possible.

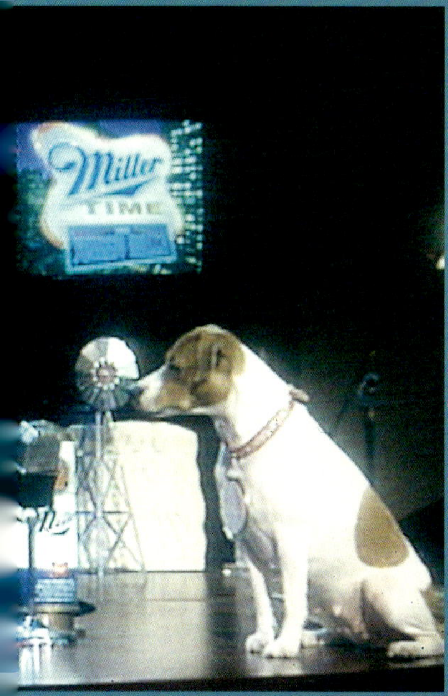

Rainey Kelly Campbell Roalfe for Scottish Courage, image courtesy of D&AD

The kinds of advertisements we watch, and our expectations of them, have progressed beyond belief. Today's teenagers live by the mantra: 'I shop therefore I am.' These same young viewers expect advertisements that are cleverer, more entertaining, and wackier than ever before. The 'cooler' the advertisement the more likelihood that the teenager will want to wear/buy/consume the product. The television advertisement has become a cultural icon and advertising reflects contemporary social concerns. Our growing consumer culture drives the demand for goods and the need to create that demand through advertising.

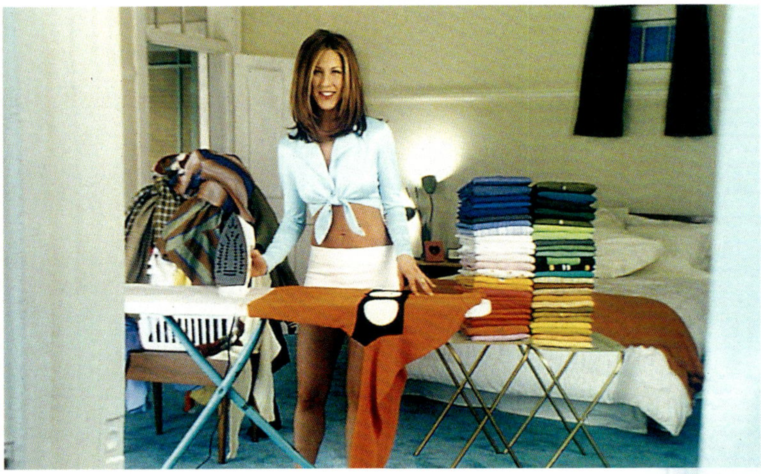

Bartle Bogle Hegarty for Elida Fabergé, image courtesy of D&AD

Jennifer Aniston, star of Friends, *was used by Bartle Bogle Hegarty to promote Lynx deodorant.*

Over the years the technology used in advertising, and the mass media as a whole, has progressed in leaps and bounds. Manual photographic cameras have become automatic, celluloid film may well be superseded by digital technology, and digital versatile disc (DVD) is technologically superior to analogue videotape. What was once possible only in dreams is now limited only by the imagination of the media producer. With technological advancements have come increased commercial opportunities. The media industries have grown into multinational global conglomerates supported in part by advertising revenue. Opportunities for making money through the media are huge and the pressure is on to keep us watching. Of course this growth of commercialism has had a big impact on the media products we consume, be they adverts, newspapers, television programmes, films or computer games.

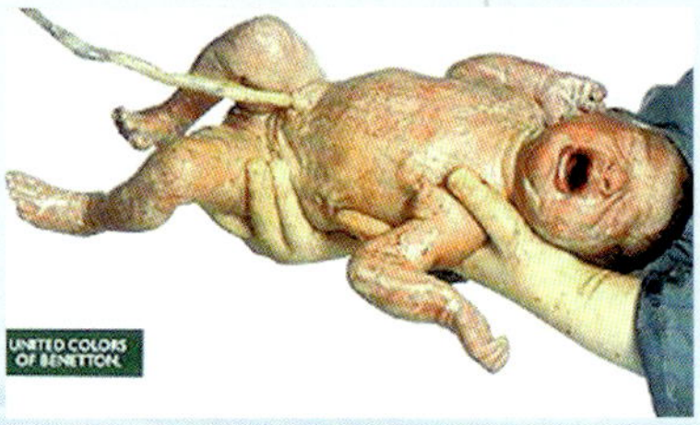

© Benetton Group/O Toscani

Advertising reflects the social concerns of the day: the burgeoning consumer culture drives the demand for goods and the need to create that demand through advertising.

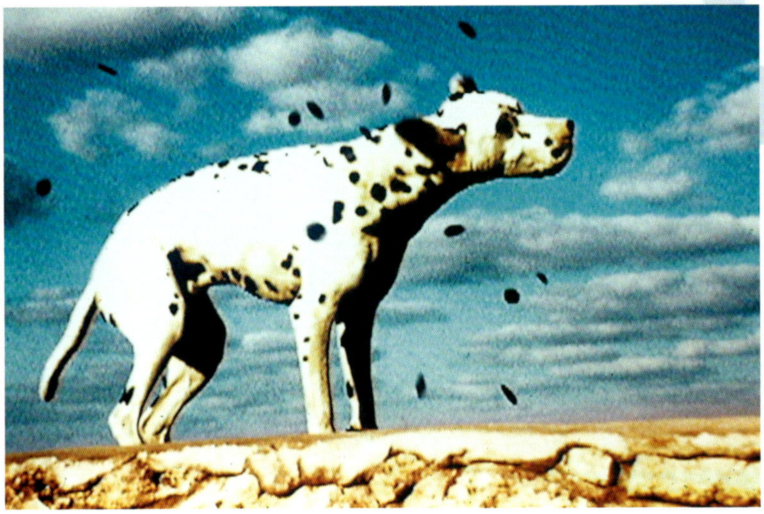

J Walter Thompson for Lever Brothers, image courtesy of D&AD

Images can now be manipulated digitally to make adverts even more memorable.

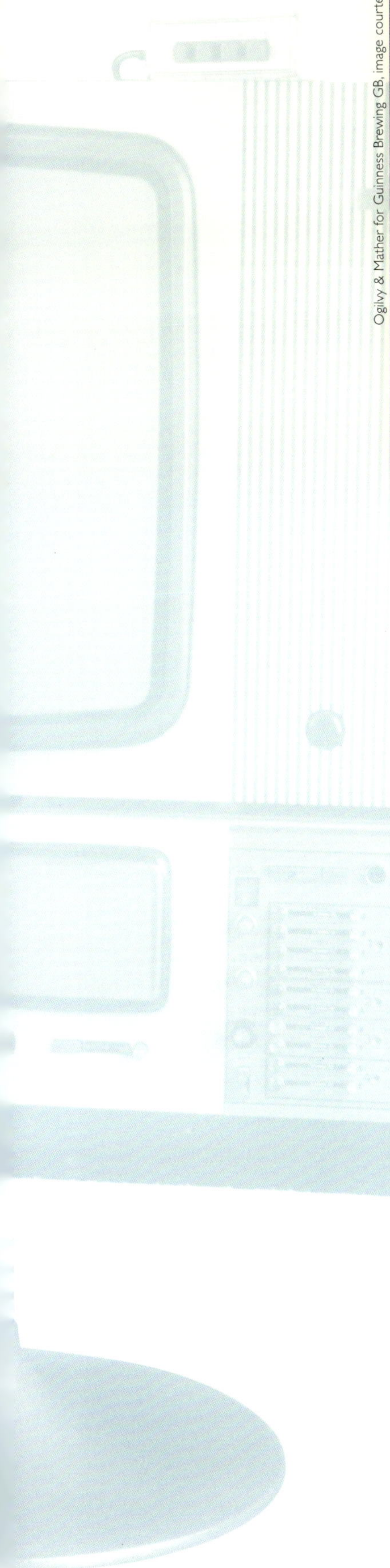

Ogilvy & Mather for Guinness Brewing GB, image courtesy of D&AD

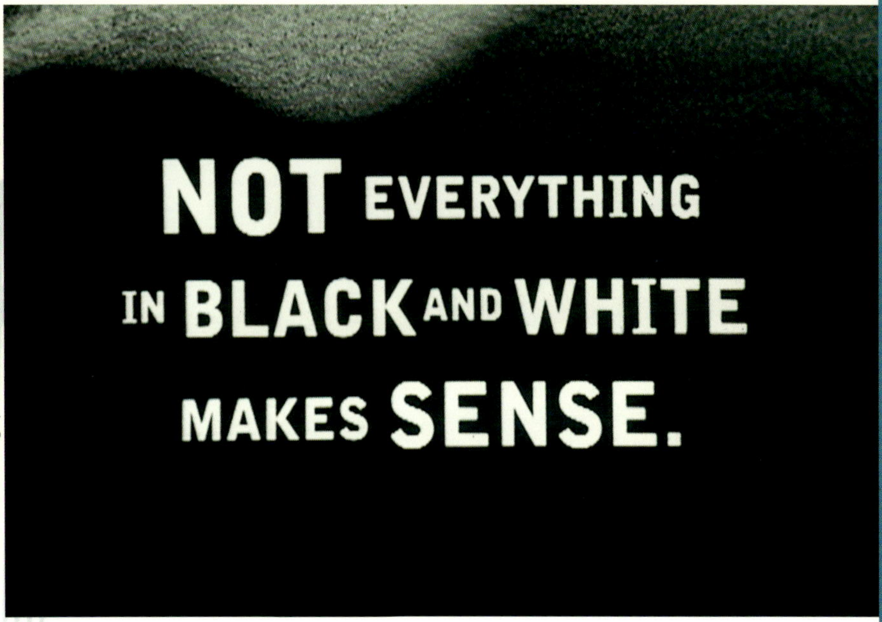

Slogans are used by advertisers to make you remember their adverts.

Increased opportunities for broadcasting have led to a growth in the number of commercial television channels, and consequently a growth in television advertising. During the 1960s ITV began to sell advertising space in 30-second slots as opposed to their original one-minute slots. More numerous and shorter slots meant more and shorter advertisements—and greater revenue for the television channels showing them. Advertisers needed to get their message across to viewers in quicker and more effective ways, and so advertisements became punchier and more succinct.

At the same time, viewers and consumers have become much more visually literate. The better we get at reading and understanding the adverts we watch, the more the advertisers are forced to develop their skills to attract, and keep, our attention. Most present-day adverts use clues and nuances to get their message across, confident that viewers will understand the finer points of the advert, if not at first viewing then definitely on the second.

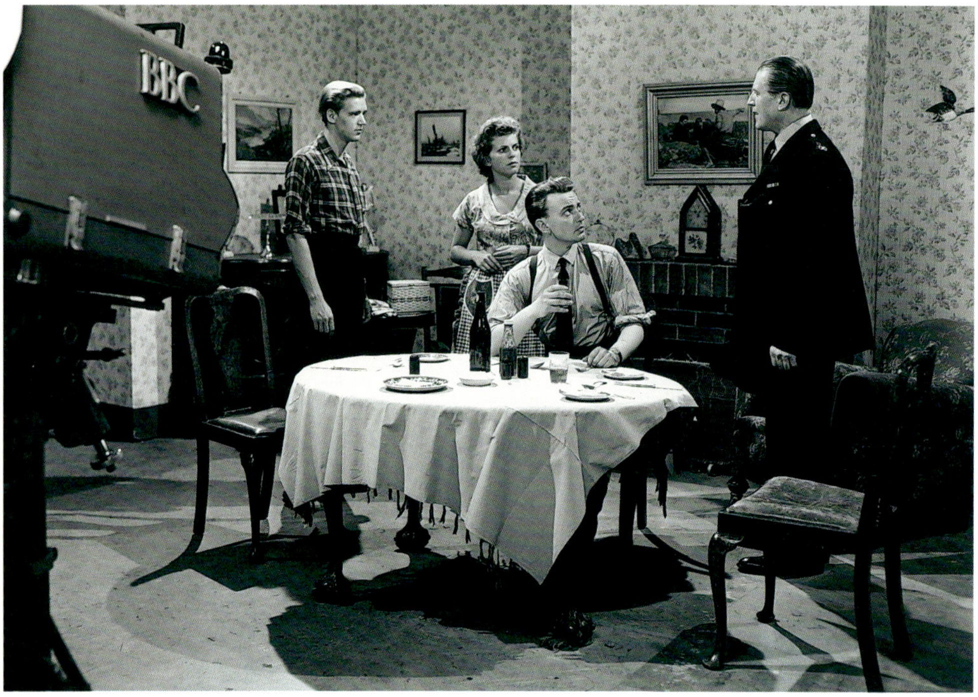

Dixon of Dock Green*—a cosy, comforting vision of policing from 1955. Television technology at the time meant the programme was made entirely in a TV studio, in a single take, like a stage play.*

Just as television advertising techniques have evolved, so have the content and quality of television programmes themselves. Let's go back to the 1950s and take the example of a typical police drama series of the time. The desk sergeant might answer the telephone and say: 'There's been a burglary? Where? The High Street, you say? Number Seven?' He asks a colleague to look in on the scene. His colleague agrees to do so and leaves the station. The desk sergeant continues to talk on the telephone. The scene changes and we see the desk sergeant's colleague knocking on the door of Number Seven the High Street. This whole process has taken a minute or more. The modern-day police drama would handle this sequence quite differently. We might not even see the phone call. We are more likely to be taken straight to the scene of the crime itself, or to hear of it on the squad car radio as we see our heroes driving to Number Seven, then cut to their arrival on the scene.

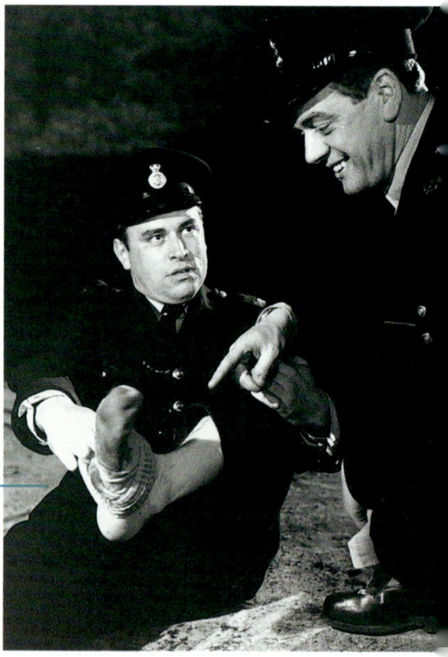

In 1962, Z Cars *gave a more relaxed and informal view of the police. Back projection and some location filming meant that stories could be more dramatic.*

'I don't think this business of television will come to much.'

Professor of Physics, Cambridge University, 1936

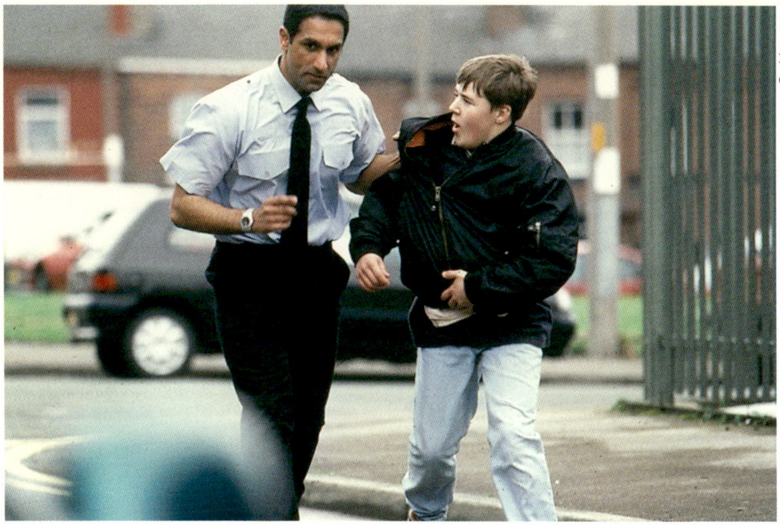

In 1998, The Cops *depicted the modern police force as a complex and diverse organisation struggling to deal with society. The series was filmed in a dynamic, fast-moving style using hand-held video cameras, giving an impression of authenticity.*

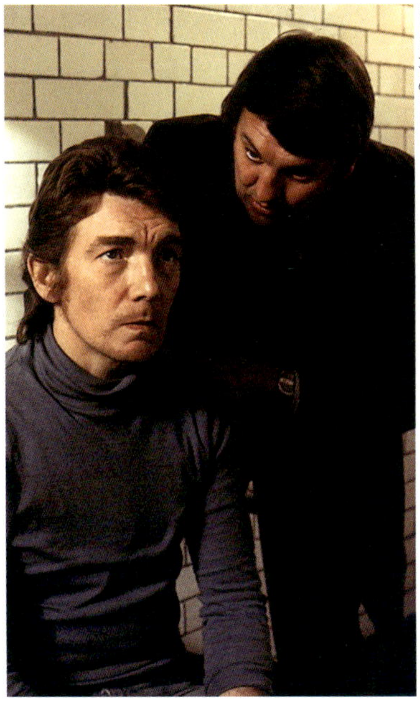

Law and Order, *a series from 1977 depicting police corruption, was made on film, allowing for a more fluid, cinematic style.*

Technological progress has freed television to move outside of the studio and into the real world. Television drama is no longer made live or with little or no editing. Time is treated more fluidly, with the action cutting from key moment to key moment rather than events being presented to us as they occur. Television is now much less like theatre and a lot more like the movies. As with advertising, the advancements in these televisual techniques have influenced audience expectations. In order to understand and follow stories constructed in this way we have had to become more sophisticated viewers. That sophistication offers its own challenges. Programme producers constantly have to look for new ways to keep us watching. An alternative channel or programme is only ever the press of a button away.

In the 1950s we had to seek out the media; at the beginning of the twenty-first century it is hard to avoid them. We are surrounded by increasingly sophisticated equipment, technology and media products. However, more choice does not necessarily equate with better quality. There has never been a greater need to be able to make an informed choice about what we want to watch, read, listen to or interact with. The National Museum of Photography, Film & Television can play a key role in this, helping to raise awareness of how today's media products are created and consumed.

The world as image

Russell Roberts
Curator of Photographs

One of the earliest uses of the term 'photography' can be found in a lecture given by the eminent scientist Sir John Herschel to the Royal Society of London on 14 March 1839. He described his own experiments with the new medium and also the two different processes that had been 'invented' that year: one by the Englishman William Henry Fox Talbot, and the other by the Frenchman Louis Jacques Mandé Daguerre. Both methods were received with fascination and wonder but only one was to have a lasting impact: Talbot's, or the *calotype* process, as it later became known. Daguerre's method produced images of high quality on polished copper plates, but these were unique objects, as they did not involve a negative from which the final image was made. In contrast, Talbot's paper-based process employed a positive–negative principle that was to become the backbone of modern photography.

'The daguerreotype is not merely an instrument which serves to draw nature... [it] gives her the power to reproduce herself.'
Louis Jacques Mandé Daguerre (1789–1851), inventor of a photographic process

Photography was welcomed as a useful and exciting new medium. In his Report to the Chamber of Deputies in Paris on 19 August 1839, François Arago suggested that the new invention would transform the realms of art, science and industry with its capacity for 'taming', classifying and interpreting the world. Artists could use photographs as reference material for their work, historians and archaeologists for exploring lost civilisations, doctors could use them as a visual aid to medicine, and scientists could use photography to map the Moon or to analyse the weather. The possibilities seemed endless. At the heart of this thinking was the belief in photography as providing a new kind of document, whose objectivity and realism was beyond doubt. Five years later, Talbot showed how photography could also be used commercially. His book, *The Pencil of Nature* (1844–46), explored some of the characteristics of camera vision and possible identities for photography, combining calotype prints with text as part of the narrative.

William Henry Fox Talbot (1800–77), The Pencil of Nature, *1844–46*

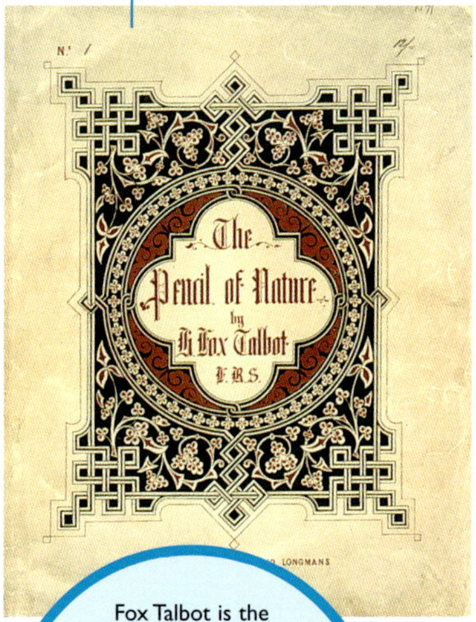

Fox Talbot is the inventor of the calotype process whereby multiple images can be produced from a single negative. This principle, upon which modern photography was founded, has only recently been superseded by advances in digital technology.

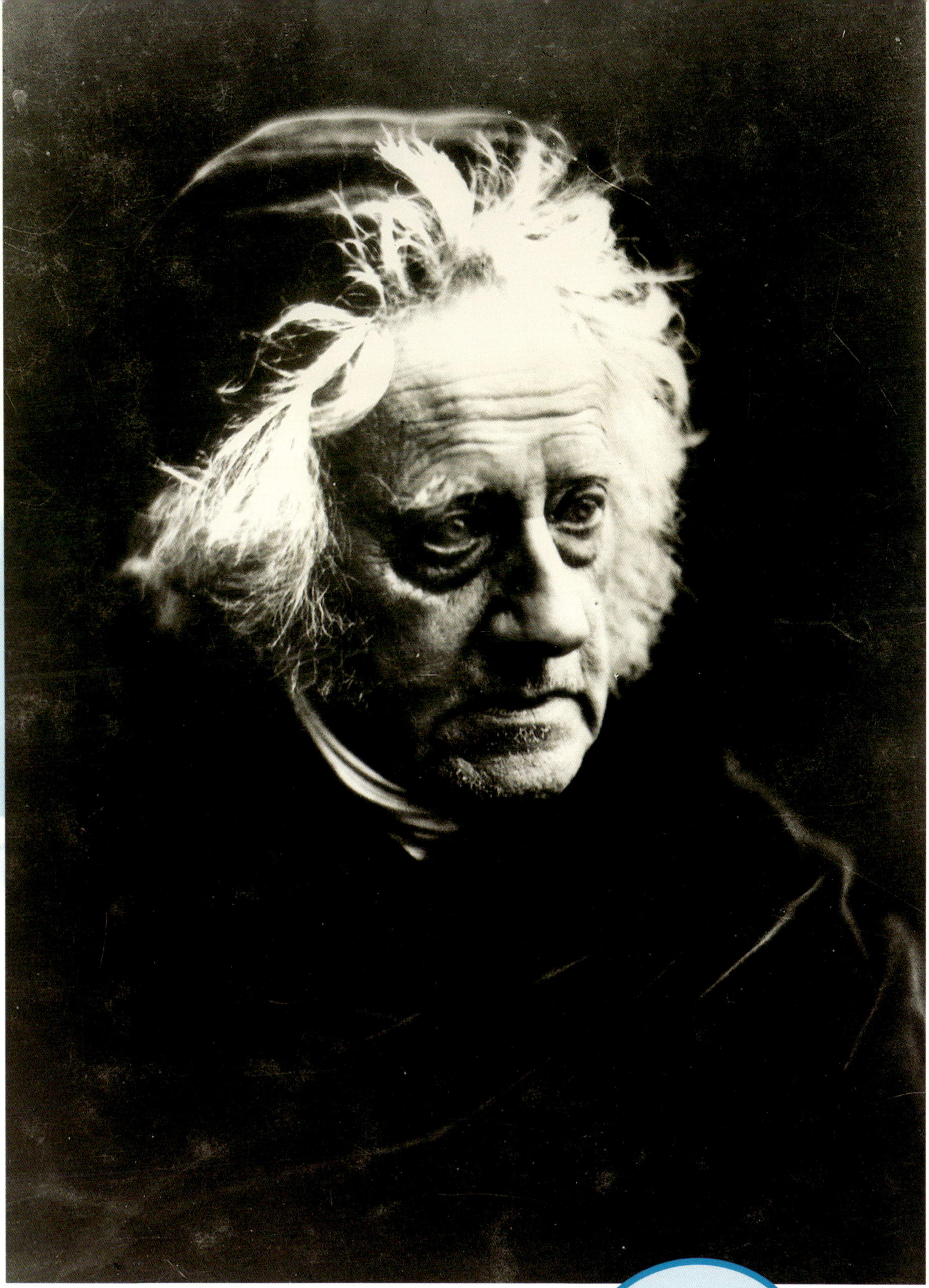

Julia Margaret Cameron (1815–79), 'Sir John Herschel', 1867

Julia Margaret Cameron used her distinguished artistic and literary friends as subjects for her photography. At the core of the Museum's holdings is an album of a personal selection of her prints, put together as a gift to Herschel to thank him for helping her to master photography.

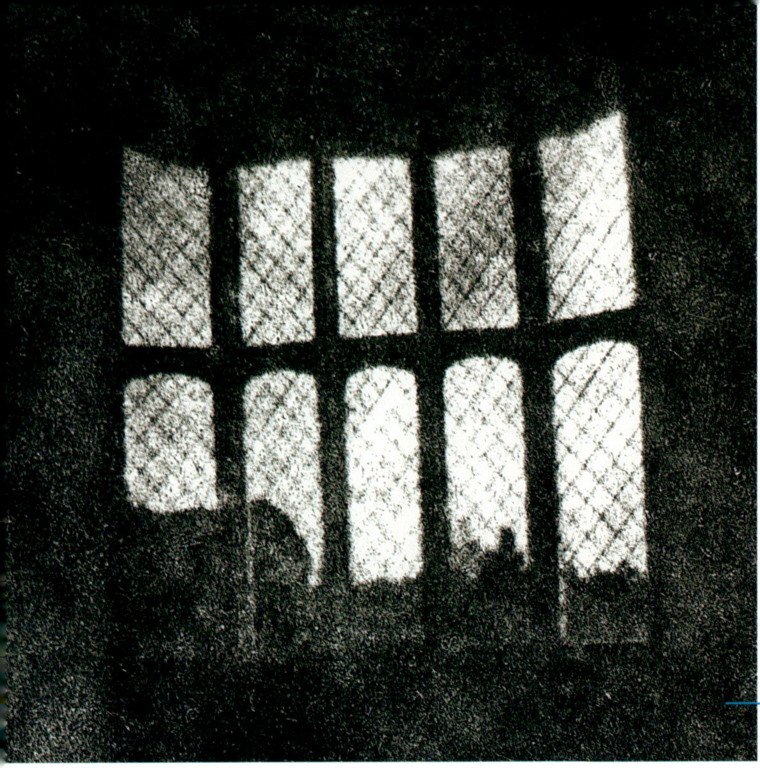

William Henry Fox Talbot (1800–77), 'The Latticed Window', August 1835

'How charming it would be if it were possible to cause these natural images to imprint themselves durably, and remain fixed upon the paper!'
W H F Talbot (1800–77), inventor of the modern photographic process

Lewis Carroll (1832–98), 'Girl in plaid skirt'. Albumen print.

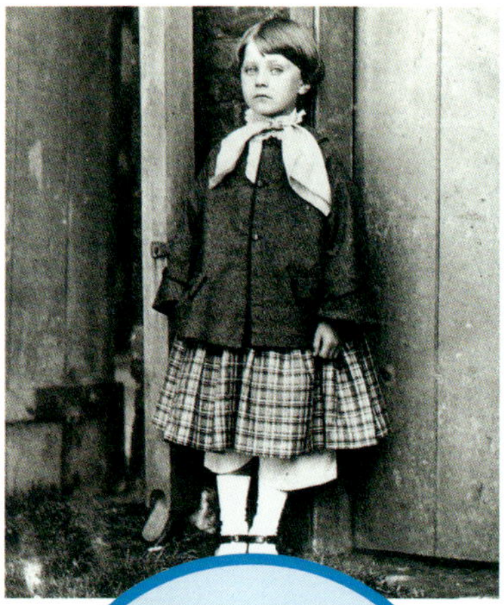

More famous as an author, Carroll was also a notable Victorian photographer. He has gained notoriety for his photographic depictions of young girls. The Museum has a small, but important collection of his work, including original glass-plate negatives. These are particularly rare, since most were destroyed shortly after his death.

The National Museum of Photography, Film & Television holds the world's largest collection of work by Talbot. As well as more than 6000 prints, the Collection includes notebooks and many of his letters describing his experiments. One of the most remarkable objects in the Collection is the earliest surviving negative: an opaque paper image of a window. Underneath Talbot wrote simply: 'Latticed Window (with Camera Obscura) August, 1835. When first made, the squares of glass, about 200 in number, could be counted with the aid of a lens.' A modest caption for one of the first examples of a process that was to have a lasting impact on culture and society.

The Collection of Photographs at the Museum has an interesting heritage. It grew out of that spectacle of Victorian commerce and applied arts, the Great Exhibition of the Works of All Nations in 1851. At the Great Exhibition, photography was displayed in two categories: fine arts and philosophical instruments. Raw materials were shown alongside techniques of manufacturing and the final product—the photograph representing the fine art of photography and the equipment—was seen as part of the interpretation of the natural world. From the Great Exhibition arose the South Kensington Museum, which in the late nineteenth century separated into two very different institutions: the Science Museum and the Victoria & Albert Museum. The Science Museum provided the base for the formation of the NMPFT in the early 1980s.

Responsible for one of the early landmarks in photographic history, Atkins produced one of the earliest photographically illustrated books in 1841 using the cyanotype process. The Museum holds examples of her work together with a bound volume of the plant specimens Atkins used to produce her cameraless images.

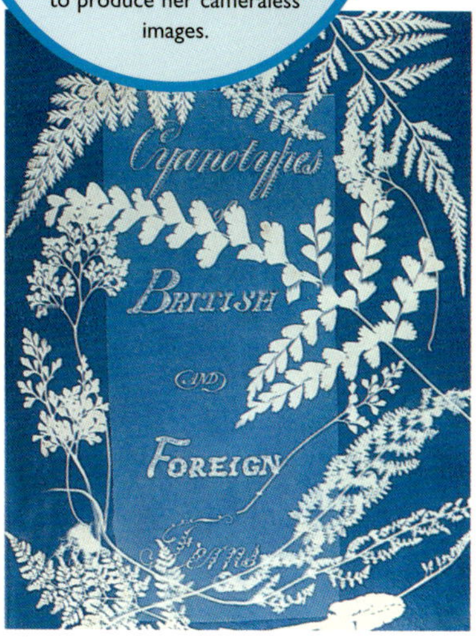

Anna Atkins (1799–1871), frontispiece to Cyanotypes of British and Foreign Ferns, *1854*

Before the establishment of the Museum, most of the Collection's acquisitions were concerned with the 'technique and process' of photography. Many photographs now recognised as important landmarks in the histories of photography began their life in the Museum as illustrations of science and technology, including photographs by Julia Margaret Cameron, Hill & Adamson, James Robertson and Roger Fenton. However, with the establishment of the Museum, the Collection expanded to embrace the diversity anticipated by Talbot and Arago in the early days of photography. The transfer of the relevant Science Museum Collections to the NMPFT was augmented by the addition of the Kodak Museum Collection in 1984, which went on display in 1989. The Museum continues to acquire, display and interpret photography across a wide range of contexts.

From the early botanical studies of Anna Atkins and the portraits taken by the Victorian author Lewis Carroll, to the landmark social documentary photography of Tony Ray-Jones and Hannah Starkey's contemporary enigmatic studies of urban life, the Museum has continued to acquire important examples of photography. These include the Ricketts Collection and archives relating to the work of Zoltan Glass, Jean Straker and the *Daily Herald*. The differences between the uses of photography as an expression of art, science or popular culture have become increasingly blurred and the Museum's Collection maps that change. The Collection also shows how photography is an important and popular medium in everyday life, from the many albums and prints of the Kodak Collection to the *Daily Herald* Archive which holds more than one million newspaper photographs from the 1920s to the 1960s.

Zoltan Glass (1902–81), 'Earl Howe reflected in the mirror of a Delage GP Straight-8 racing car', c.1935

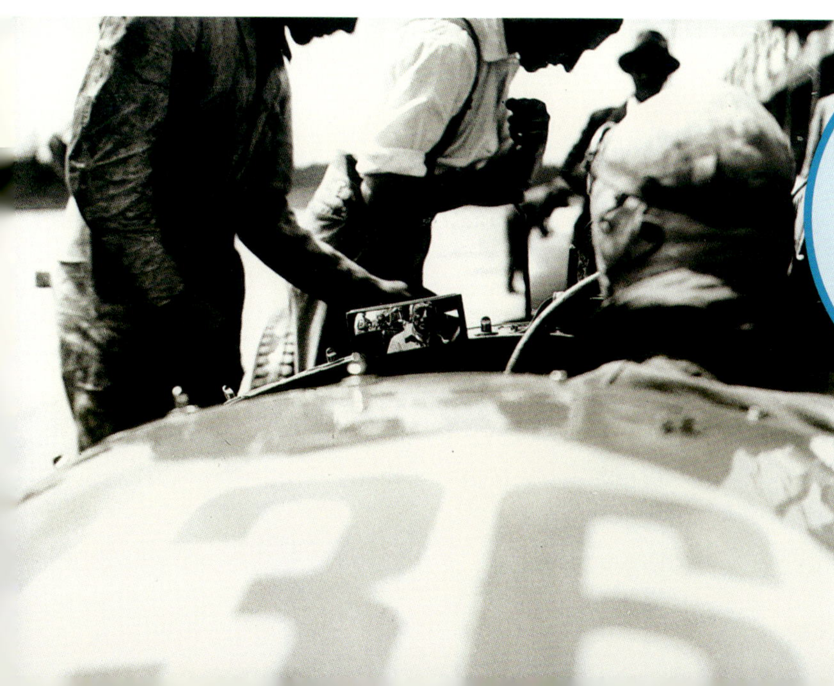

One of the wave of photographers who fled the rise of fascism in Germany during the 1930s, Zoltan Glass came to London in 1936. Throughout the 1940s and 1950s he contributed to a variety of magazines, including *Picture Post* and *Lilliput*, and eventually became a very successful advertising photographer. The Collection includes his early studies of German motor racing, as well as examples of his advertising and glamour photography.

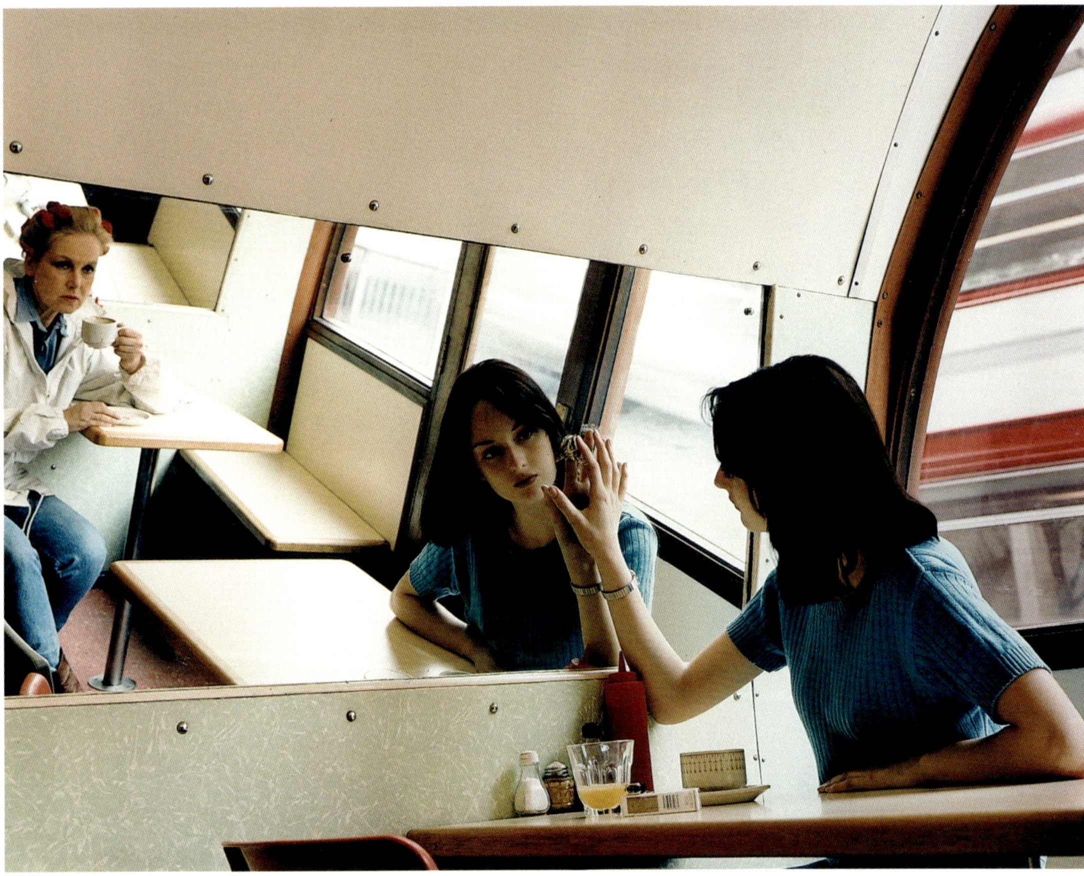

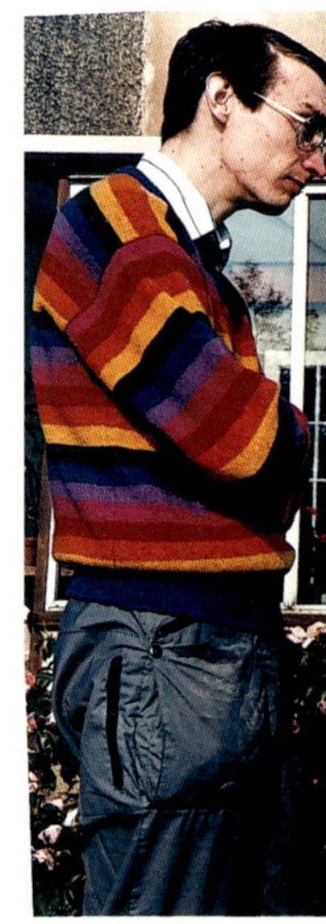

Hannah Starkey (b.1972), 'Untitled', 1997

Starkey's photographs are staged, narrative-based images of urban life. These photographs convey mundane and private moments that are familiar but rarely photographed. Mirror images and doubling are a source of fascination for her. These themes occur throughout this series; they evoke questions about identity and social space.

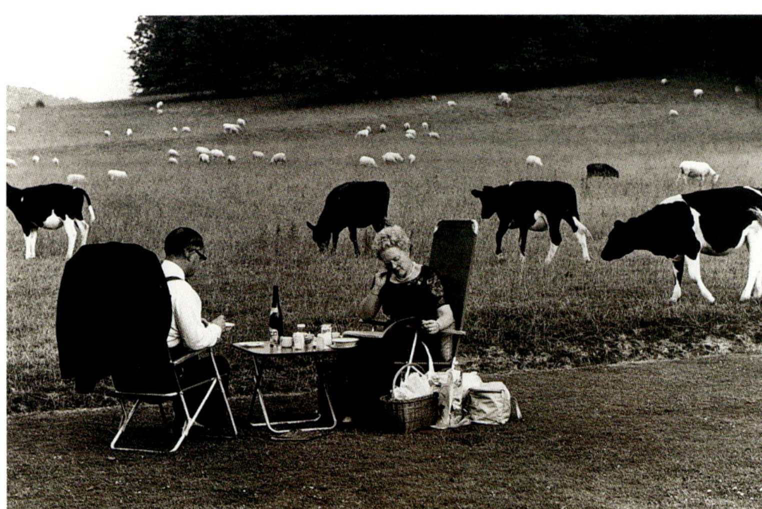

Tony Ray-Jones (1941–72), 'Glyndebourne', 1967

Ray-Jones is an influential but previously little-known photographer. He is best known for his work in documenting the English at leisure, published in the book *A Day Off: An English Journal* (1974). The Museum holds an important collection of his work.

Parr is a leading figure in the 'new colour documentary' school of British and European photography of the 1980s. His photographs have at times caused consternation among his subjects, mainly because his style is often seen as confrontational. The Museum holds a considerable body of his work, including the maquette of his book, *The Cost of Living, 1989.*

It was during the 1960s that photography began to find greater currency in visual arts. Subsequently, museums and art galleries began to take a greater interest in collecting and exhibiting photography. This sparked a renewed enthusiasm for photography in Britain and marked a break with the dominant tradition of painting in the visual arts. The traffic in art and documentary photographic styles between the United Kingdom and the USA intensified during this period, continuing up until the 1980s. The work of Tony Ray-Jones is a good example of this merging of different cultural styles, as are the challenging and sensitive documentary photographs of Chris Killip. Both of these photographers are represented in the Collection alongside significant work by other photographers including Oscar Rejlander, Peter Henry Emerson, H P Robinson, Edward Steichen, Alvin Langdon Coburn, Weegee, Henri Cartier-Bresson, Fay Godwin, Don McCullin, Helen Chadwick and Jo Spence.

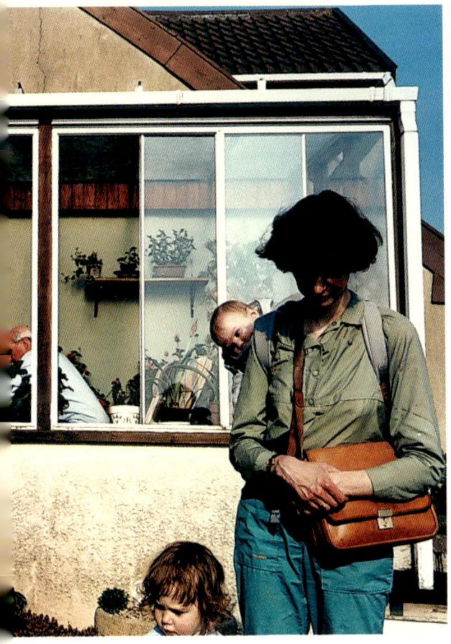

Martin Parr (b.1952), 'Garden open day', from The Cost of Living, *1989*

During the 1990s photography played a significant role in British contemporary art. Work by Richard Billingham, Nick Waplington and Hannah Starkey approaches everyday life with an aesthetic that is a combination of photographic styles. This approach reflects the ongoing interest in the diverse uses of photography that is central to the identity of the National Collection.

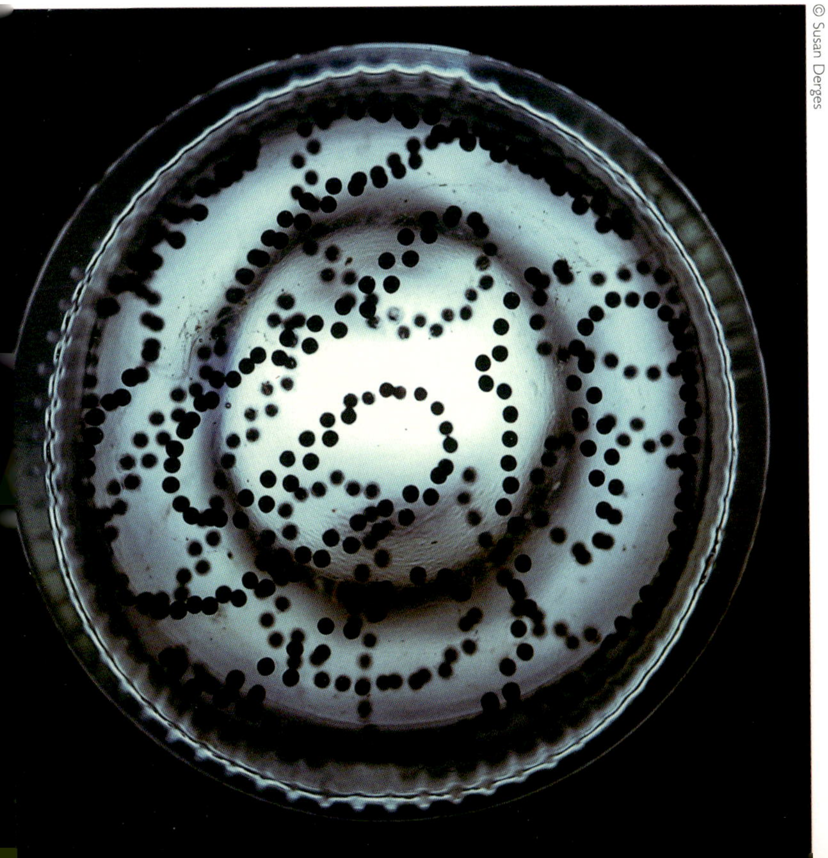

Derges' work has explored different aspects of photography as an art and science. The subject matter for her photographs and the way the image is made often relate to scientific observation and the natural world. Boundaries between nature and culture are areas that are continually shifting in her work. 'Vessel No. 3' is from a series that records the developmental changes from egg to young toad.

Susan Derges (b.1955), 'Vessel No. 3'

The Gandolfi camera: a romantic tale of timber

Amanda Nevill
Head of Museum

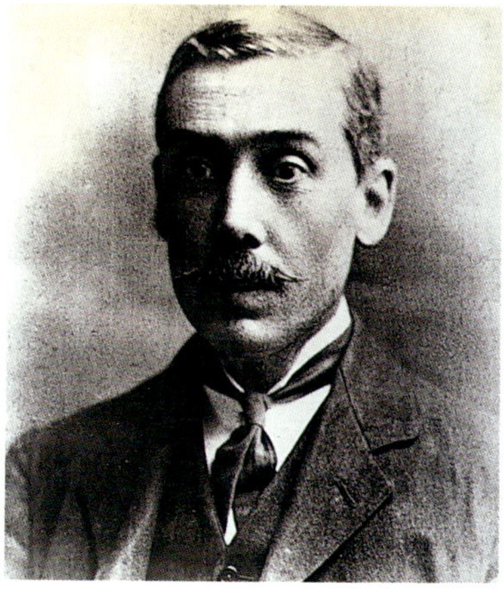

Louis Gandolfi (1864–1932), founder of the family business which for over 100 years produced a meticulously hand-crafted range of cameras and stubbornly refused to bow to the gods of mass production. Louis played the concertina, which he had made himself. Whether or not the shape of the concertina influenced the design of the classic camera is unknown.

With very few exceptions, the history of photography is dominated by discussion of and admiration for the work of photographers. The camera, although important, is relegated to the status of an enabling tool. However, cameras were essential to the evolution of photographic techniques, and the creators of cameras demand a better billing! The care, dedicated craftsmanship and tenacity of the Gandolfi family deserve this recognition.

Louis Gandolfi set up his own camera-making business in 1885, during a time of transition in photography. The complicated and cumbersome technical requirements were giving way to a photography which could be practised with relative ease by the 'push-button' consumer. Setting up a precision-crafted business at this point could have been financial folly.

The Gandolfi camera designs were initially very simple, and no attempt was made to take on the newer 'hand-held' camera. Gandolfi concentrated on a folding bellows type, based on a traditional dry plate apparatus, the process by which photographs were captured on a specially coated glass plate, instead of the roll films used today. Focal lengths were fixed by the choice of lens.

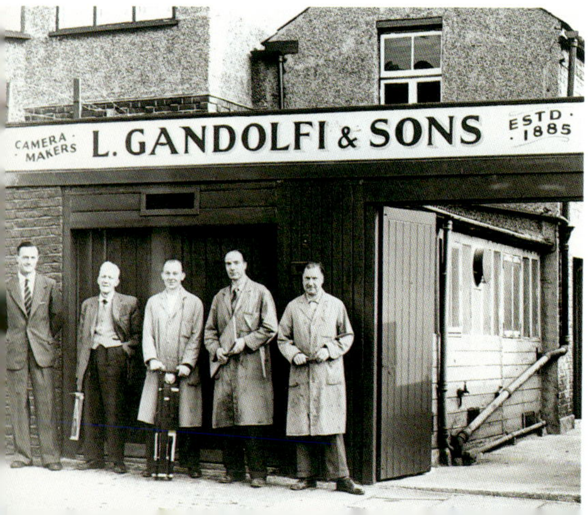

The Gandolfi workshops in Borland Road, Peckham (south-east London). The business moved to these premises in 1928. Gandolfi have continued to produce bellows camera designs up to the present day, crafted in mahogany, teak and even—on special occasions—such exotica as rosewood, walnut and ash.

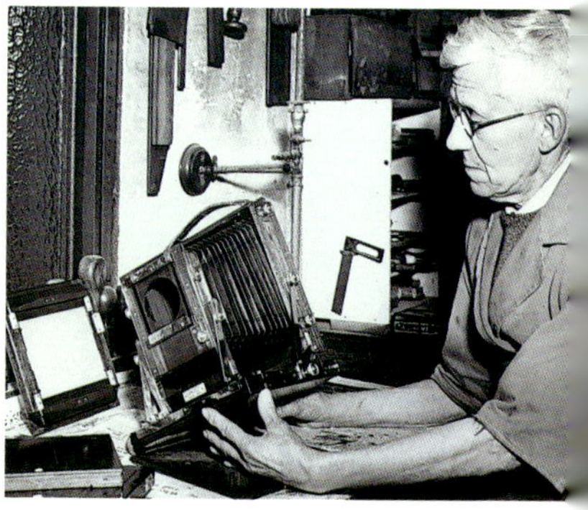

Thomas Gandolfi, who died in 1965, was Louis' eldest son. At a time when mechanisation and mass production moved the emphasis away from the individual and objects lost their personalised characteristics to become mere merchandise, wood came to symbolise a caring past when each object is imbued with the spirit of its maker.

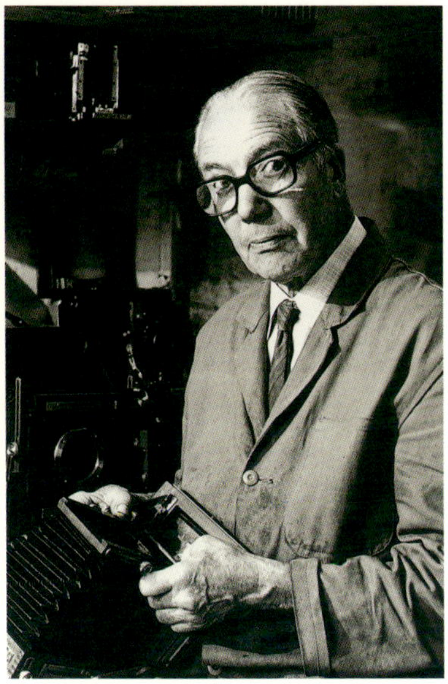

Portrait of Frederick Gandolfi by Ronald Franks, FRPS. Fred described camera-making as '... eight different tasks—entirely different. You've got to understand history, and a bit about photography generally, so that you know how to talk to your customer. You've then got to be able to select timber, then of course, you've got to be a wood machinist ... then metal workers, and finishers, platers, polished brass work and lacquer work.'

The market for Gandolfi cameras appears eccentric. They were used not just by the dedicated photographer, but—possibly because of their hand-crafted robustness—were fixed to aeroplanes during the First World War, presumably for reconnaissance. Lord Carnarvon commissioned a Gandolfi camera which was taken to record the findings at Tutankhamen's tomb. The cameras were also, on one occasion, used to photograph atom-bomb explosions. The cameras' charred remains (probably highly radioactive!) were returned to the Gandolfi workshops for restoration.

The business has depended on special one-off orders, with an emphasis on detail and craftsmanship, each item produced as though it might be the last. It was this philosophy which was passed on by Louis to his sons before he died in 1932, and which continued up until their death in the late 1980s.

To the Gandolfi brothers the knowledge of materials, particularly wood, for a successful camera, was paramount. Wood was their obsession. In recorded verbal memoirs made by the celebrated photographer Ken Griffiths, Fred talks nostalgically about a publication entitled *Timber* which he describes as being all about the 'romance' of special timbers. He talks inspiringly of woods used by pirate-ship builders in Cuba, Sir Francis Drake's preference for mahogany and, quaintly, of an aristocrat who, in preference to the more traditional offering of roses or chocolates, sent his mistress a board of wood, to which Fred adds: 'and, of course, she was charmed with it'.

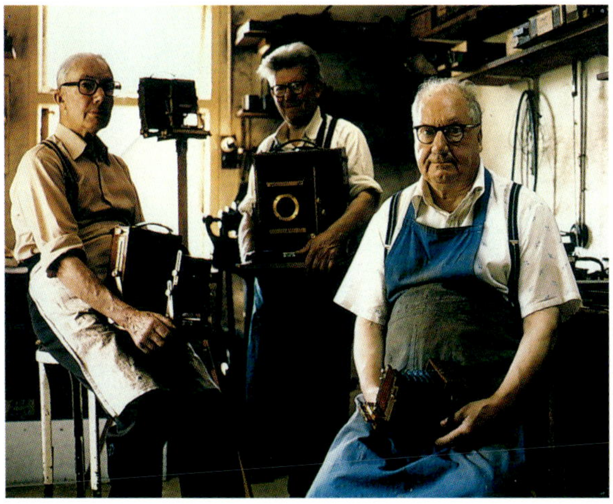

Thomas, Frederick and Arthur Gandolfi with some of their meticulously crafted cameras. The emphasis on wood signifies lasting quality, conveys comfort and reassurance.

Ken Griffiths, a devotee of Gandolfi cameras, is similarly seduced by the idiosyncratic charm of the 'tactile' wooden cameras. They appear old-fashioned, evoke nostalgia and, particularly in the case of portraiture, break down the barriers between photographer and sitter. The the length of time taken to set up allows the photographer and sitter to become accustomed to each other. Griffiths also cites the benefits of the surprise factor when, from this apparently antique camera, a very modern Polaroid print appears, something which never fails to intrigue.

To infinity and

Alison Roden
IMAX Programming & Marketing Manager

'To infinity and beyond . . .' Buzz Lightyear's words from *Toy Story* go some way towards expressing the scope offered to audiences by large-format cinema. Imagine venturing far into outer space, flying so close to the *Discovery* shuttle that you can see every rivet, or crawling over the seabed in search of the *Titanic* wreck. The world's largest film medium, 15 perforations/70 mm, offers you both those experiences, plus hundreds of others.

Since 1983, when the National Museum of Photography, Film & Television opened the doors of Europe's first permanent IMAX® cinema, millions of visitors have been transported to locations beyond their wildest dreams. In 1999, we were again at the cutting edge of large-format technology as Europe's first IMAX® SR 3D projector was unveiled to the public.

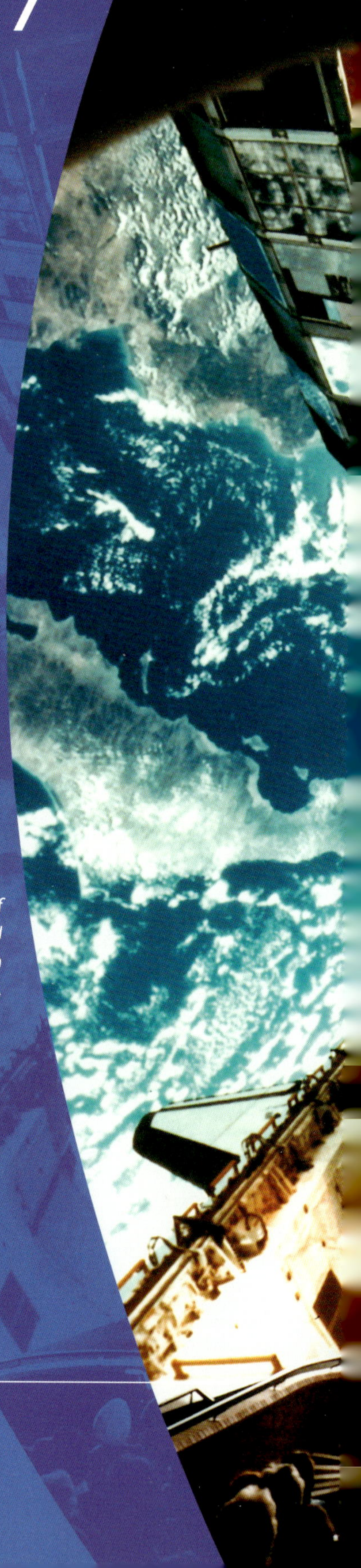

Spectacular images of space have proved particularly successful on the giant screen.

> *'The original and still the greatest home of the image—both still and moving.'*
> Independent

beyond . . .

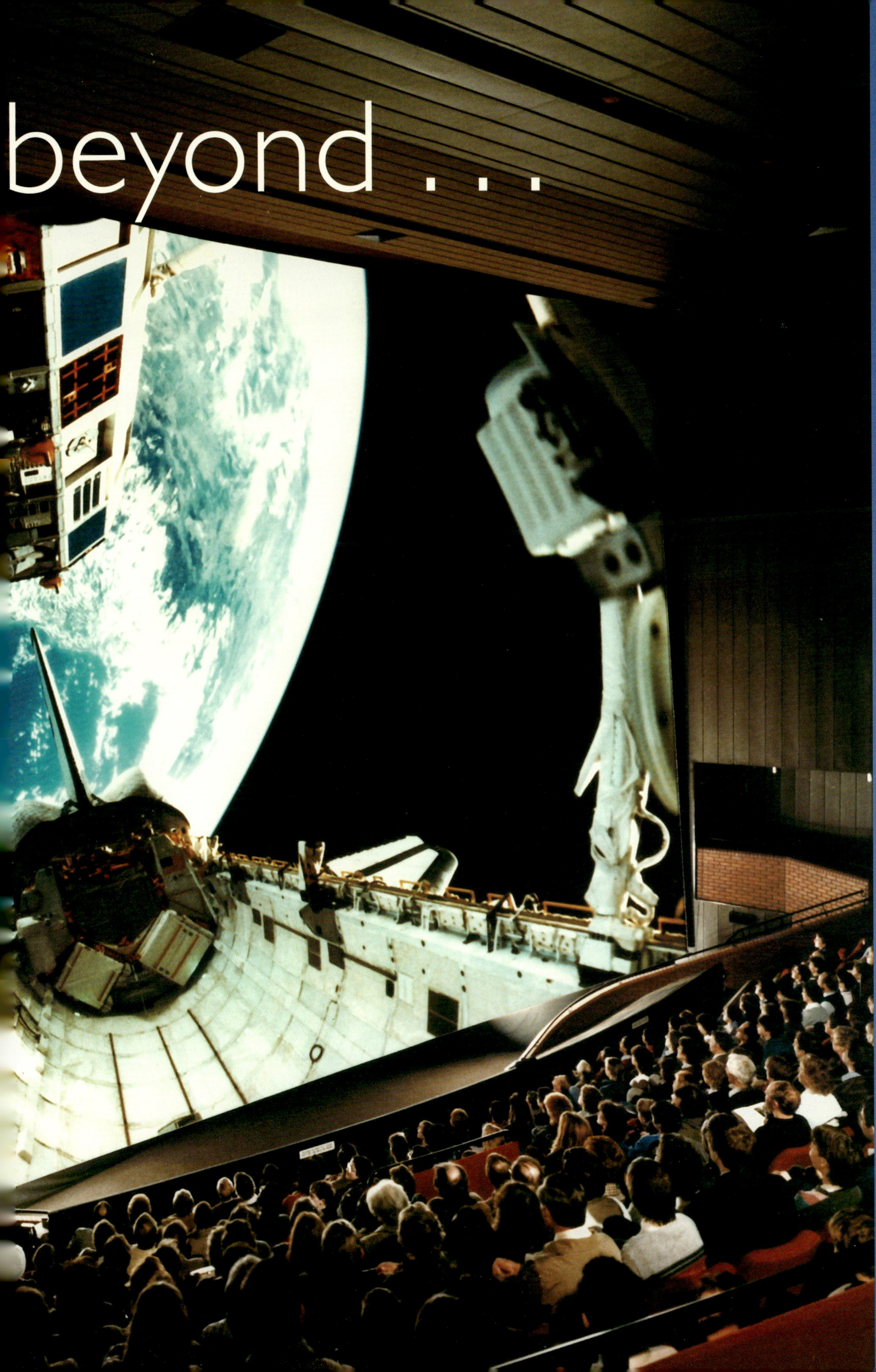

Shuttle image © Imax Corporation

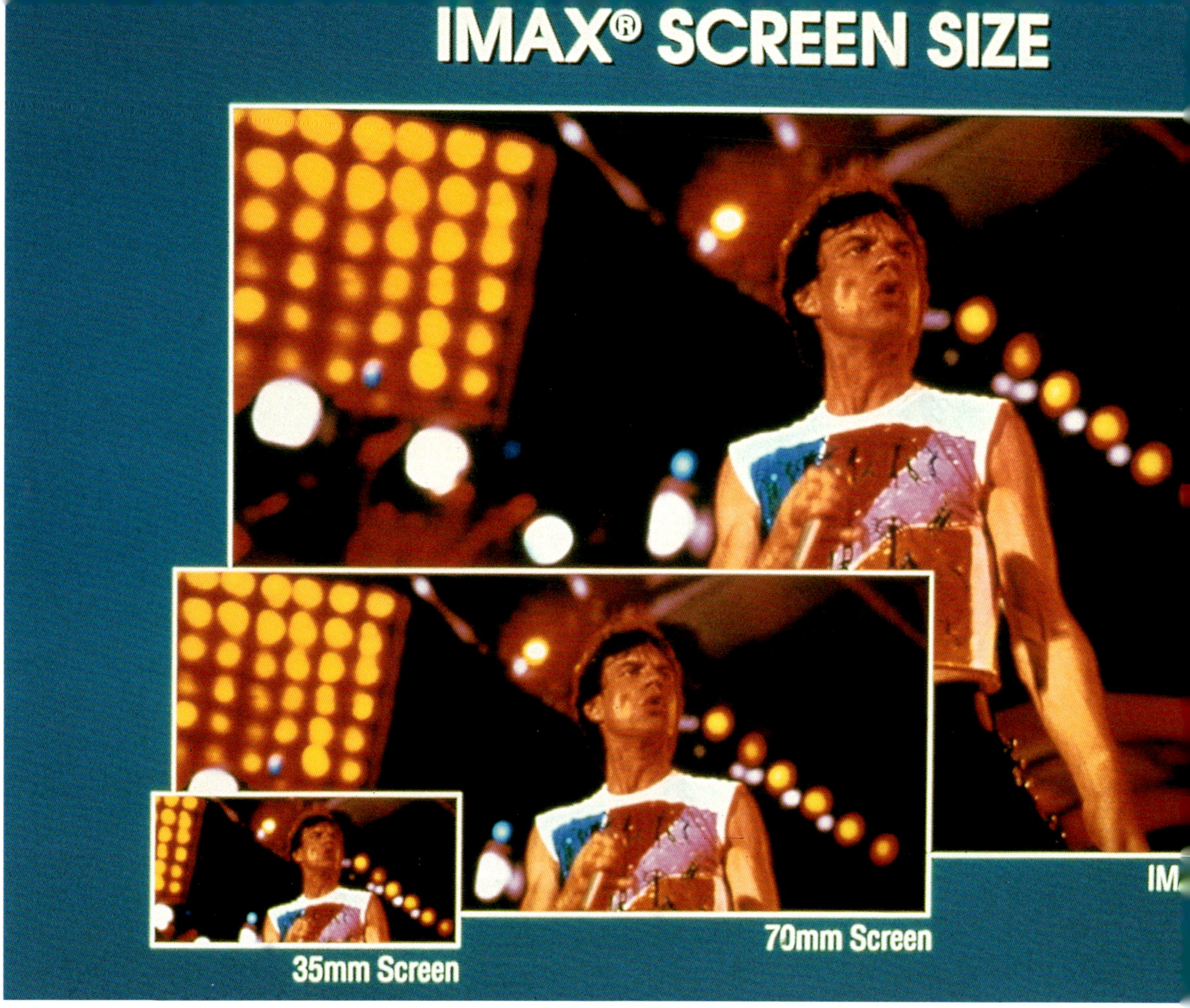

The IMAX cinema screen is up to ten times larger than a regular 35 mm cinema screen.

The giant format was developed at the close of the 1960s and grew out of the frustrations of a group of young Canadian documentary film-makers, as they struggled to produce spectacular images for Expos and World Fairs. Roman Kroitor, Graeme Ferguson and Robert Kerr hit upon the idea of turning the projector on its side and running film through it horizontally rather than vertically. They also upped the rate at which the film travelled through the projector to 24 frames per second, to produce a strobe-free image. Chance then brought them news of Australian Ron Jones' invention of a device which created a 'rolling loop' of film as it entered the projection gate, keeping the film at constant, even tension and alleviating all shredding problems. The rest, as they say, is history.

Since the Museum opened its IMAX cinema, the large-format industry has grown tremendously. At the close of the 1990s more than 500 million people worldwide had seen a large-format film at some time in their lives. The network has grown to over 200 cinemas. The style and subject matter of films shown in these cinemas have changed too as the industry has attempted to draw closer to its Hollywood cousin.

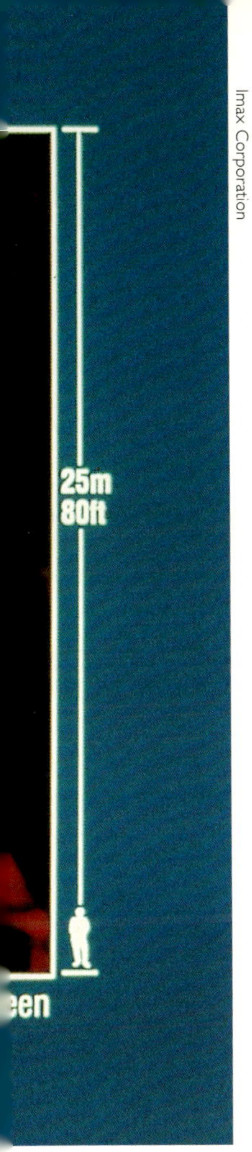

Imax Corporation

The catalyst for many of the changes we are currently seeing in large-format film-making has been two recent developments: the advent of 3D and the growth of multiplex cinemas with a large-format screen attached. As competition between multiplex chains for audiences has increased, a giant screen has proved the perfect means to differentiate one chain from the next. This in turn has brought a new audience into large-format cinemas: people used to the exploits of Stallone and Schwarzenegger, and hungry for more than wildlife documentaries. Alongside this commercialisation of the marketplace has come a dramatic step forward in 3D technology. The red/green cardboard spectacles of the 1950s have now been replaced by glasses producing full-colour images, so convincing in their three-dimensionality that entire audiences reach to grasp at objects apparently floating less than 1 metre from their noses.

Despite such boundary-pushing technology, however, the large-format industry still resembles mainstream cinema in its infancy in many ways. Large-format cameras are large, heavy (it takes two people to carry the regular model), noisy and unwieldy. The giant film frame used demands high levels of light. The size of the film stock and the speed at which it runs through the camera necessitate cartridge changes every three to five minutes. Thankfully, the recent exciting developments in computer-generated imagery and digital image capture have given the film-maker a much broader palette from which to paint. Digital cameras can now capture and output images to a sufficiently high resolution for projection on the large-format screen, whilst being small and light enough to manoeuvre into the tightest corner.

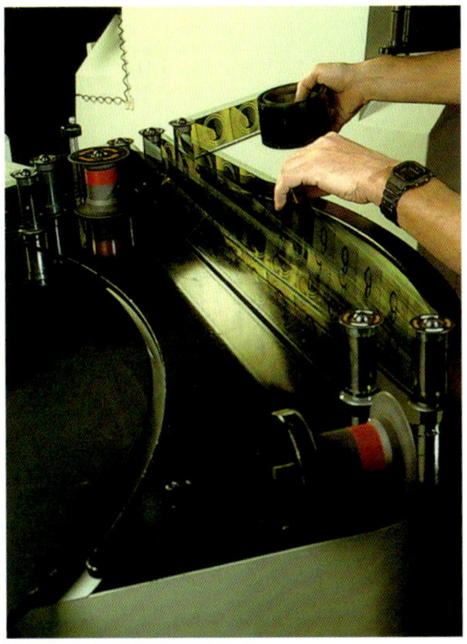

A series of gears and guide wheels keeps the giant 15 perf/70 mm film (each film frame is 70 mm high and carries 15 perforations top and bottom) at constant tension as it travels through the projector.

Other problems remain, however: the fact that the projected image fills the viewer's peripheral vision both vertically and horizontally demands that the pace of cutting and any movement within the frame be relatively slow if audiences are not to fall prey to motion sickness. The use of close-ups remains a thorny question: can audiences read emotions on a face seven stories high? On-screen dialogue is complicated and expensive to achieve: the intrusive noise of the camera prevents voices being captured 'live', and to recreate them in a studio demands painstaking accuracy as any lack of lip-synch is immediately obvious to the audience. Film-makers are still struggling to find the creative language which will unlock the full potential of this giant medium.

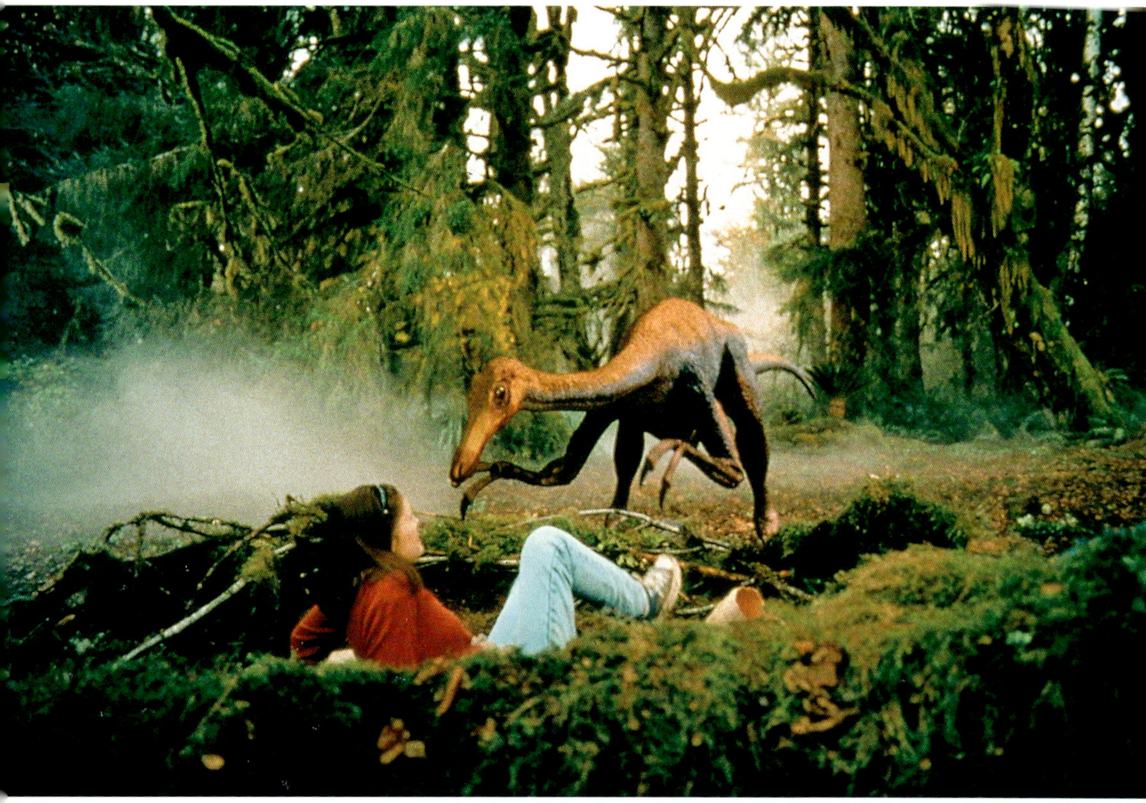

Blue Sky/VIFX, Imax Corporation

T-Rex. Back to the Cretaceous combines spectacular computer-generated images and live action to thrilling effect.

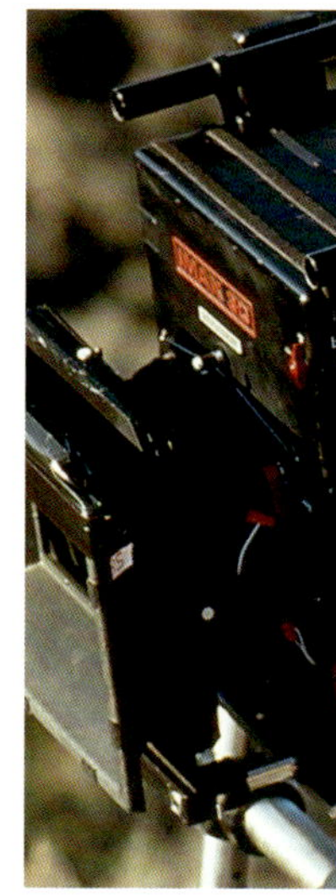

There are signs however that a new type of large-format film is in the process of emerging. Directors from the mainstream movie world are moving into large-format production—first Jean-Jacques Annaud (director of *The Bear, Quest for Fire* and *The Lover*) in 1995 with *Wings of Courage* and latterly Brett Leonard (director of *Lawnmower Man* and *Virtuosity*) with *T-Rex* in 1998. Film-makers are increasingly taking the tools of the feature film—dramatic action, character development, and a strong storyline—and finding ways to translate them to the giant screen.

Much of the most exciting development and experimentation of late has been in the field of animation. Imax Corporation has developed the SANDDE system, which allows animators to 'draw' in 3D and then uses a computer to turn their sketches into fully formed, animated figures. Their first short, *Paint Misbehavin'* is a hilarious cartoon caper, which introduces audiences to the 3D system. Equally ambitious work has taken place in the field of stop-motion animation. Award-winning Russian animator Alexander Petrov has worked on a 25-minute version of Ernest Hemingway's *The Old Man and the Sea*, which he has painstakingly hand-painted, frame by frame, and recorded using a specially modified 15 perf/70 mm camera—some 36,000 frames of animation. The results are breathtaking.

The twenty-first century has exciting things in store for the large-format industry. Successes such as the film *Everest* have increased both public and industry awareness of the giant format. The growing number of theatres means that production finally becomes increasingly viable. As the financial sums start to add up, so the involvement of mainstream directors and Hollywood talent will become a reality. Many are now seeing 15 perf/70 mm as the future of cinema exhibition, in the face of shrinking multiplex screens and improved in-home entertainment. For an outing to the cinema that truly transports its audience into another world, large-format film looks the way to go.

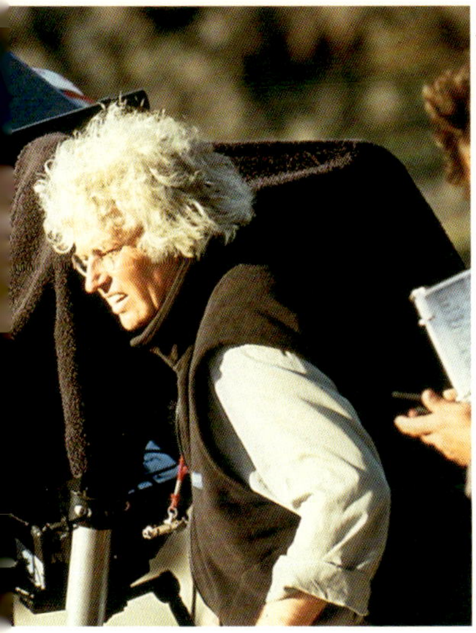

Sony Pictures Classics

Jean-Jacques Annaud during the shooting of Wings of Courage.

Everest, *from MacGillivray Freeman Films, gained over US$57 million worldwide up to 1999, bringing new audiences to the large-format world.*

MacGillivray Freeman Films

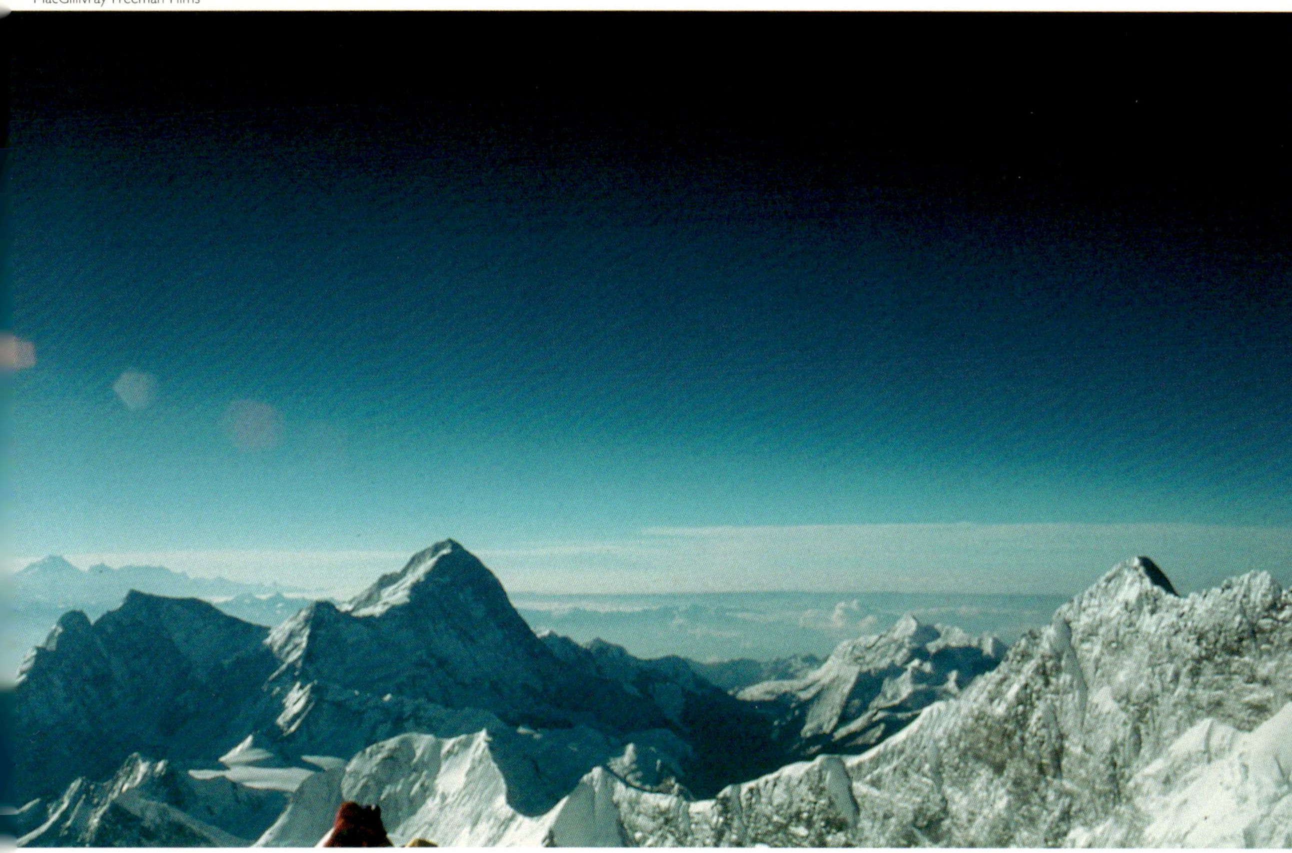

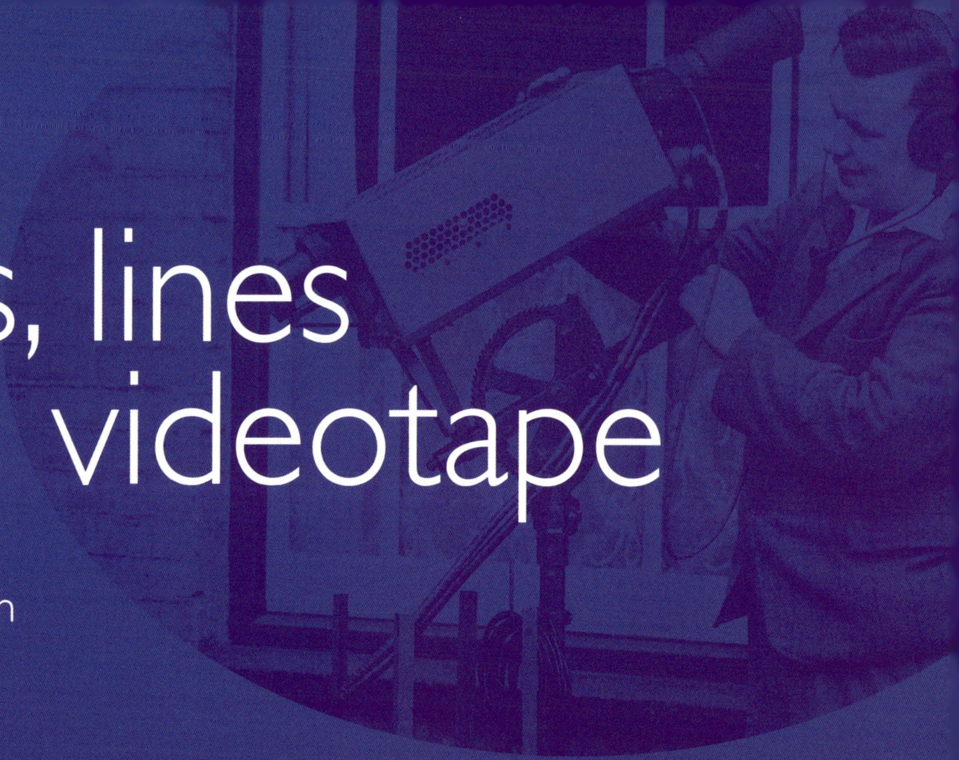

Sets, lines and videotape

John Trenouth
Curator of Television

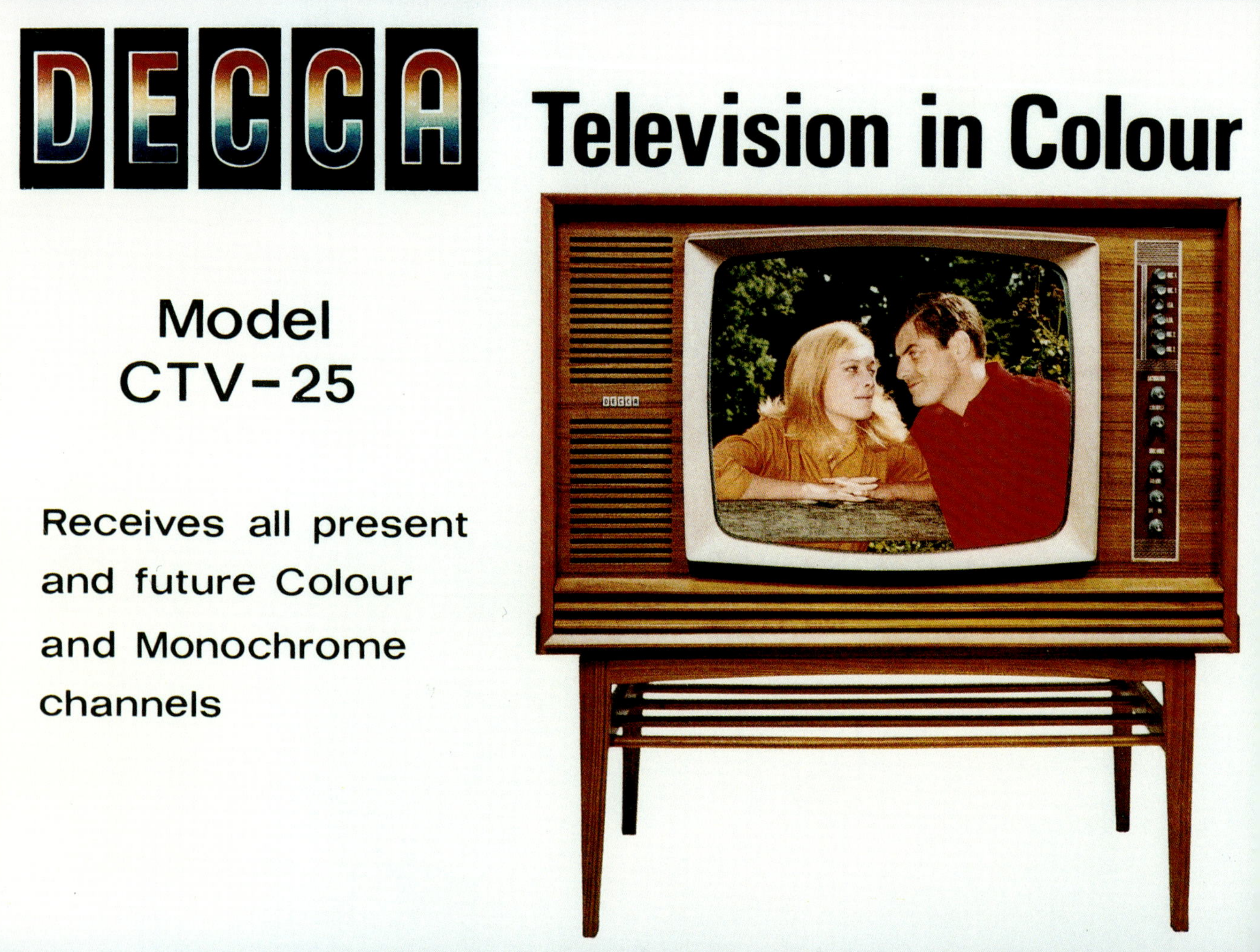

When 625-line UHF colour television was introduced, advertisements such as this 1968 image tried to persuade the customer that buying a very expensive new set was a good investment.

and future Colour
and Monochrome
channels

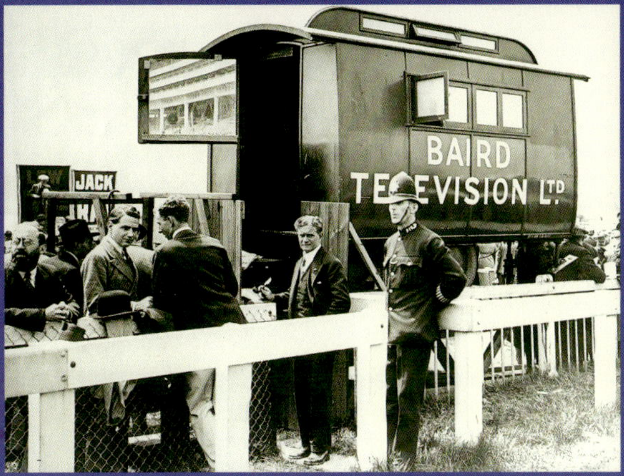

The 1931 Derby was televised using the Baird mechanical 30-line system—this was the world's first television outside broadcast. The large 'scanner' (as Baird called his camera) was housed in the wooden caravan. It had to be immobile when it was working, so the image was reflected using a mirror on the door, and this could be moved to follow the action.

In 1934 a series of classes in television theory and operation was held at the Borough Polytechnic, London. An enthusiastic group of students got to grips with a Baird 'televisor'.

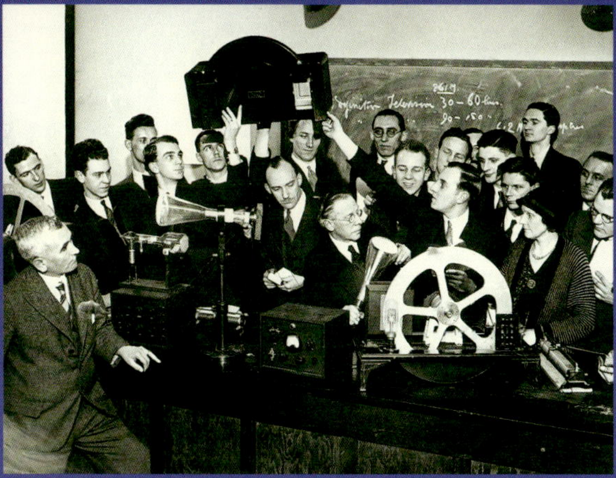

'Television? No good will come of this device. The word is half Greek and half Latin.'
C P Scott (1846–1932), erstwhile editor of the Manchester Guardian

An eminent scientist, a member of the Royal Institution, had been intrigued by the urgent request for his presence on this winter's evening. He had even overcome his fear of heights to toil up a succession of cold, dark and narrow stairways, with only a thin metal handrail for guidance and support. He had stood patiently, the freezing cold wind whistling around his ankles, waiting for his turn to enter the tiny room. A major scientific breakthrough, a stunning new invention, was about to be demonstrated—and why not? After all, this was 1926—though the 'flickers' had not yet learnt to talk, other inventions were already on offer to the public: wireless, aeroplanes, electricity, the motor car and lasting peace . . . But the anticipation was almost worth more than the viewing. He could not help his outburst: 'Well, what's the good of it when you've got it? What useful purpose will it serve?'

This was the start of television, an invention which would dramatically change the world and become the most powerful tool of mass communication. Two days later, on 28 January 1926, *The Times* published a short article outlining the visit of the Royal Institution to John Logie Baird's laboratory in Soho, where members had witnessed an image showing 'the recognisable head of a person speaking' although 'faint and often blurred'. On the whole, the 40 scientists were not impressed, but their comments as they left the demonstration—'Nothing much', 'Doesn't know what he's about', and 'Absolute swindler'—did not appear in *The Times*' article.

Only ten years later those crude, faint, flickering images had been turned into something which would surely have impressed the Royal Institution. On 2 November 1936 the BBC started the world's first regular high-definition television service, broadcasting from Alexandra Palace in north London. For the would-be viewer, however, there were problems: as well as the huge expense of buying a receiver (about the cost of a saloon car), there was also the choice of system to be made. The BBC transmitted alternate weeks on two different and incompatible systems. The Baird 240-line system transmissions could not be seen by viewers who had purchased the rival EMI 405-line system receivers, and vice versa. Even worse, viewers who had purchased the earlier Baird 30-line 'televisors' found themselves saddled with an expensive piece of redundant technology. Across Europe the picture was even more confusing with 60-line and 180-line transmissions giving way by the late 1940s to 405, 441, 625 and 819 lines.

Mass-producing televisions in the 1930s was very labour intensive. The rows of valves on the heavy chassis were all hand-wired. This is a 1938 staged publicity photograph, and the young woman is using a most unsuitable screwdriver for the job.

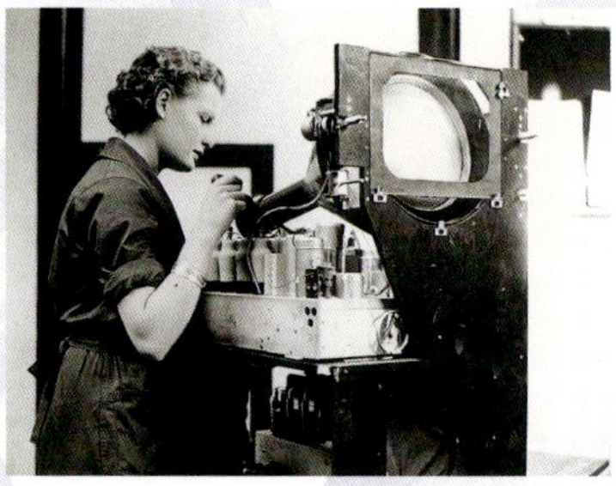

Advertising poster from 1949. Early television sets had small screens, because the technology did not exist to make large cathode ray tubes. As an alternative, some manufacturers, such as Philips and Decca, made projection sets. A 2.5-inch television tube produced a brilliant picture which was then projected on to a large screen.

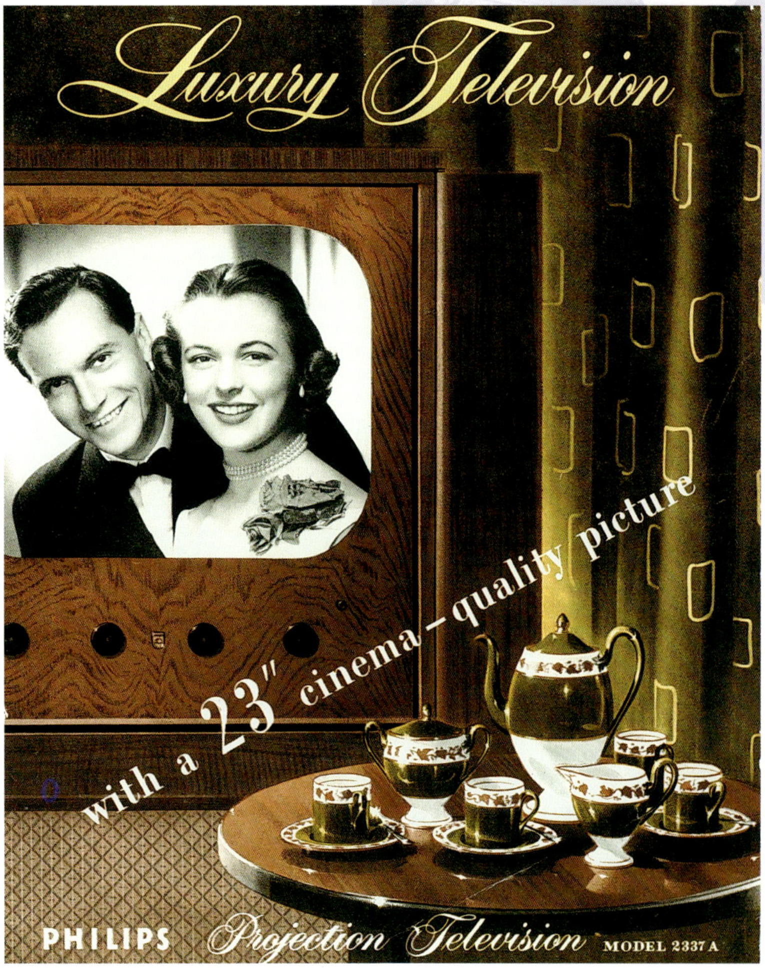

'More than half of those questioned are interested in digital TV . . . A word of warning, though: we have also learnt from questionnaires that 50 per cent of men also believe in UFOs.'

Michael Connor, European Business News

In 1955 commercial television (ITV) started in Britain. Several million proud owners of television sets suddenly discovered to their horror that their sets could not receive the new channel. Consequently the set-top box was born. Usually called a 'Band III convertor', it sat on top of the television set and received the higher-frequency signal on which ITV transmitted. All new sets on sale by this time had the ITV receiver built in, but you still needed a different aerial for each channel. In a number of towns and cities where the ITV signal was poor, enterprising television dealers erected large aerials on nearby hilltops and piped the signal to subscribers via cable. However, government legislation at the time prevented local programming, and most of these early cable-TV networks had fallen into disuse long before the introduction of multi-channel cable TV in the 1980s.

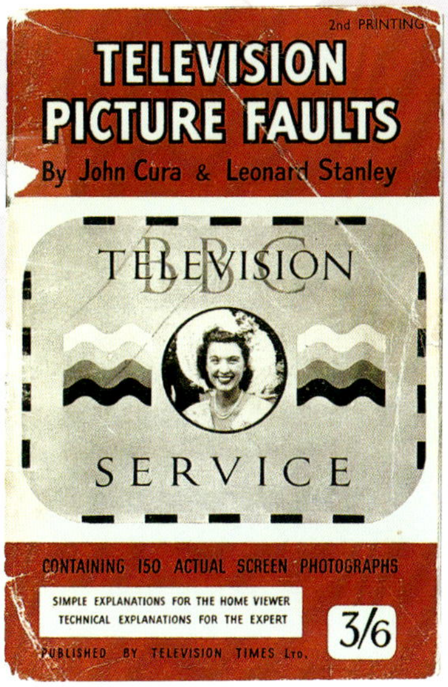

Early television sets were very temperamental. People did not want to call out an engineer every time there was a fault, so booklets like this were popular in about 1950, because they explained which of the many controls on the television set should be adjusted to get a better picture.

By the early 1960s viewers were confident that their much-loved TV set could travel with them as they moved house and be tuned into the local BBC and ITV transmitter wherever they lived. Then in 1964 a third channel (BBC2) opened. This time a set-top box was not enough: a completely new set was required to cope with the increase to 625 lines as well as higher transmission frequency. Within three years many BBC2 programmes were in colour, requiring the purchase of a colour TV which was very expensive and unreliable (many early colour sets were known in the television trade as 'curtain burners', because that's what they did best). By the time Channel Four Television started in 1982, cheap and reliable colour receivers were in common use, with no real dilemma facing the viewer buying a new set—that is, until satellite TV arrived. In 1990 you could either buy Sky Television or the rival BSB system. Both were totally incompatible with each other, and experience from way back in 1936 suggested that only one would survive. And only one did: Sky Television.

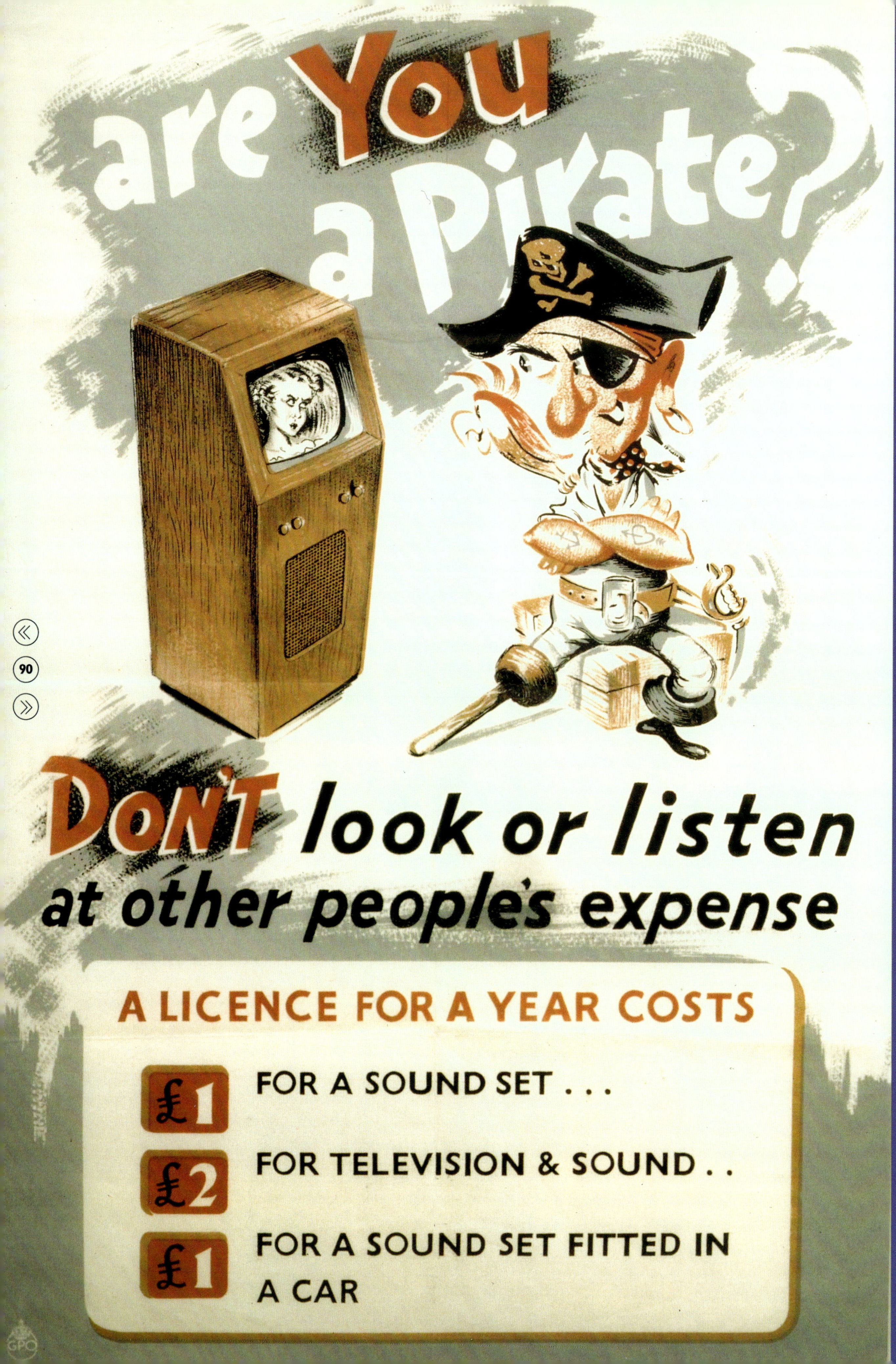
are You a Pirate?
DON'T look or listen at other people's expense
A LICENCE FOR A YEAR COSTS
£1 FOR A SOUND SET . . .
£2 FOR TELEVISION & SOUND . .
£1 FOR A SOUND SET FITTED IN A CAR
GPO

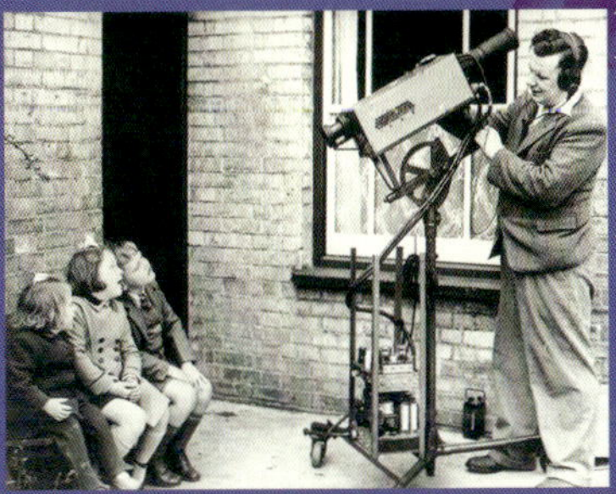
(Daily Herald Archive)

In 1950, if you were interested in home video, you had to build it yourself. This man made his own broadcast-quality camera and stand using surplus parts. It certainly impressed the neighbours' children.

In 1980 an invention made during the early 1950s was poised to revolutionise the way in which we viewed television, in the same way it had earlier revolutionised television programme-making. Since the late 1940s the race to develop video recording had been gaining momentum in Britain, Japan and the USA. It was won by a team from the American Ampex Corporation led by Charlie Ginsberg and Ray Dolby (who later found fame with his tape noise-reduction process). Working in Ginsberg's garage, the team perfected the VR1000 recorder which weighed over a ton, was the size of five telephone kiosks, consumed vast quantities of electricity and required compressed air and a vacuum pump as well as a full-time engineering crew to operate it. The price tag at the time was equivalent to buying ten semi-detached houses, so all in all it is not surprising that its use was confined to the television companies. However by 1980 two rival domestic video recorders were available in the high-street shops. Again the consumer was faced with making the choice and again the two systems, VHS and Betamax, were totally incompatible. And, once again, the marketplace would in the end support only one of them. Which one did you choose?

Digital television promises us lots of extra channels, lots of extra facilities and superb picture and sound. It does, however, have a major drawback: it's available in three different non-compatible forms—digital satellite, digital terrestrial and digital cable. Which one will you choose? Would it help if we pointed out that, since the start of television, if you had chosen between rival systems purely on technical merit, you would have made the wrong decision nearly every time?

In 1951 there were no television detector vans, so the General Post Office relied on poster campaigns to get people to pay their television licence fee.

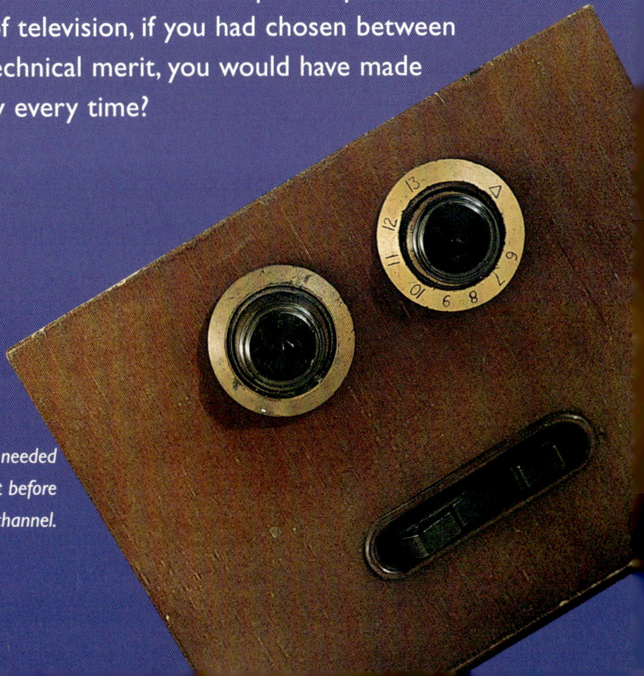

When ITV started in the 1950s, you needed this 'Band III adaptor' on your TV set before you could receive the new channel.

Good neighbours

Professor Colin Bell
Vice-Chancellor, University of Bradford

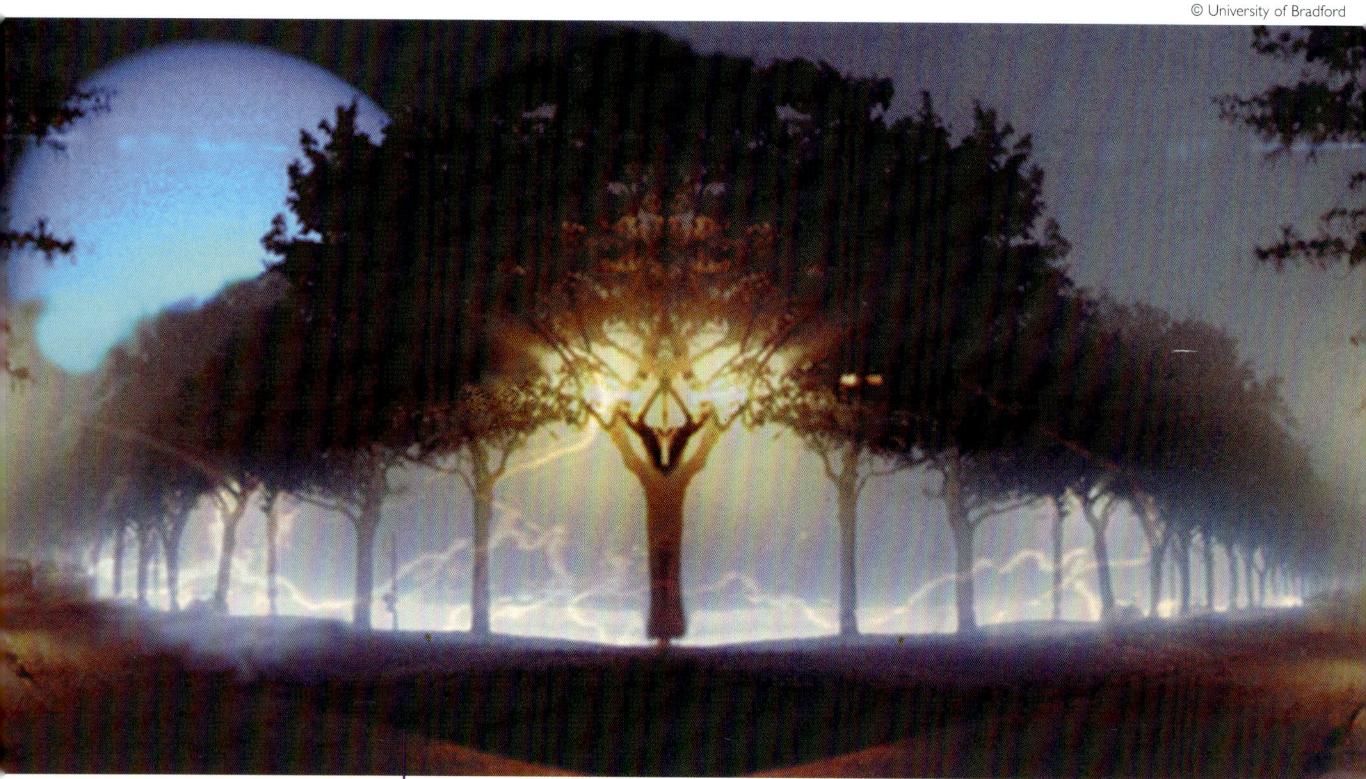

'Mind Out inner booklet design', photograph manipulated by Holly Irvine, second-year student on the Electronic Imaging and Media Communications course, University of Bradford.

'There is only one place where you can see the greatest special effects technicians in the world creating movie magic beyond your wildest dreams—Bradford!'
Impact magazine

One of the National Museum of Photography, Film & Television's neighbours in the city centre is the University of Bradford. The University's evocative motto is 'Making knowledge work'. It is useful and interesting to apply that motto to the Museum's central materials.

Knowledge is *shaped* in at least five ways:

- directly by the people and institutions who produce it
- by the 'science' that underlies it
- by the technology through which it is made
- by its social context
- and above all by its reception by its audience.

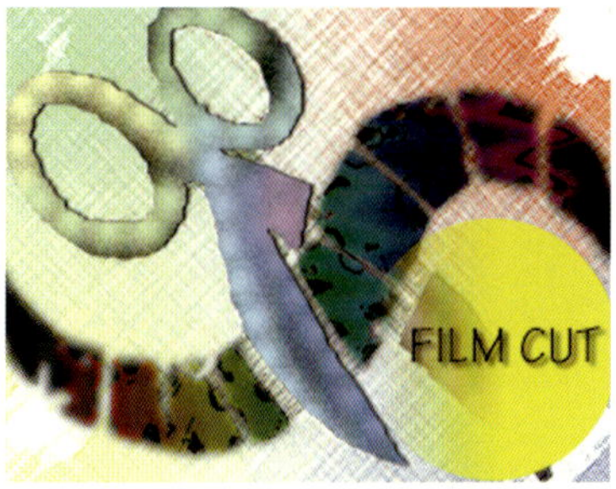

'Film Cut', artwork by Eleni Spyridou, student on the Electronic Imaging and Media Communications course, University of Bradford.

It is well known that no publication, no reception and no audience equals no science. This applies every bit as much to photography, film and television. As with science it is possible to analyse the shaping of knowledge in such a way as to make possible for us all to understand much more about the images we see. As this shaping is active and artful and usually conscious and deliberate rather than passive, naive, unconscious and accidental it *can* be studied and displayed.

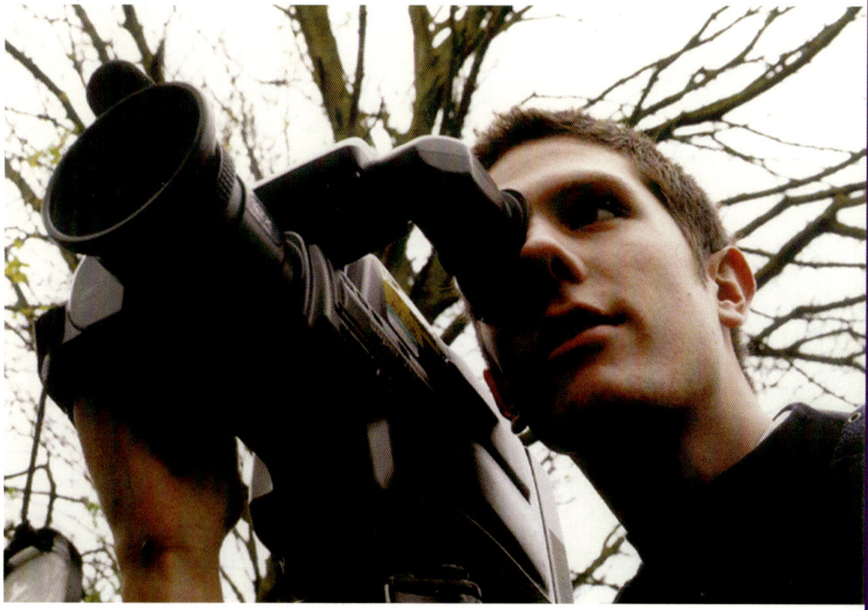

'Ground Roots', photograph by Jim McEwen, third-year student on the Electronic Imaging and Media Communications course, University of Bradford.

What the Museum does so brilliantly is to make that shaping tangible. This is an essentially empowering experience. Science is often thought to be how and why are things the way they are, as opposed to judgements about whether they are any good or whether we like them. The evaluation of the aesthetical aspect of a photograph must be associated with some scientific comprehension if we are to truly understand what is seen. What makes this all the more exciting is that, because we rarely agree about a photograph, film or television programme or advertisement, we become self-conscious about the critical process. And so we come to know more about ourselves too.

The Museum, now more than ever, gives us the material basis to develop this critical process and so simultaneously to become more aware of ourselves. Our use of the Museum can shadow that of views of photography. On the one hand we can be minimalist (passive, or just plain lazy!). This is the view of photography where the influence of the photographer's hand and eye is belittled. You come, you see, but you do not engage. Alternatively, you can be very engaged and do active shaping work on what you see.

'Traffic Lights', photograph by David Campbell, second-year student on the Electronic Imaging and Media Communications course, University of Bradford.

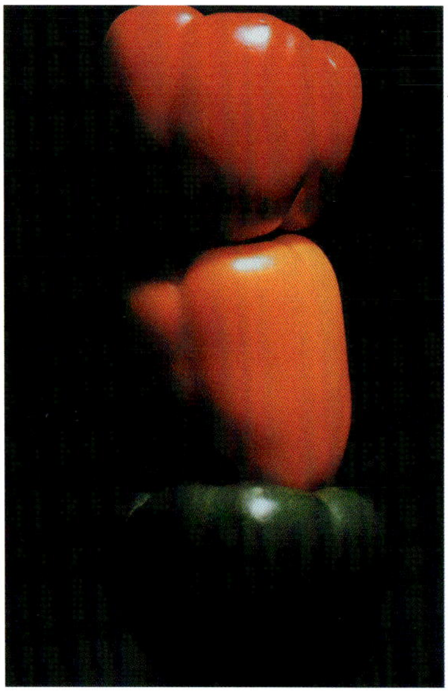

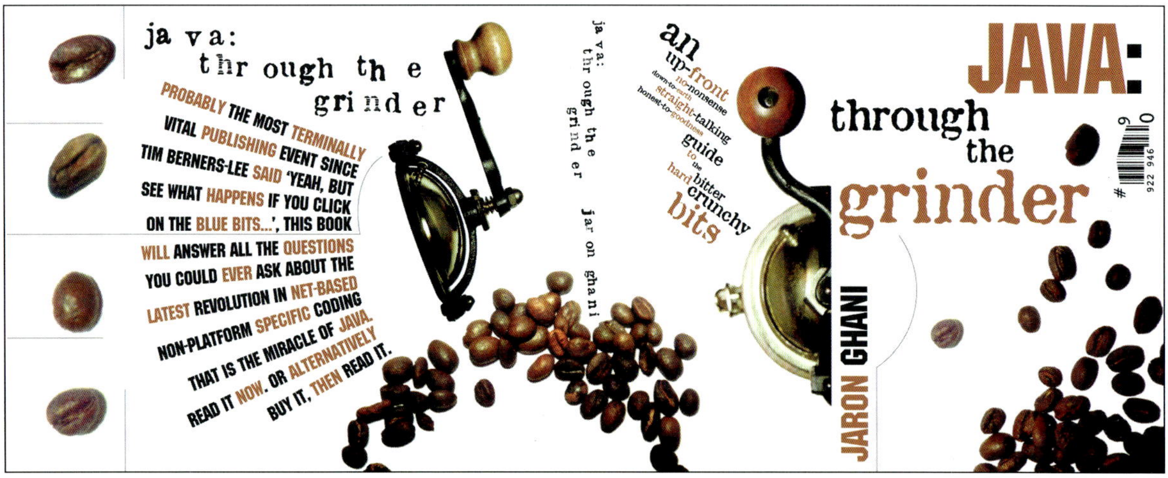

'Java: through the grinder', artwork for a book cover by Jaron Ghani, second-year student on the Electronic Imaging and Media Communications course, University of Bradford.

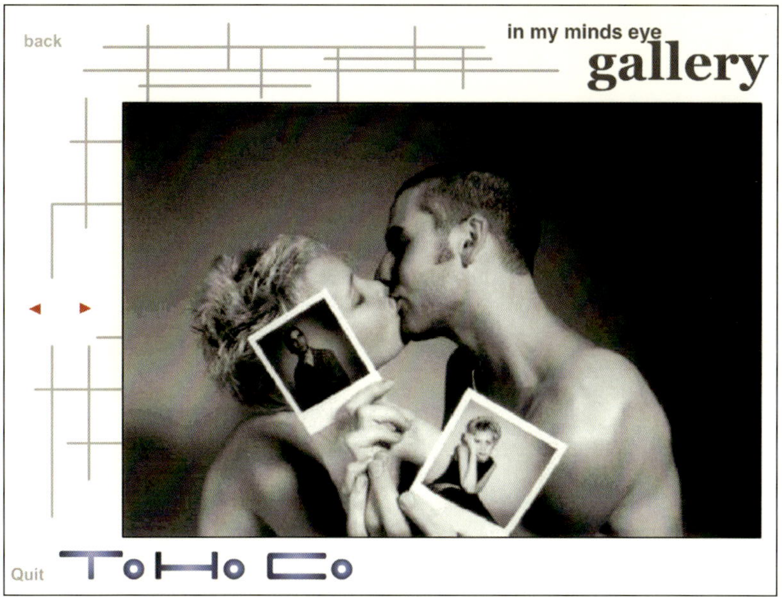

© University of Bradford

'In My Mind's Eye', photograph by Thomas Harmer, third-year student on the Electronic Imaging and Media Communications course, University of Bradford.

Great universities now insist in their mission statements that students be literate in a number of ways—the latest being with computers and information technology. Less emphasis has been placed on visual literacy as a general and universal ambition for undergraduates. With the greatly enhanced Museum as our close neighbour we look forward to developing programmes together that will support the growth of just such a literacy. If universities need to produce active citizens for the future, and Bradford University most certainly does, then a critical understanding of the workings, through images, of modern media is required. With Pauline Kael, the famous film critic, we want them to say more than 'Wow' after seeing a movie.

'A knowledge of photography is just as important as that of the alphabet. The illiterate of the future will be ignorant of the use of camera and pen alike.'
Laszlo Moholy-Nagy (1895–1946), artist and photographer

The great sociologist of modernisation, Max Weber, puts the growth of bureaucracy and above all the rationalisation of everyday life at the centre of that process. This is a progressive disenchantment of the world, the eradication of mystery, emotion, tradition and affectivity and its replacement by rational calculation. Just because so many of the images, and the image mongers, aim to re-enchant and mystify in order to entertain and to sell, it is an important purpose of the Museum (and the University) to (re)disenchant and (re)demystify. Educate in other words. It is a great comfort to me, as head of a major, national educational institution located in Bradford that there is another: the National Museum of Photography Film & Television.

Sponsors

The new National Museum of Photography, Film & Television, launched in spring 1999, was created with generous support from its project partners:

Supported by the Heritage Lottery Fund

SUPPORTED BY THE NATIONAL LOTTERY THROUGH THE ARTS COUNCIL OF ENGLAND

EUROPEAN COMMUNITY
European Regional Development Fund

Major funders:

Kodak

City of BRADFORD METROPOLITAN DISTRICT COUNCIL

Foundation for sport and the arts

· The Gandolfi Foundation ·

Dana and Albert R. Broccoli Charitable Foundation

Gallery sponsors and technology partners:

Bradford & Bingley

saville AUDIO VISUAL

SiliconGraphics Computer Systems

TRIMENSION SYSTEMS LTD

iBase

SONY

REUTERS

D&AD

Founding partners:

Bradford & Northern Housing Association

Canon

Deepend

Interbrand Newell & Sorrell

Leach Colour Limited

Provident Financial

Rex Procter & Partners

Walker Morris